COMPREHENSIVE TREATISE

ON

LAND SURVEYING,

COMPRISING

THE THEORY AND PRACTICE

IN ALL ITS BRANCHES;

IN WHICH

THE USE OF THE VARIOUS INSTRUMENTS EMPLOYED IN SURVEYING,
LEVELLING, &c. IS CLEARLY ELUCIDATED

BY

PRACTICAL EXAMPLES.

ILLUSTRATED BY FORTY COPPERPLATES, CONTAINING UPWARDS OF
ONE HUNDRED AND SEVENTY FIGURES.

BY JOHN AINSLIE, LAND SURVEYOR.

EDINBURGH:
PRINTED FOR SILVESTER DOIG & ANDREW STIRLING, EDINBURGH;
CRADOCK & JOY, LONDON; AND MARTIN KEENE, DUBLIN;
BY JOHN BROWN.

1812.

TO

JOHN RENNIE, ESQ.

CIVIL ENGINEER.

SIR,

I am induced, from a consideration of your profound knowledge in the Art which the following pages are intended to illustrate, as well as in testimony of the numerous acts of kindness which I have received from you in the line of my profession, to prefix your name to the following TREATISE ON PRACTICAL LAND SURVEYING.

With the greatest respect,

I am, SIR,

Your very humble Servant,

JOHN AINSLIE.

PREFACE.

FLATTERED by the favourable reception given to a work of mine published some time ago by Messrs. Constable & Co. Edinburgh *, and urged by repeated and earnest solicitations from various quarters, I have been induced to offer the present Work to the Public.

I have in this Treatise attempted to exhibit a comprehensive view of the whole art of Land-surveying, both in theory and practice, and have illustrated its application upon different scales, in the measurement and delineation of private properties, and in the surveys of counties or large districts. I have endeavoured to explain, in the most easy, intelligible, and familiar manner, the uses of the various instruments employed in land-surveying, viz. the chain, the cross staff, the plain table, the circumferenter, the sextant, and the theodolite; and have shewn the readiest modes of their application to the measurement of boundary lines of different figures, and to every variety of surface which may occur in practice.

The importance of this branch of the subject must appear obvious, when it is considered that many who are well versed in mathematics, and completely masters of the theory of land-surveying, are often strangely bewildered when on the field, from a want of readiness in adapting the use of

* The Gentleman and Farmer's POCKET COMPANION and ASSISTANT, a new Edition of which, with Improvements, is lately published.

instruments to the occasion ; a facility which can only be acquired by practice and a thorough knowledge of their use. .

The Author flatters himself, that the experience which he has had in
the discharge of his professional duties, has enabled him to render this part
of the subject peculiarly simple and intelligible.

The reader is here furnished with a number of plain and easy directions
for using the various instruments employed in measuring surfaces of different kinds, or taking levels for constructing drains, rail-ways, canals, &c.

Nor has less attention been paid to what may be called secondary objects
in the art of surveying. The learner will here find an account of the readiest and most approved methods of keeping field-books, and of making
eye-sketches ; of the different modes of protracting and plotting the angles
and bearings ; of equalizing and calculating areas ; of delineating, copying,
and reducing plans ; and of dividing lands. Directions are also given for
beautifying and adorning plans with Indian ink and colours ; and the
whole is illustrated by 40 copperplates, exhibiting upwards of 170 different figures. In short, no pains have been spared to render this work ex-
tensively useful, both by the variety and novelty of the matter which it
contains.

CONTENTS.

SECTION FIRST.

ARTICLE I. AND II.

SECTION SECOND.

Art. I. Of the Chain.

Art. II. The Cross Staff.

Art. III. Of the Plain Table.

SECTION THIRD.

Art. I. Of Areas.

Art. II. Of Equalizing Different Figures.

SECTION FOURTH.

OF LEVELLING.

SECTION FIFTH,

COUNTY SURVEYING.   219

SECTION SIXTH,

OF MILITARY SURVEYING.   231

SECTION SEVENTH,

OF REDUCING PLANS.

1

Art. II.   Of Delineating Plans.

TREATISE

ON

PRACTICAL LAND SURVEYING.

SECTION FIRST.

ART. I. DEFINITIONS AND PROBLEMS.

In this TREATISE, which is strictly practical, the mathematical demonstrations are omitted. The Surveyor may, however, be assured, that the principles upon which the problems are wrought are susceptible of strict demonstration. A facility in performing these problems is of the greatest use in practise. But before proceeding to the problems, it may be proper to lay down the following definitions:

LAND-SURVEYING has for its object the discovering of the extent of area contained in horizontal surfaces; for no greater number of poles could be planted perpendicularly upon the surface of a hill, than what can find room to stand upon the plane of its base: of course, no greater number of plants, all of which grow upright, could find room upon the hill's surface than what there is room for on its base.

Surfaces consist of mere length and breadth, and do not, like solids, infer their constitution from the three dimensions of length, breadth, and thickness.

A

Lines, whether right lines or curved, are the mere boundaries of surfaces; and as such are to be considered as having only length without breadth in the mere termination of a line. A *Point* is the termination of a line; and as such, has neither length nor breadth.

Parallel lines are lines placed equidistant from each other, and which, however far extended, can never meet; as the lines A B and C D in *Plate* I. *Fig.* 1.

Angles are formed by the meeting of lines drawn in different directions When a line, as A D in *Plate* I. *Fig.* 4. falls penpendicular upon the line B C, so that the two angles on the opposite sides of the line A D, at the point D, are equal, then these two angles are each of them right angles. *Fig.* 6. *Plate* I. represents a right angle; *Fig.* 7. is an acute angle, which is less than a right angle; *Fig.* 8. is an obtuse angle, which is greater than a right angle. The rates at which the two lines forming the angle diverge from the point where they meet, characterise the nature of the angle, as consisting of a certain number of degrees; which will be explained when the circle is treated of. It may be proper here to observe, that when only two lines, in different directions, meet at a point, and of course form only one angle at the point of junction, the angle is marked and designed by a single letter, as in *Fig.* 6. 7. 8. *Plate* I. But if three or more lines meet a point, and form two or more angles, three letters are used to mark and name these different angles; and in naming them, the letter at the point of junction is named in the middle. Thus, in *Fig.* 9. *Plate* I. the angle formed by the junction of the lines C A and B A, is designed the angle B A C or C A B; and that formed by the lines C A and D A, is named the angle D A C or C A D.

Figures are the portions of surface completely inclosed and bounded by lines, either right or curved; those bounded by the former being designed *Rectilinear* figures, those bounded by the latter *Curvilinear.*

I. *Rectilinear Figures* comprehend *Triangles,* or spaces bounded by three right lines. Of these there are three kinds, as characterised by their bounding lines: the *Equilateral triangle,* of which all the three sides are equally represented by the triangle B C A, *Fig.* 12. *Plate* I.; the *Isosceles triangle,* of which two sides are equal, *Fig.* 13. *Plate* I.; the *Scalene tri-*

angle, where the three sides are unequal, *Fig.* 14. *Plate* I. Triangles are also characterised by their angles—*N. B.* All the three angles of a triangle are equal to two right angles; so that if one angle is a right angle (or greater than a right angle), none of the other two can be so great as a right angle.—If one of the angles is a right angle, the triangle is a *right angled triangle*, as *Fig.* 15. *Plate* I.; if one angle is obtuse, it is an *obtuse angled triangle*, as *Fig.* 13. and 14. *Plate* I; if all the three angles are acute, it is an *acute angled triangle*, as *Fig.* 12. *Plate* I.

II. *Quadrilateral figures*, or spaces bounded by four right lines. These comprehend the *Square*, in which all the four sides are equal, and the opposite sides parallel; and all the angles are right angles, as *Fig.* 16. *Plate* I.; the *Parallelogram*, or oblong, as *Fig.* 17. *Plate* I. of which the two opposite sides are equal and parallel, and all the angles are right angles, but all the four sides are not equal; the *Rhombus*, of which all the sides are equal and parallel, but none of the angles are right angles, *Fig.* 18. and 19. *Plate* I.; the perfect *Rhombus* has two of its angles of 120 degrees and two of 60; the *Rhomboid*, which is to the rhombus what the parallelogram is to the square, *Fig.* 31. *Plate* I.; and in which the opposite sides are equal and parallel, but the sides are not all equal, and none of the angles are right angles; the *Trapezium*, *Fig.* 21. *Plate* I. in which the four sides are unequal, none of them parallel, and none of the angles right angles; the *Trapezoid*, *Fig.* 20. *Plate* I. in which two of the sides may be parallel but not equal, or two sides may be equal but not parallel, and two of the angles may be right angles, but neither of the other two.—*N. B.* In every quadrilateral figure the four angles are equal to four right angles. All quadrilateral figures, which are neither squares, parallelograms, rhombuses, nor rhomboids, are called *Trapeziums*. As every four-sided figure contains four angles, they are also named *quadrangular*. If the figure is bounded by more than four sides, it is called a *polygon* or a *multilateral figure*.

Curvilinear figures. These comprehend the *Circle* and the *Ellipsis* or *oval*. Several of the principles of the art of surveying are referable to the properties of the circle; and the practical surveyor may sometimes be called upon to trace out an oval upon pleasure grounds.

The *Circle* may be considered as a figure traced by a point moving round

a centre, and keeping always at the same distance from the centre, till it
arrives at the place from whence it set out.   It may be traced upon a slate
or paper with a pair of compasses, by fixing one foot in the centre, and
making the other revolve round it, extending the compasses to the width
required in the circle, whilst a writing or slate pen, fixed to the moving
foot, traces the line of its course.   In tracing a large circle upon the ground,
a convenient way is to fix a pin in the centre, to put the end of a cord
with an eye over the pin, and, at the distance required, to move round
with the other end of the cord, marking the line it makes by pins at short
distances.   A right line, drawn in any direction from the centre of the circle to its circumference, is called the *Radius* of the circle; and from the
mode in which a circle is formed, it is self-evident that all the radii of a
circle are equal.   Any right line drawn across the circle, and passing
through its centre, is called the *diameter of the circle*, and divides it into two
equal parts ; each of these parts is named a *semicircle :* the part of a circle,
cut off by any right line drawn across it, which does not pass through the
centre, is called the *segment of a circle.*   In *Fig. 22. Plate* I. A F B D E is
the circumference of the circle ; C is its centre, the line A B is its diameter ; the lines drawn from the centre to the circumference A C, F C, D C,
and B C, are radii of the circle ; the line D C, perpendicular to A B, if
prolonged to E, would divide the circle into four equal parts; the portions of the circle A C D, or B C D, are named *Quadrants* of the circle.

The circle is used to measure the rate of divergence of the two lines forming an angle : for this purpose the circumference of the circle is conceived to
be divided into 360 equal parts, called *degrees ;* the semicircle contains 180
of these degrees ; the quadrant A C D, (*Fig. 22. Plate* I.), contains 90 degrees ; the divergence of the two lines forming an angle, is ascertained by the
number of degrees of the circumference of a circle, which these two lines would
intercept, were we to form the circle from the point, as its centre, where these
lines meet ; and the angle receives its name from the degrees so intercept-
ed : thus the lines A C and C D (*Fig. 22. Plate* I.) intercept the 4th part
of the circumference, or 90 degrees ; and the angle A C D is called an
angle of 90 degrees, or a right angle ; the line F C intercepts with the line
D C one half of these, or 45 degrees, and the angle F C D is called an an-

gle of 45 degrees. It is the same thing whether the circle, by the intercept-
ed portions of whose circumference circles are measured, be a greater or lesser circle; for m n is just the eighth part of the circumference of the lesser
circle, as F D is of the larger one, drawn from the same common centre C.

The *Ellipsis* is regularly formed as a circle of two centres, as represented *Fig.* 30. *Plate* I. Two pins are planted as in the figure; a thread
or cord, with its ends fastened together, is then thrown over the pins; a
black lead pencil, or other marker, is then held upright in the hand, with
the double of the cord, and is carried round the pins at the full stretch of
the cord, from the two planted pins or centres, and marks the progress
round the centres of the angle formed in the cord by the marker. Ellipses,
it is evident, may thus be formed with any proportion of their length to their
breadth; the nearer the distance of the two centre pins, with the same
length of cord, the more nearly will the ellipsis approach to the form of
a circle; and the same thing will take place, in proportion to the length
of cord, with the same distance of the centre pins,

We now proceed to describe the mode of performing a few Geometri-
cal Problems; in the exercise of which the practical surveyor should en-
deavour to acquire a readiness.

ART. II. GEOMETRICAL PROBLEMS.

PROBLEM I. (*Plate* I. *Fig.* 1.)

To draw a line parallel to a given line A B. With a pair of compasses
take the distance you want to make one line distant from another; then
set one foot of the compasses in A, and describe an arch with the other foot
at C; remove the compasses with the same extent, and put one foot of the
compasses at B, and with the other foot describe an arch at D; draw the
line C D, which will be parallel to A B.

PROB. II. (*Plate* I. *Fig.* 2.)

To divide a line into two equal parts. Let A B be the line to be divided.
Stretch the compasses to any extent, exceeding half the length of the line

A B; fix one foot in A, and sweep the arch C D; then with the compasses at the same extent fix one foot at B, and cut the former arch in the points C and D; draw the line C D through the points of intersection, which will divide the line A B into two equal parts. This is the best mode of raising a perpendicular upon the middle of a line, if you have room below at D.

Prob. III. (*Plate* I. *Fig.* 3.)

From the end of a line, as A B, *to raise a perpendicular at* B. With any extent in a pair of compasses set one foot in B, and describe an arch d e b; with the same extent put one foot of the compasses in d, and turn the compasses twice upon the arch, marking the points e and b; and from these points describe the arches, bisecting each other at g; then draw the line g B, which will be perpendicular to the line A B, at the end of the line at B.

Prob. IV. (*Plate* I. *Fig.* 4.)

To let fall a perpendicular from a point at A *upon the given line* B C. With any extent greater than the distance from A to D, put one foot of the compasses in A, and describe the arch H B; then put one foot of the compasses in the intersection at H, and describe an arch at K; with the same extent, on B as a centre, bisect the arch at K; then draw the line A D in a straight direction from the point A to the point of intersection at K, and the line A D will be perpendicular to the line B C.

Prob. V. (*Plate* I. *Fig.* 5.)

To raise a perpendicular from the end of a line, when there is not room on one side to extend the arch d e b, *as in figure 3.* With any extent you think proper between your compasses, put one foot at the end of the line at B, and describe an arch at D; with the same extent, put one foot of the compasses in any part of the line A B, suppose at L, and bisect the former arch in D; with the same extent in D as a centre sweep the arch L E C; draw a line from L through the centre D to the arch at C; lastly, draw the line C B, which will be the perpendicular to the line A B at B. Various other methods might be shown how to raise and let fall perpendiculars; but what has been pointed out is thought sufficient.

PROB. VI. (*Plate* I. *Fig.* 10.)

From a given point, to make an angle equal to a given angle. Let B A C be the given angle; set one foot of your compasses in the point A, and with any extent sweep an arch e d, intersecting the two lines B A and C A, which form the given angle; then with the same extent fix one foot in the point A D, where the required angle is to be formed, and sweep the arch E F; take the arch e d in your compasses, and apply it to the arch E F, marking those points; then draw straight lines from the points E and F to the angular point D, and you will have the angle E D F equal to the angle B A C.

PROB. VII. (*Plate* I. *Fig.* 11.)

To divide a right angle in three equal parts. From the angular point A describe an arch B C, and with the same extent set one foot of your compasses upon the arch at B, and make a mark upon the arch at m; then with the same extent set one foot of the compasses on the arch at C, and make another mark with the other foot at k; draw straight lines from the points m and k to the angular point A, which will divide the right angle into three angles of 80 degrees each.

PROB. VIII. (*Plate* I. *Fig.* 12.)

To make an equilateral triangle whose base is A B. Take the length of A B with a pair of compasses, and with that extent set one foot of your compasses in A, and describe an arch at C; then with the same extent set one foot of the compasses in B, and with the other foot bisect the arch in C; draw lines from the point C to the points A and B, and A B C will be an equilateral triangle.

PROB. IX. (*Plate* I. *Fig.* 13.)

To construct an isosceles triangle upon the line D E. With the extent of the line D F set one foot of the compasses in D, and describe an arch at

F; then with the same extent set one foot of the compasses in E, and intersect the arch at F; draw the lines F D and F E, and it is formed.

PROB. X.   (*Plate* I. *Fig.* 14.)

To construct a scalene triangle whose sides are all unequal, as A B, C B, *and* C A. Take the length of A B, and lay that distance off upon a line drawn at pleasure; then with your compasses take the length of the line A C, and with one foot in A describe an arch at C; then take the length of the line B C, and with one foot in B bisect the arch at C; draw lines from the point of intersection at C to A and B, and it is made.

PROB. XI.   (*Plate* I. *Fig.* 15.)

To form a right angled triangle on the line GH. At the point G raise a perpendicular G I, as described in *Plate* I. *Fig.* 3. and draw the line H I, and it is finished.

PROB. XII.   (*Plate* I. *Fig.* 16.)

To form a square whose sides shall be equal to K L. Raise a perpendicular from K to N, and another from L to M, both of an equal length with K L; join M and N, and it is done. Or you may draw K N perpendicular to L K, from the point K; then take the length of L K, and prick off that distance at N; and with the same extent in your compasses put one foot in N, and describe an arch at M; and, with the same extent, put one foot of your compasses in L, and with the other foot bisect the arch in M; and from the point of intersection at M draw the lines M L and M N, which form the square L K N M.

PROB. XIII.   (*Plate* I. *Fig.* 17.)

To form a parallelogram whose sides shall be equal to the given lines A B *and* A D. Lay down a line equal to the length A B; at the point A raise a perpendicular of the length of A D; then with your compasses, extended to the length of A B, put one foot in D, and describe an arch at E; then with the extent of A D fix one foot in B, and bisect the arch at E; from the point of intersection draw the lines E D and E B, and it is done.

PROB. XIV.　(*Plate* I. *Fig.* 18.)

To construct a rhombus upon a given line A B. Take the length in your compasses, and with one foot in B describe the arch D E C; with the same extent on A as a centre describe an arch cutting the former; and on D as a centre describe an arch cutting D E C in C draw the lines A D, B C, and C D, which form a rhombus.

PROB. XV.　(*Plate.* I. *Fig.* 19.)

To form a rhombus of any angle given, suppose B A C. First make an angle equal to B A C; take any length you please between your compasses, suppose A B; with the same extent make a mark on the line from A to C; and with the same distance on B as a centre describe an arch at D; then with the same extent, and on C as a centre, cut that arch in D; lastly, draw the lines B D and C D, and it is formed.

Plate I. *Fig.* 31.

A rhomboid has its opposite sides equal and parallel, but not perpendicular.

PROB. XVI.　(*Plate* I. *Fig.* 20.)

To construct a trapezoid upon the line C E, *whose parallel lines shall be as the lines* C D *and* E E. With a pair of compasses lay off the distance of C E; then at the end of the line at C raise a perpendicular of the length of C D; at the other end of the line at E raise another perpendicular of the length of the given line E F; join those lines, and it is done.

PROB. XVII.　(*Plate* I. *Fig.* 21.)

To construct a trapezium equal to a given trapezium, suppose the trapezium ADBC. From any angle of the given trapezium draw a line to its opposite angle (which is called a diagonal), suppose the line A B; lay down a line of the same length as A B, and extend your compasses to the length of the line A B of the given figure; fix one foot in the end at B, and with the other foot sweep an arch the length of B D; then take the length

B

from the given figure A D, and put one foot of the compasses in A, and bisect the arch at D, draw in the lines A D and D B ; then take the length of the line from the given figure A C, and put one foot of your compasses in A, and describe an arch at C; then, with your compasses extended to the length of B C, and in like manner from the point B, bisect the arch in C ; draw the lines A C and B C, and the trapezium is formed equal to the one given.

Note, the dotted line D e in the Plate has no connection with the above construction, nor has the dotted lines from D and C to the diagonal. Their use will be explained in another place.

PROB. XVIII.   (*Plate* I. *Fig.* 23.)

To construct an equilateral triangle within a circle, let D E F G *be the circle, of which* H *is the centre.* With the same radius as the circle is drawn by, set one foot of the compasses on any part of the circumference you please, suppose on E, and with the other foot bisect the circumference in D and F, and draw the line E D ; then take the distance of the line F D, and set one foot in F, and with the other bisect the arch in G ; draw the lines G F and C D, and it is formed.

PROB. XIX.   (*Plate* I. *Fig.* 24.)

To construct a square within a circle. Divide the circle into quadrants ; first, by drawing a line through the centre, suppose from I to L, and another line perpendicular through the centre (See *Plate* I. *Fig.* 2.) from K to M ; then draw lines from I to K, K to L, L to M, and M to I, and the square is formed.

PROB. XX.   (*Plate* I. *Fig.* 25.)

To construct a regular hexagon in a circle. The radius of a circle being transferable six times on its circumference, take the same radius the circle is drawn by, put one foot of the compasses on any part of the circumference, and divide the circumference into six equal parts ; lastly, draw lines from every point to the one next it till you have gone all round, and the hexagon is finished.

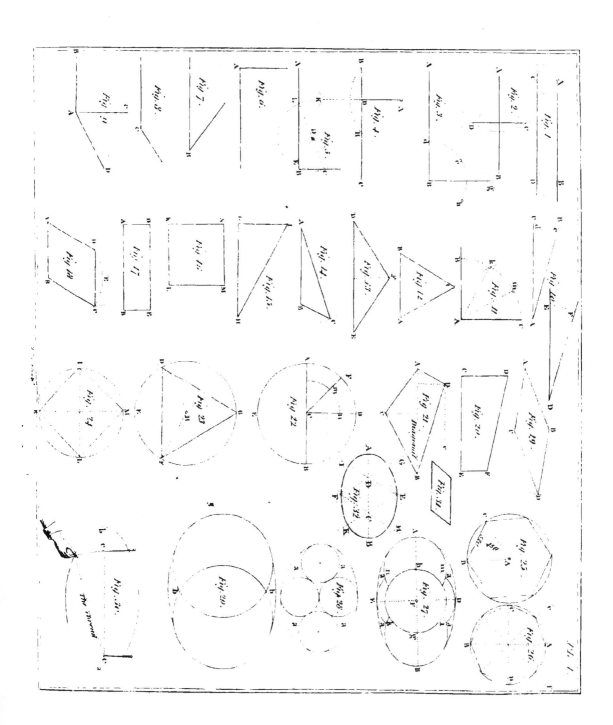

Prob. XXI. (*Plate* I. *Fig.* 26.)

To construct an octagon, or eight-sided figure.   Describe a circle, and divide it into four equal parts by two diameters perpendicular to one another (as in *Fig.* 24. above); then set one foot of the compasses in A, and with any distance you please sweep an arch at e, and another at f; then set one foot of the compasses in C, and with the other bisect the arch in e, and with the same extent on D as a centre; bisect the arch in f; then draw the dotted lines from the points e and f exactly through the centre to the other side of the circumference, which will divide the circle in eight equal parts; lastly, draw right lines from every point where the above straight lines touch the circumference to the next point touched, and the octagon is formed.

Prob. XXII. (*Plate* I. *Fig.* 30.)

To describe an ellipsis.   The ellipsis is formed by a curve drawn about two centres, as represented in *Plate* I. *Fig.* 30. Two pins are fastened at the points c c (which points are termed the foci of the ellipsis); a thread or cord is to be doubled, and the ends fastened; the thread is then thrown over the pins; and with a pen or pencil, by keeping the thread equally tight about the pins (taking care to hold the pen or pencil upright) the figure may be easily described. It is evident, the nearer the two pins approach to one another, the nearer does the figure approach to a circle.

Prob. XXIII. (*Plate* I. *Fig.* 32.)

By the following method a figure may be formed with arches of circles only, and which will nearly resemble the ellipsis. Draw any line, as A B, and upon it describe two isosceles triangles, D E C and D F C; produce their sides to H, G, I, and K; then on the vertex (of each triangle) E and F, with the distance E F, describe the arches G H and I K; lastly, on C and D as centres, with the distance C H or D G, describe the arches H K and G I, and it is done. This figure is generally preferred for a grass plot, and sometimes in the construction of arches.

Prob. XXIV.   (*Plate* I. *Fig.* 27, 28, and 29.)

Easy modes of forming elliptical figures by compasses, Fig. 27.   Draw a line the length of the oval, as A B, and let fall a perpendicular through the centre F from D to E; with one foot of the compasses in E, describe a circle, the diameter of which shall be half the length of the line A B; then put one foot of the compasses where the arch intersects the line A B at g, and with the same radius as the circle already made describe the arch i B k; remove the compasses to h, and put one foot in h, and sweep the arch m A n; then take a stretch of half the breadth you wish to give to the oval, and put one foot of the compasses in the centre F, and with the other foot describe an arch at D and another at E; and then with your hand cut off the four corners a a a a, and the figure is formed.

Plate I. *Fig.* 28.   A figure somewhat resembling the ellipsis, made by drawing four circles, and with the hand, cutting off the four corners a a a a.

Plate I. *Fig.* 29. represents also a figure which is formed by two circles, the part of it marked b b being drawn with the hand.

Prob. XXV.   (*Plate* II. *Fig.* 1.)

To divide a line into two parts, which shall be in the same proportion to each other as two given lines.   Let A A be one line and B B the other; let C D be the given line, to be divided into two parts bearing the same proportion to each other as A A does to B B.

First, from C draw a line at pleasure, as C F; then with a pair of compasses take the length of the line A A, and lay that distance off upon the line C F, which will reach to a point at E; likewise take off the length of the line B B, and set that distance off from E, which will reach to a point in F; then draw a line from E to D; lastly, draw a line parallel with E D, from the point at E, this last line will cut the line C D at G, and will make the line C G, in the same proportion to G D that A A is to B B.

Prob. XXVI.   (*Plate* II. *Fig.* 2.)

To divide a line into any number of equal parts, suppose eight.   Lay down a line of any length at pleasure, suppose A B; from one end of it lay off any small angle you please above the line, and another parallel to it below, as D E, with any short distance ; lay the distance off eight times upon the upper line, and with the same extent eight times upon the under line, and draw lines from point to point, from the upper line to the under one, which will divide the middle line F into eight equal parts. This mode is very useful in dividing scales into equal parts.

PROB. XXVII. (*Plate* II. *Fig.* 3.)

To construct a diagonal scale, suppose one fourth of an inch to each primary division. Draw a line at any length you wish to make your scale, suppose an inch and a half in length ; raise a perpendicular at both ends of an equal breadth, which divide into ten horizontal parallel lines, at equal distances, the whole length of the scale ; then divide the length into six equal divisions, and draw vertical lines parallel with the perpendiculars, which will be one fourth of an inch each division ; then divide the left hand division into ten equal parts, both at the top and bottom ; draw a diagonal line from o to the first of the small divisions at the top of the scale ; then draw another line from the first division at the bottom to the second division at the top of the scale, and go on in this way till the whole of the ten lines are drawn ; then insert the figures, as represented on the *Plate* 1. 2. 3. 4. 5. ; the first figure is sometimes called *ten*, the second *twenty*, the third *thirty*, &c. In the first case, each of the small divisions is one : the first figure is sometimes called 100, the second 200, the third 300, the fourth 400, the fifth 500. In that case, each small division is called *ten*, two is termed *twenty*, and so on in proportion.

Diagonal scales may be made of various dimensions, in the same way as above.

To take off a distance from a diagonal scale, suppose 446 links, when the figure *one* upon the scale is termed 100. Place one foot of the compasses in the fourth vertical line, at the sixth line up, and extend the other foot along the parallel line to the fourth diagonal, which will be the distance required.

SECTION SECOND.

DESCRIPTION AND METHOD OF SURVEYING WITH VARIOUS INSTRUMENTS.

ART. I. OF THE CHAIN.

THE Chain in general is made 100 links in length. The Measurer should also be provided with ten pins, made of wood or strong iron wire; a piece of red cloth should be tied to the head of each pin, so as they may be easily found. Chains are divided by pieces of iron or brass, at the end of every ten links, for the conveniency of numbering the odd links at the end of stations, and where offsets are taken; and it is very requisite to be provided with three or four poles, called station staffs, about eight or ten feet in length, with a red or white flag tied to the top of each, for their being seen when they are placed at a distance; and if shod with iron, they will be easier stuck in the ground. The Measurer ought also to have an offset staff ten links long, and divided and numbered from one to ten, for taking offsets into the bends and angles in the fences; or a tape, which is better, divided into links in place of feet, such as carpenters, masons, and painters use for measuring their work. These tapes can be bought at most of the hardware shops.

Being provided with the above articles, place one of the poles where you intend to measure to, and leave the other at the mark you begin at. Let the foremost assistant take one end of the chain and the ten pins; and the other assistant, when the chain is stretched out, must direct him in a line with the pole they are to measure to. If he is not exactly on the line at first, the hindmost assistant must cause him to move to the right or left till he is exactly on the line with the station staff, where he is ordered to stick down one of the pins at the end of the chain. The foremost chain-man goes forward and the hindmost one follows, and stands with his hand above the first pin, and moves the foremost assistant to the right or left, till he is exactly on the line; when he is ordered to stick in his second pin. The hindmost chain-man lifts the first pin at the same time the other sticks his second pin. The one chain-man goes forward, and the other follows to the second pin; the foremost man then sticks in his third pin by the direction of the hindmost man. It will be proper to observe, that each of the chain-men should be very careful, in keeping the line very correct, which they can both know exactly; the foremost assistant will always see the back pole and the hindmost assistant in a line, and the hindmost assistant never allows the foremost one to stick in his pin till he sees that he is exactly on the line to the pole they are measuring to; and the one assistant should always lift the pin with the same hand that he has the chain in, and the other should stick down his pin with the same hand that he draws the chain with. The chain-men can now direct each other; but if they should deviate in the least from the line, they can put themselves exactly upon it again, by moving a little to the right or left till they are exactly upon it again, which they can easily ascertain when the hindmost assistant sees the foremost assistant in a line with the pole, and the foremost assistant observes the hindmost assistant in a line with the pole left at the place where the measuring began. If great care is not taken to keep the line, particularly where offsets are taken, none of them will be right, but either too short or too long, according to the distance they are to the right or left of the line. The foremost man always sticks in his pins, and the hindmost lifts them up, till they are all spent, which should be counted to see if none are lost. This is what land-surveyors call a change, or 1000 links. The hindmost man gives the whole of the pins to the foremost chain-man, and proceeds measuring as before. They may either change at ten pins or eleven: if they change at eleven, the hindmost man sticks in one of the pins, and gives the foremost man only nine. They now continue measuring till the pins are all spent a second time. This is called two changes, or 2000 links. But we shall suppose the foremost chain-man comes to the pole before it was necessary to change pins the second time; in that case, the hindmost assistant's pins are counted, which we shall suppose eight chains and twenty-five links. You insert for the length of that line in the field-book 1825. A land-surveyor never thinks of setting down in his field-book, or eye-draught, chains or links at the end of his figures, as every one that measures with the chain generally inserts their distances in links.

Some surveyors, in some of the counties in England, survey with a chain ten yards in length; in Scotland, some measure with a chain ten ells in length, each ell being 37 inches; and in Ireland with a chain of 2 perches, or 42 feet in length.

Plate II. (Fig. 12.)

Shews the method of taking an angle with the chain, when you have no other instrument to take angles with in the field; it saves the trouble of measuring the diagonal. Many surveyors prefer taking an angle with it, on account of its simplicity, to any other instrument. Suppose the angle B A C is wanted from the corner of the hedge A; measure one chain or 100 links from A on the line A C, and order the chain-man to leave a pin at a; then measure another chain's length from A to b; when that is done go up to the mark at b, and measure to a, which is 76 links, which note down on your field-book.

To protract the angle B A C, draw a line at pleasure, representing the dotted line A B; then take the length of one chain from a larger scale than the one you intend to plot the field by, and with one foot of the compasses in A sweep an arch, as a b; then take off 76 links from the same large scale the arch was described by, from a to b; then put one foot of the compasses in b, with the extent of 76 links, and make a mark upon the arch at a; draw the line A C through the point a, which will give the angle B A C. Suppose you want to lay off another angle from C towards D, lay that angle off as above directed, and take off 100 links from a large scale, suppose four times larger than you intend to plot the field by, the larger the scale the better; then draw an arch from the point, and make a prick upon the dotted line C A at e; then take off 160 links from the same scale the arch e d was described by; then put one foot of the compasses in e, and bisect the arch in d; lastly, draw a line from the angle C through the point d, and the angle A C D will be formed. Observe, when the fences are measured, that you measure the distance from the hedge to where you stand, on each side of the fences; and if a pole is placed at the same distance from the hedge, it will be exactly parallel. In *Plate* II. *Fig.* 9. an angle was taken with the chain into the middle of the hedge, in the trapezium at A to a and b, and the distance across from a to b was 147; but it is the same thing, and answers the purpose better, to measure parallel with a fence, suppose from 5 to 10 links. The reason of having represented the dotted lines a little from the fence is, that obstructions are frequently met with when the measure is taken close to the fence. All other angles that are taken with the chain are taken in the same way in the field; which insert either upon an eye-sketch or in a field-book.

Plate II. (*Fig.* 13.)

A B C D E F is a field of six sides, surveyed with the chain, the fences of which are all straight. The best method of measuring this field is to divide it into triangles on the spot, which is represented with dotted lines on the figure, and represent the lines that were measured to divide it into four triangles. Begin the measurement at any angle you please, suppose A, and measure to B, which is 1000 links, which insert in an eye-sketch; then measure the fence from B to C, 1500, and from C to D, 650, from D to E, 1200, from E to F, 800, and from F to A, 710, to where you began; all of which distances set down carefully in an eye-sketch or a field-book; then go to A, and measure across the field to D, which is 1420; then measure from D to F, which is 1200; then return to D, and measure to B, which is 1400, which finishes the survey; and insert all the distances in an eye-sketch or a field-book, whichever you choose to keep.

To plot and delineate a plan of Fig. 13. Draw any one of the lines you choose to begin at by random with a black lead pencil, to represent either of the fences or dotted lines across the enclosure. Suppose you begin at A, take 1000 links from a scale of equal parts, and lay off that distance upon the black lead line, which will reach to B; then take the distance 1420 from the same scale, and put one foot of the compasses in A, and describe an arch

c

D; then take the distance of 1400 from the scale, and put one foot of the compasses in B, and bisect the arch in D; then take the distance from D to C, 650, and set one foot of the compasses in D, and sweep an arch at C; then take the distance from B to C, which is 1500, from the same scale and put one foot of the compasses in B; bisect the arch in C; then take 1200 from the same scale, which is the length across the field from D to F, and put one foot of the compasses in D, and sweep an arch at F; then take the distance from A to F, which is 710, from the same scale, and put one foot of the compasses in A, and bisect the arch in F; then take the length from F to E, which is 800, from the scale, and with that extent put one foot of the compasses in F, and sweep an arch at E; then take the distance from D to E, which is 1200, from the same scale, and put one foot of the compasses in D, and cut the arch at E; then draw in the fences A B, B C, C D, D E, E F, and F A, which gives the exact shape of the enclosure, if the lengths are all right measured in the field, and the distances taken exact from the scale of equal parts with the compasses. Let a field consist of ever so many sides, they must all be divided into triangles and trapeziums, either in the field or on a plan, before the area can be obtained.

Plate II. (Fig. 14.)

There are numbers of enclosures that have their sides very crooked and irregular, as *Fig. 14.* Let this enclosure be divided into a triangle, as A B C, whose side A B is 540, the line B C 760, and the side C A 900. Great care must be taken in measuring each line, and taking offsets into all the bends and angles, which are represented by dotted lines. On the figure where they are taken, not only the distance of each offset must be marked by an eye-sketch, but the distance where each offset is taken at. Suppose you begin the measurement at C, at 250, you take an offset to the bend of 50, and at 560 you take another offset of 60, and the length of the line C A is 900. Begin again at A, and measure to B; at 120 an offset is taken of 60, at 250 another is taken of 5 to the fence, at 400 another offset is taken of 80 to an angle in the fence, and the whole distance of the line A B is 540. In measuring the line B C, an offset is taken at 400 of 90,

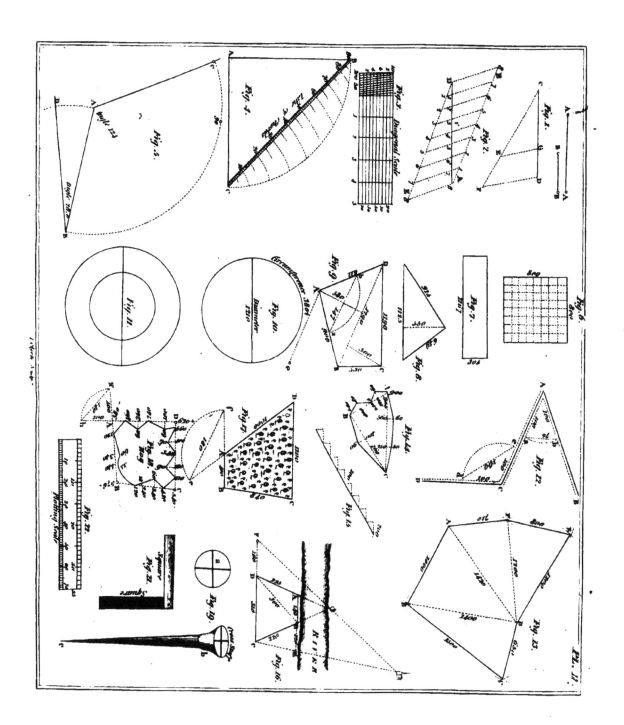

Pl. II.

to an angle in the hedge, and the whole length of the line B C is 760. The above distances being all carefully marked in the field upon a field-book or eye-sketch, it is now to be delineated and laid down by scale and compasses. Draw a line at pleasure to represent the longest side A C with a black lead pencil, and take off the distance 900 from a scale of equal parts, which is the distance from A to C, and make a mark at C and another at A; then take the distance, which is 540, from the same scale, and put one foot of the compasses in A, and describe an arch at B; then take the distance 760 from B to C; put one foot of the compasses in C, and with the other foot bisect the arch at B; then draw the line A B and B C with a black lead pencil, which will form the triangle A B C.

The different offsets are now to be laid off where each of them were taken. Some surveyors, for quickness, use a feather edged scale (see *Plate II. Fig.* 22.); others use a scale of equal parts and a pair of compasses. First, on the line A B, make a mark at 120, another at 250, and another at 400; at 120 lay off the offset 60, at 250 lay off 5, at 400 lay off the offset 80; then draw in the fence to the offset 60, from thence to the offset 5, from thence to the offset 80, and from thence to B, which will give you the boundary line from A to B; then either use the feather-edged scale or a pair of compasses, and prick off 400 upon the line B C, and opposite it prick off the offset 90 to the corner of the fence; then draw in the boundary from B to the offset 90, from thence to C; lastly, lay off 250 and the offset 50; also 560 and the offset 60; then draw in the fence from C to the offset 50, from thence to the offset 60, from thence to A, which closes the inclosure. After inking it in, rub out the black lead lines, and you have the exact shape of the ground, if you have measured the lines correct.

Plate III.

Is the field-book of the farm of *Longlee*, also a plan of said farm, laid down upon a scale of 10 chains in an inch; which plan is made out to give an idea how to measure and plot the farm. The survey was begun at A, and poles placed in A, B, C, and D, exactly in a line; the distances were then measured from A to B C and D, and pits dug in the ground where each pole was placed. It will be proper to observe, that a pit must be dug with a spade at each station, where a pole stood. The poles were then removed from A and B, one of which was placed in E and the other in F, exactly in a line with the poles C and D, and the same line measured forward to E and F. The poles were then removed from C and D; the one was placed in G and the other in H, exactly in a line with F and E, and the distance measured forward to H. The poles were then removed from E and F; the one was placed in I and the other in K, and the line measured forward to I and K, which finishes the first long line. By the above method of measuring, a line may be continued for miles, by letting two poles stand, and advancing the other two poles in the same line. Poles were put up in L and M, and the distance measured from K to L and M. Poles were then placed up at M N O P, all in a direct line, and the distance measured forward to N O and P. The poles were then removed from M and N, the one was placed in Q, and the other in R, in a line with P and O. The pole was then removed from Q, and placed in A, in a line with R Q, and the distance measured forward to A, which makes a closing. Poles were then placed in A T U and V, and the distances measured forward to T U and V, which finishes the line along the road. Poles were then placed in W X Y and Z, and the line continued and measured from V to F, where it joins the first long line from A to K.

Before proceeding farther, I shall now point out the method used in plotting the survey of what is done, and afterwards describe the way how to finish the enclosures.

First draw a line at pleasure, to represent the long line ABCDEFGHIK; and with a pair of compasses prick off the distance 7090, which is the distance from A to K, from a large scale, suppose two chains in an inch, with a pair of large compasses; then take off from the same scale 8000, which is the length of the line K L M; put one foot of the compasses in K, and describe an arch at M; then take off the distance 6450, which is the distance from M to A, and put one foot of the compasses in A, and bisect the arch at M; then, with a sharp pointed black lead pencil, draw the line K L M and the line M N O P Q R A, which will form the triangle A K M; then take off from the same scale 4800, which is the distance from A to F, and make the mark o at F upon the line A K; then take off from the same scale 2620, which is the distance from A to V; put one foot of the compasses in A, and sweep an arch at V; then take 4460, which is the distance from V to F; put one foot of the compasses in F, and bisect the arch in V; then draw the lines A V and V F, which will form the triangle A V F.

All the intermediate distances and offsets, and where the hedges were crossed, having previously been inserted in the field-book, the next thing to be done is to prick off the distances from A to B, A to C, A to D, A to E, A to F, A to G, A to H, and from A to I; make the mark O where each pole was placed, and insert the letter of reference at each mark; do the same upon the other lines; then begin and lay off the offsets taken to the different angles and bends, and prick them all off from the same scale, and also where the hedges were crossed in measuring the different lines.

In measuring the line A K, the road was left 2150, and an offset on the left at 2500 of 430 to g; which distance lay off, and draw in the road 40 wide from A to g; then lay off the distance 3680, where the hedge was crossed between D and E, and draw in that fence from g; then prick off the distance 4820, where the hedge was crossed between F and G; then lay off the distance 6050, where the hedge was crossed at the road, and also 40 for the breadth of the road; and an offset to the river of 110, to the end of the bridge; draw in the fence from the end of the bridge to K, and lay off the distance from K to L, which is 1600; draw in the fence from K to M; then lay off the offset 20 from N to the fence, and make a mark that a hedge goes off, and draw in the fence from M to the mark; then lay off the offset 80 from O; draw in the fence from N to the offset 80. In measuring the line from M to A, the boundary was crossed at 2430, which mark, and also where the hedge was crossed at 3100; and lay off the offset of 150 on the right to the boundary; then draw in the fence from the offset of 80 to where the boundary was crossed; from thence to the offset of 150, taken between P and Q; from thence to where the boundary was touched at 4100; then prick off from the scale 4190, and an offset of 200 to the corner of the boundary; lay off an offset of 180 at R; another of 120 at 5080, another of 270 at 5100, another of

270 at 5310, another of 200 at 5320, and another offset of 200 at 5520, and mark the corner of the boundary; then draw in the crooked boundary from the offset at R, to where the boundary was touched at the sharp angle, from thence to the offset of 20 at A; then draw in the road from A to V, 30 wide. In measuring the line V F, cross the hedge at 15, at the corner of the planting, and prick off an offset of 15 to the river; at 1700 prick off an offset of 10 to the river; at W prick off an offset of 60 to the river; then draw in the river from the road, about two chains wide, to the offset of 60 at W; and prick off 1850, where the hedge was crossed, between W and X; and prick off 3420, at crossing another hedge, between Y and Z.

I now come to show how to finish the measurement of the inclosures. Go to the mark at G, and measure to a, from thence to H, and take the off-sets to the river, and from H measure a diagonal to b, and from H to c, and from c to b, and from b to G, which finishes enclosure II.; then measure a diagonal from K to c and from c to L which finishes enclosure I.; then measure the diagonal from L to N and from N to c, which finishes enclosure III.; then measure the diagonal from c to O, then a line along the hedge from O to b, which finishes the measurement of enclosure IV.; then measure the diagonal from b to P, and measure from P to g, which finishes enclosure V.; then measure the diagonal from Q to C, and measure from C to R, which finishes enclosure VI. and VII. Begin again at Z and measure, and take four offsets to the river, which finishes enclosure VIII.; then measure from X to d, and take three offsets to the river, and measure from d to Y, and take two offsets to the river, which finishes enclosure IX.; then go to B, and measure a diagonal to e, and from e measure to C, also from e to f and from f to B, which finishes enclosure X.; then measure the diagonal from e to V, and from V, by the side of the planting, to f, which finishes enclosure XI.; then measure a diagonal across the yard from T to s; (in measuring that line an offset was taken to the corner of the planting); then measure from S to U, and take the length and breadth of the house at f, which finishes the house, yard, and plantings.

The triangle A K M, and the triangle A V F, being already plotted, I have now to show how to plot the different enclosures. Take the distance B 70, which is the length from G to a, from the scale, and put one foot of the compasses in G, and describe an arch at a; then take 1080, which is the length from a to H, from the scale, and put one foot of the compasses in H, and bisect the arch in a ; then draw in the fence from the mark near G to a ; then lay off the offset 10 at a to the river, also an offset of 100 at 280, likewise an offset of 80 at 540, and the offset of 70 at 900 to the river, and the offset of 130 at H to the river; then draw in the river about two chains wide from the first offset to the others; then take 1700, which is the length of the diagonal from H to b, from the scale, and put one foot of the compasses in H, and sweep an arch with the other foot at b; then take 1170, which is the length from H to c, and put one foot of the compasses in H, and describe an arch at c; then take 1160 from the scale, and put one foot in b, and bisect the arch in c; then draw in the road, 40 wide, from b to c, also the road from c to the bridge, and the fence from b to the mark between F and G, and the fence from the corner of the road at c to L; and if the diagonal answers to 1800 between K and c, it is right, which finishes enclosure I. and II.; then take off from the scale 1700, which is the length of the diagonal from L to N; and if the distance from N to c answers to 1440, it is right; then draw in the fence from the offset at N to the corner of the road near c, which finishes the plotting of enclosure III ; then take 1820 from the scale, which is the length of the diagonal from c to O; if that distance answers, draw in the fence from the offset at O to the road opposite b, which finishes the plotting enclosure IV.; then take from the scale 1590, which is the length of the diagonal b P; if it answers, draw in the road from b 40 wide to g, and also the fence from the mark between P and Q to g, which finishes enclosure V.; then take from the scale 1730, which is the length of the diagonal Q C; if it answers, draw in the fence from R to C, which finishes the plotting of enclosures VI. and VII.; then take 1170, which is the distance from Z to a; at 140 lay off an offset of 110 to the river; at 300 lay off an offset of 100 to the river; at 410 lay off another of 180 to the river; and at 600 lay off another of 290; then draw in the river from one offset to the other, and the river about two chains wide, which finishes the plotting of enclosure VIII.; begin again at X, and take off from the scale 870, which is the distance from

X to d and put one foot of the compasses in X, and sweep an arch at d; then take 860 from the scale, and put one foot of the compasses in Y, and bisect the arch in d; then lay off an offset of 60 at X, also one of 50 at 340, and another of 60 at 600, and draw in the river from offset to offset, from X to d, and from d lay off the offsets taken to Y, which finishes enclosure IX; then take 2150 from the scale, which is the length of the diagonal from B to e, and put one foot of the compasses in B, and describe an arch at e; then take 550 from the scale, and put one foot of the compasses in C, and bisect the arch at e; then take 1300 from the scale, and put one foot of the compasses in e, and sweep an arch at f; next, take 1000 from the scale, and put one foot of the compasses in B, and bisect the arch in f; then take off from the scale 2200, which is the length of the diagonal from e to VI; if it answers, draw in the fence from C to e, from thence to the mark between W and X to the river, and the fences from e to f, from f to V, and from f to B; which finishes the enclosures X. and XI; then lay off from the scale 680, which is the length of the diagonal across the yard from T to S, and put one foot of the compasses in T, and describe an arch to the corner of the planting at S; then take from the scale 480, and put one foot of the compasses in U, and bisect the arch in S; (in measuring from T to S, an offset was taken on the left of 800 at 280 to the corner of the planting, which lay off, and also 200 by 80, the length and breadth of the house); lastly, draw in the house, and also the fences; which finishes the planting and the yard, and also the plotting of the whole; which should be carefully inked in, and the black lead lines rubbed out with a piece of bread or Indian rubber.

Different surveyors have objected to measuring with the chain, and assert, that there are many things that cannot be done with it, such as measuring the horizontal distance of a steep bank, the distance across a wide river, or measuring a plantation that cannot be entered on account of brushwood, brambles, &c. A land-measurer that is well acquainted in measuring with the chain, can overcome all those difficulties, notwithstanding its being more tedious than with a theodolite. I shall now suppose a steep bank is to be plotted upon a horizontal plane, upon paper, which must be done correctly, otherwise it will not join to other parts of a plan.

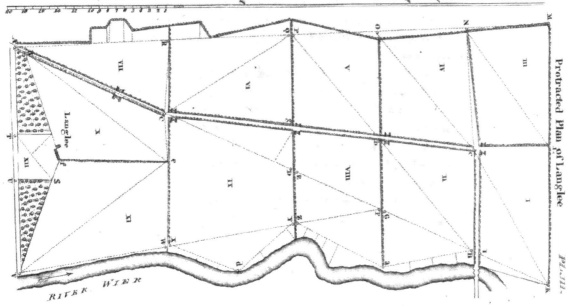

Protracted Plan of Langlee

Pl. III.

Scale of Chains

RIVER WIER

Langlee

Plate II. (*Fig.* 15.)

Represents a steep bank. The method used is by taking a short length. If the bank is not very steep, take half a chain's length; or, if very steep, take 25 links, or less. The foremost chain-man ascends the bank, and the hindmost chain-man takes 25 links, or a quarter of the chain, and orders the foremost man to stick in a pin, while the hindmost man holds the chain as nearly level as he can guess. Some surveyors, who wish to be still more correct, have a plumb, which they allow to hang over a mark, which makes them certain that the hand is exactly over the mark when the chain is held up to the level with the pin stuck in the bank by the foremost man. The plumb is made with a piece of lead with a small cord fastened to it, about seven feet in length, and is held in the same hand that the chain is held with, which the hindmost man carries with him, and observes that the lead always hangs over the pins which the foremost man sticks in the face of the bank. By the figure, it will be observed that there were eight different pins stuck in the bank, which is two chains horizontal measure, whereas the measurement of the slope of the hill is two chains and 40 links. This shows the necessity of plotting plans by horizontal measure. If that measure is not allowed, it gives too little measure for the adjoining fields.

Plate II. (*Fig.* 16.)

Is a river which it is requisite to have the exact width of, and which cannot be measured across on account of its width and depth; and we will suppose the surveyor to have no other instrument but the chain. I shall suppose one of the stations is at A, nearly opposite a tree close by the river side. The method of obtaining the breadth of it is to put a pole in at the station A and another at B, nearly opposite the tree; then go any length you please, and put in a pole at D, exactly in a line with the pole in A and the tree; then put in a pole at C at any distance you please, provided it is in a line with B and the tree on the opposite side of the river. When the poles are all placed, measure the distances from one pole

D

to another, and insert each distance on an eye-draught, and measure a diagonal from A to C, or from B to D. First lay off the distance from A to B 140 links; then take the distance 225 from A to D from the same scale, and put one foot of the compasses in A, and describe an arch at D; then take the length of the diagonal, from B to D, which is 300, from the same scale, and put one foot of the compasses in B, and bisect the arch in D, which fixes that point; then take the distance from B to C, which is 220, and put one foot of the compasses in B, and describe an arch at C; then take the distance from D to C, which is 310, and put one foot of the compasses in D, and bisect the arch in C; then lay a ruler upon the marks C and B, and draw a line across the river from the point C through the point B; then draw another line from the point D through the point A, across the river; and where the one line intersects the other, is the distance across the river to the tree; or if there be any other distance you want to know, suppose the church, which stands a considerable way off the river, continue the line C D 160 to F; then draw a line from F, which is in a line with the tree and the church; produce the line A B to E, and measure to E 120 links; lay a ruler upon C and E, and draw a line towards the church; and the intersection of the other line is the distance from the tree to the church. If you apply a pair of compasses to the tree and the intersection at the church, and lay the extent upon the same scale the rest of the work was plotted by, then you will have the number of chains and links the church is from the tree. Thus it is evident, that inaccessible distances may be ascertained with a chain only.

Plate II. (*Fig.* 17.)

A B C D represents a coppice of wood, which we will suppose very much run over with brushwood and brambles, so that it cannot be measured through. In that case, take an angle with the chain, by measuring 100 links from A to e, keeping yourself in a line with the fence A D, and put in a mark at e; then measure 100 links from A to f. in a line with the fence A B, and measure the distance from f to e, which is 180; then measure on the outside of the wood from A to B, which is 400, and from B to C, which is 840, and from C to D, which is 1100, and from D to A, which is 1000; all those distances being carefully inserted either on an eye-draught or a field-book. To plot the wood, draw a line at pleasure, to represent the line e A D; then put one foot of the compasses in A, and sweep an arch from e to f, after having taken off 100 links from a large scale; then take off 180 links from the same scale, put one foot of the compasses in e, and bisect the line at f; then lay a ruler upon the point of intersection at f and the angle of the wood at A; and draw the fence A B, and with the distance 400 lay off from A to B, by any scale you want to plot the wood by, which you may make much smaller than the scale used for laying down the angle; then take the distance from A to D, which is 1000 links, which lay off upon the line from A to D by the same scale you used from A to B; then take the distance of the line B C, which is 840, and put one foot of the compasses in B, and describe an arch at C; then take the distance from D to C, which is 1100; next, put one foot of the compasses in D, and bisect the arch at C, which gives the exact shape of the wood.

Plate II. (*Fig.* 13.)

Is a very irregular bog or marsh, which is very wet. First put up poles at A B C and D. It is necessary that an angle be taken with the chain, it being impossible to measure a diagonal across the marsh. First measure 100 links to h, in a line with the poles A and D; then measure out 100 links in a line with the pole in A and the pole in B, and put in a mark at g; measure from g to h, which is 140 links; then take the distance from g to h from the scale, and with one foot of the compasses in g bisect the line at h; then lay a ruler upon the point in A and the point g, and draw the line A B; then lay a ruler upon the point h and the point A, and draw the line A D, which forms the angle D A B. The distance from A to B is 576, from B to C 540, C to D 620, and the distance from D to A is 580. Those distances being all laid off from the field-book upon a plan, you have then to lay down the offsets, which you also take from the field-book, in the same way as described in *Plate* II. *Fig.* 14. After all the offsets are pricked off, draw the outline of the bog from offset to offset, all round till it closes, and you will have a plan of it.

Many more examples might be given for taking angles with the chain, and for measuring very irregular pieces of land; but what has been already said on the subject shews, that pieces of land, however irregular, may be measured with the chain, a few poles, and ten pins, without the aid of any other instrument.

ART. II. OF THE CROSS STAFF.

Plate II. (Fig. 19.)

Is the representation of a cross staff; a very simple but useful instrument, and can be easily procured. Some surveyors, particularly in the inland counties of England, have the top very finely mounted in brass; others, that are very partial to this small instrument, have them mounted with plain sights, resembling those on a common theodolite, and prefer it to the best instruments that are made, and use no other. A cross staff, made of boxwood, plaintree, or ash, answers the same purpose as well as those that use them mounted in brass. The circle marked a, with two lines crossing one another at right angles, should be three or four inches in diameter, and sawn across with a common saw about half an inch deep, and about the sixteenth part of an inch wide; b is a socket for fixing the staff to the cross; c is the point of the staff, shod with iron for sticking it in the ground, which must be done at every observation that is taken with it It will be found very useful in taking the perpendiculars to offsets, and for keeping the chainmen in a line between two objects or poles in measuring from one station to another. The cross staff always gives a right angle, and points out exactly that part of the chain when you are opposite any bend or angle to a fence or boundary you want to take an offset to; the angle which the fences make with one another can be ascertained with great precision; and any field, however intricate, can be measured with it and the chain; although in some fields it is more tedious and laborious to measure with, and draw a plan from, the dimensions taken in the field, than either the plain table or theodolite; yet any piece of ground can be surveyed with the cross staff and the chain with great accuracy.

Plate II. (Fig. 21.)

Represents a rectangular square; which is made use of when you protract the survey taken with a cross staff, as by laying one edge of it upon any line, the other edge gives a right angle, or perpendicular, which the cross staff gives in the field ; it is commonly made about eight or nine inches in length, but if longer so much the better.

Plate II. (Fig. 22.)

Is a feather-edged scale, made use of for pricking off distances that are taken in the field when the survey is protracting; which is much quicker than taking off the distances with compasses from a scale of equal parts.

Plate IV. (Fig. 1.)

Suppose you want to take the angle B A E in the field with the cross staff, stick it in at the corner of the fence, and look through one of the slits upon the head of the staff parallel with the fence A B ; then look through the opposite slit, having previously sent one of your assistants forward with a pole a few chain lengths, suppose 500 links; sign to him to move to the right or left hand till you see him ; there cause him to place up a pole at C : measure to that pole : then remove the cross staff, and stick in a pole where it stood at A, and set up the staff at C, where your assistant's pole was placed; look through one of the slits to the pole left at A, and order your assistant to go to the fence A E ; and cause him move to the right or left till you see him through the other slit ; then measure from C to the fence at E, which is 160 links.

To protract that angle upon paper, draw the line A B at pleasure, and apply the square (see *Plate* II. *Fig.* 21.) to the line A B; and draw the line A C, which is perpendicular with A B; with the feather-edged scale, or a pair of compasses, prick off 500, the length from A to C ; then lay one edge of the square upon the line A C, and the other edge at C will give the perpendicular to E ; then lay off the distance from C to E, which is 160, and make a mark at E ; then lay a ruler or the edge of the square upon the angle A and the mark at E, and draw the fence, which gives the angle B A E.

Plate IV. (*Fig. 2.*)

Suppose it is required to take the angle E D H with the cross staff, which is less than a right angle ; stick in the cross staff at any convenient distance upon the fence E D, suppose at G, and measure from G to D, which is 205 links ; look through the sight or slit parallel with the fence D E ; then look through the other slit, and cause one of your assistants to go with a pole towards the fence D H, and cause him to move either to the right or left till you see the pole which he fixes at H ; measure to H, which is 326 ; then upon your paper draw a line at pleasure, to represent the line D E ; then prick off 205 from D to G, and lay the square upon the line D E and the angle of the square at G, and the other edge will be the perpendicular to H ; lastly, draw in the fence from D through the mark at H, which gives the angle E D H.

Plate IV. (*Fig. 3.*)

Is three enclosures measured with the chain and cross staff, and a plan made out of those enclosures.   The cross staff was placed at A, and a distance of 270 links measured into the corner of the fence at e ; another line was measured from A to g 560, the other corner, which is perpendicular with the line A B ; in measuring the line A B, crossed a hedge at 720, and continued the same line to B, which is 1220. The cross staff was set up at B, and a backsight taken to A, and a fore sight taken to C, by looking through one slit to A and the other slit to C, which is perpendicular with the line A B, and the distance measured to C, which is 660.   The staff was set up at C, and a back sight taken to B, and a fore sight to D, which is perpendicular with the line B C; an offset was taken at C of 262 to the corner of a hedge at h.   In measuring the line C D, crossed a hedge at 300, (where a mark was left) ; at 700 an offset was taken of 80 to the corner of a straight hedge, which was crossed on the line A B, and the distance to D is 1120, and an offset of 100 was taken to the fence on the right, and another to the fence opposite of 80; which set down on an eye-draught, as well as all the other offsets and distances that are taken.

Set up the cross staff in D, and take a back sight to C, and a fore sight to E, by looking through the slits, which are perpendicular with the line C D; measure to E, which is 980; then measure to F, which is 1000; from thence to the mark left where you crossed the hedge at 300 on the line C D, which is 870; at F an offset was taken of 100, which is in a line with the line B C. All the above distances being inserted on an eye-sketch, I now have to shew the method of making out a plan from the eye-draught that was kept when the survey was taken.

Draw a line at pleasure to represent the line A B; choose any scale you think proper, suppose two chains to an inch; lay the interior angle of the square upon the point A; and by laying one edge of it upon the line A B, the other edge will give the perpendicular to g; then with a pair of compasses take off 560 from the scale, and lay that distance off from the point A to g; then lay off 270 from A to the corner of the hedge at e; draw in the fence from e to g; then lay off the distance of 720, and make a mark where the line A B crossed a hedge; then lay off 1220, which is the whole distance from A to B; then lay the edge of the square upon the line A B, and the interior angle of it upon the point B, and the other edge will give the perpendicular to C, which draw in with a black lead pencil; then lay off the distance upon the line B C, which is 660, and also the offset of 262 at h to the corner of the inclosure; then draw in the fence from e close by A to B; from thence to h, and lay the edge of the square upon the line B C, and with the other edge draw the perpendicular to D; then lay off the distance by the scale and compasses from C to where the line crossed the hedge at 300, which mark with the point of the compasses, or a black lead pencil; then lay off 700, where an offset was taken to the corner of a hedge of 80, which offset mark; then from the same scale lay off the distance from C to D, which is 1120; and also the offset of 80, and another of 100 to the fence; draw in the fence from the corner at h to g; you also draw-in the fence from the offset at 80 to the mark made at 720 on the line A B, which finishes two of the enclosures; then lay the edge of the square upon the line D C, and the other edge gives the perpendicular to E; lay off the distance from D to E, which is 980; then draw the fence from g to E, and take off with the compasses 1000, which is the distance from E to F, and on E describe an arch at F; then take the distance from the scale from F to the mark left at 300 on the line C D, which is 870; by placing one foot of the compasses in that mark the other will bisect the arch in F; then draw the fence from E to F, and from F to the mark at 300 on the line C D, which finishes the outline of the three enclosures. A short line of 100 was measured from F to i, merely to try how the line corresponded with the line B C; and it was found to be right. The fences ought to be drawn in with ink, and all the pencil lines rubbed out with bread or Indian rubber.

Plate IV. (Fig. 4.)

Represents the farm of Monklaw, which consists of twelve enclosures, measured with the chain and the cross staff. Began at A on the line A B, and a perpendicular taken to F of 400, an offset of 200 at 400 on the line A B to the brook; at 930 a perpendicular was measured to a to the corner of a hedge; in measuring to a crossed the brook or rivulet; at 140 an offset was taken of 120, opposite 880, to a corner of an enclosure; and the whole distance to a is 1420 to the angle of the inclosure No 1. (all of which distances insert in your eye-draught). Returned to 930, and continued measuring the line A B; at 1130 an offset was taken of 100 to the brook, where a hedge goes off, and crossed the brook at 1600; at 1900 crossed a straight fence, where an offset was taken of 220 to the brook, which is the boundary of the farm; at 2405 an offset to the brook of 30, at 2700 one of 170 to the brook; and the whole distance from A to B is 3106, where another offset was taken to the brook of 150. The cross staff was placed at B, and a back sight taken to A and a foresight to C, by looking through one slit to A, and through the other to C, which gives the perpendicular from the line AB to C; at B an offset of 160 to the river; at 830, close by the river Frome, where a fence is crossed upon the line B C, and crosses another hedge at 1620, and an offset of 50 to the river at 2800, another offset of 20 to the river, and the whole distance to C is 3100 (which insert in your field-book or eye-sketch). Again,

1

an offset was taken of 160 to the river at C, and another of 400 to the corner of the river and a fence ; the cross staff was placed at C, and a back sight taken to B, and a foresight or perpendicular to D (which is always known when your assistant is seen through the other slit), where he fixes his pole, by the observer's directions, either to the right or left, till he is exactly perpendicular, when he is desired to stick in his pole. In measuring the line C D a fence is crossed at 200, at 420 an offset of 300 is taken to an angle in the fence, at 620 a perpendicular is taken to the river, which is 1130, and an offset to the fence of 200 ; at 1220 set up the cross staff, and take a perpendicular along the road to the river, which is 1240 ; at 1250 crossed the fence, at 2140 the cross staff is set up, and a perpendicular taken to the river at 330 crosses a fence, and it is 920 more to the river ; at 2400 crosses a fence, and the whole length of the line C D is 3600, which insert, and all other distances that are taken in measuring the different lines ; set up the cross staff in D, take a back sight to C, and a perpendicular to E, also a perpendicular to the river Frome ; crosses a fence at 120, and it is 1070 more to the river, where the fence leaves it ; at D is an offset to the boundary of 280. In measuring the line D E, crosses a fence at 700, where there is an offset of 90 ; crosses another fence at 1400, and an offset 200 taken to the boundary ; the whole distance from D to E is 2700 : fix the cross staff in E, and take a back sight to D, and a perpendicular to F, and measure the distance to F, which is 500, which enter in the eye-draught, and write Closes at F. Set every distance carefully down in the field-book or eye-sketch ; you need not mind whether the eye-sketch is very like the ground, only make it in such a way as to give yourself a just idea of what you are doing, and be careful to make the figures legible, and to mark the offsets distinctly and where they were taken at.

I shall now point out the method of making out a plan from the dimensions taken in the field, and inserted in the field-book ; and afterwards the manner in which the inclosures are to be finished that are not already completed.

The mode of laying off the perpendiculars having been already particularly mentioned in the last three figures, a repetition in what immediately follows would be superfluous.

First, a perpendicular was taken from A to F, and the distance 500 measured to F ; 500 must be taken from a scale of equal parts, and laid off from A to F ; a perpendicular was taken upon the line A B at 400, an off set of 200 to the brook, another at 930 to the corner of a hedge, where the brook was crossed at 140, and an offset taken at 880 of 120 to the corner of a hedge, the whole distance to a is 1420 ; lay all those distances off, also 1130, and the offset of 100 to the brook ; then sketch in the brook with a black lead pencil from F to the offset of 200, from thence to where the brook was crossed at 140, and to the offset of 100 at the corner of the fence ; then draw in the fence from that corner to a, and make a mark ; then lay off 1600 at crossing the brook, and 1900 where the line crossed a straight hedge, and an offset of 220 to the brook ; lay off those distances, and draw in the brook to where it was crossed at 1600, from thence to the offset at 220 ; then lay off 2405, and the offset 80, also the offset of 170 at 2700, and the whole distance from A to B 3106, and the offset of 150 to the brook ; then sketch in the brook from 220 to 80, from thence to 170, and from thence to the offset taken at B to the brook of 150 ; then lay off upon your plan a perpendicular line with the square from B, and lay off the offset to the river of 160, and make a mark where the line crosses the hedge at 830, and draw in the river from 160 to 830, which river is about 150 links wide ; lay off 1620, and make a mark where you crossed the fence and the offset of 50, also lay off 2800 and the offset 20 ; then the whole length of the line B C, which is 3100, and the offsets 160 and 400 ; next, draw in the river from 830 to the offset 50, from thence to the offset 20, thence to 160, and from thence to 400 ; observe the sand bank on the other side of the river opposite the offset of 20, that was taken at 2800 ; from C lay off a perpendicular to D, on the line C D lay off from the same scale 200, where you cross a fence at 420 ; lay off the offset 800 to the fence ; at 620 a perpendicular was taken to the river of 1130, and an offset to the fence of 200 ; draw in the fence from the water to where the fence was crossed at 200, from thence to the angle of the fence at 800 ; then to the offset of 200 taken at 620 ; you may also sketch in the river from the corner of the hedge to the mark left at the river at the end of the perpendicular, which measured 1130; lay off 1220, and a perpendicular to the river, and the distance 1240 along a road which is 20 links wide, and draw in the river from the mark at the end of the perpendicular at 1130 to the mark at 1240; lay off another perpendicular from 2140 to the river, and mark 830 at crossing the hedge, and lay off 920 more to the river; then lay off from the scale 2400 at crossing a hedge, and lay off the whole length of the line from C to D, which is 3600, and the offset 280 to the boundary; lay off another perpendicular from D to the river, which is exactly at where the boundary joins the river; and from the scale take first off 120 where it crosses the hedge, and 1070 more to the edge of the river; you may now draw in the river from the bottom of the road to the mark at 920, from thence to where the boundary joins the river Frome, which is about 150 links wide; [also draw in the fence from 1220 to the offset 330, from thence to 120, and continue that line forward to the boundary, which is 300 beyond where the hedge was crossed; at 120 lay a perpendicular off with the square from D to E, lay off from D 700, where the fence was crossed, and also an offset of 90 to the boundary; then lay off from the scale 1400 at crossing the fence, and an offset of 200 to the boundary; then lay down the whole distance from D to E, which is 2700; you may now draw in the boundary from the river to the hedge at 300, from thence to 280, and from 280 to the offset at 90, from thence to the offset at 200, and from 200 to E; then lay off a perpendicular and the distance 500 from E to F, where the line closes; then draw in the brook to F, which finishes the whole of the outline of the farm. If the distance meets, which it will do if all the distances has been right measured, and the lengths taken exactly from the scale with the compasses, you may rest assured all is right, so far as is done.

I now come to point out how to finish the measurement of the enclosures which were not finished in going round the farm.

First, look out for the mark you left at a, which is in the corner of the enclosure No 1. and walk along that hedge, and put up the cross staff along the fence, and try it several times, till the perpendicular cuts the corner of the fence at b; then measure from the cross staff to a, which is

180, and the distance to b is 740, both of those distances set down on your eye-draught ; then stick up the cross staff near the fence, so as you can see parallel with it as far as the boundary ; if you cannot see the angle of the enclosure at d at the first trial, move yourself along the fence till you do see it ; then measure the distance into b, which is 280, and the perpendicular to the cross hedge at d, which is 1035, insert these distances ; then go to the mark at 1220 on the line C D, and measure up towards the houses, which is 980, to the end of the building, which mark, and also the breadth of the house, which is 30 links, and the breadth of the road 30, and the far end of the house is 1070 ; insert 1275 to the next house, and 1300 to the upper side of it, and an offset of 190, which is its length ; at 1430 crossed a hedge, and at 1820 an offset was taken across the yard of 200 ; at 2200 crossed a hedge, and 3260 is the length of the whole line from the mark at 1220 to the brook ; then go back to the houses, and measure 30 for the breadth of the road, 30 more for the breadth of the house, and 90 for the whole width of the yard, all of which distances being inserted on the eye-sketch.

I now come to point out what way to plot upon the plan the enclosures which were not plotted when the outline of the farm was made. Begin at the corner a in No 1. lay off 180 from a to where a perpendicular was taken, to the cross hedge b ; lay off that perpendicular, and the distance 740 upon it ; then lay off the distance from b, 230, to where a perpendicular was taken to d, which distance, 1035, lay off with the scale ; then lay a ruler upon the points a b and d, and continue that line to the river ; then lay a ruler upon the corner a, and the mark upon the line D E at 1400, and draw that line into the angle of the boundary at 200 ; then lay a ruler upon the point b, and the mark left at 700 on the line D E, which will reach to the boundary at the offset 90 ; lay a ruler upon the point d, and see if it answers the former line ; if it does, this finishes No 1. 2. 3. and 4. ; then draw a line from the house, on the opposite side of the road, at 980 to b, which finishes No 7. ; then draw a line from 1420 above the house, to where the hedge was crossed at 1620, and an offset taken of 50 on the line B C to the river ; then lay a ruler on the point where an offset was taken of 120 at 880, on the perpendicular to a, from the line A B at 980, and draw the fence through the mark where it was crossed on the line B C at 880; this will finish enclosure No 9. 10. 11. and 5. Next, lay off 200 from the scale, from the road at the underside of the house towards b; then draw a line from the offset of 200, that was taken across the yard from 1820, and draw in the line of the yard, which finishes No 6; lay off all the short distances about the houses from the dimensions on the eye-draught, and it is completed. The enclosures 8. and 12. were done when the perpendiculars and offsets were taken on the line C D. After having drawn all the fences, the brook, and river, &c. with ink, rub out all the black lead lines, and you will have an exact outline of your plan.

Particular care should be taken, if the assistants at any time should get hollow into ground, where they may lose sight of the poles (or station staffs). In measuring a long line, which frequently happens, the cross staff being easily fixed in the ground, by looking back to one pole through the slit, and forward to the other from a rising ground, where the poles are both seen, the assistants measure forward to the cross staff till they perceive the poles. This instrument is of great service to land-measurers who make use of a the-odolite, for laying off the perpendiculars in the field, to the bends and angles of fences, which saves them the trouble of inserting the bearing that they otherwise would have to take, had they no cross staff: this instrument invariably gives a right angle. It has another property, that I have frequently found, of saving much time in the field; for example, when I have been using a theodolite, a bush or small height sometimes prevented me from seeing a pole which could not be perceived from one station to another; by ordering one of my assistants to go forward, and put himself in a line with the two poles with the cross staff (which he can soon do, by removing it to the right or left, till both station staffs are seen through the slit), I then measure the distance which is in a line with the pole I am measuring to. More might be advanced in favour of the utility of the cross staff; but what has been already explained is deemed sufficient for an attentive student.

Art. III. Of the Plain Table.

Plate IV. (*Fig. 5.*)

Is the representation of a plain table. A represents the upper side
of the table, 20 inches by 14, upon which a sheet of paper is fixed, containing the representation of a reduced plan of figure 6th. B is a compass box with a magnetic needle, K is the index, and I I the sights, which
are fixed at each end, D is the junction of the legs which support the
table, fastened with three brass screws at the head to keep them together;
but at the same time, not so tight but to allow the legs to move easily
out and in; the head to which the legs are attached is commonly made
of boxwood, the table and legs of mahogany. The paper is fixed to the
table with a frame. C represents the underside of the table, d is a brass
socket fastened with three screws, the socket projecting out about 2 inches,
which goes on to the cone at the top of the legs, and is made fast to them
by the screw e. The index I I is moveable, and only laid upon the view
of the table, to represent the method of using it when an angle is taken;
it is commonly made of brass, about 18 or 20 inches long; the sights are
also of brass, about 5 inches high. From the end of the index, in each of
the sights, there is a small and large aperture, or slit, one over the other.
If the aperture be undermost in one sight, it will be uppermost in the opposite, and *vice versa*. The plain table can be purchased, with all its ap-
paratus, from any of the mathematical instrument makers, from four to
five guineas. The wood work may be made by any carpenter, and the
other work by a brass founder; the magnetic needle may be had at any
of the watch-makers in any sea-port town that are in the practise of re-
pairing mariners compasses; but it is commonly much more complete
when had from a mathematical instrument maker. Surveying by the
plain table is a very expeditious method, as every angle taken is plotted
in the field, and all the distances laid off by scale and compasses, even
the fences may be all drawn with a pencil upon the paper (that is put upon
the table); at the same time, and such lines only might be inked as you wish
to insert upon the plan.

This useful instrument is so simple in itself, that any person with a little practise may survey with it. However, a further explanation, including the method of using it, will be essentially necessary to the young surveyor.

The table is made of a smooth board, in the form of a sheet of demy paper, and sometimes made as large as to hold a sheet of royal. The frame that is made to keep the paper fast upon the table is taken off, and the paper should be made wet with a sponge previous to its being laid upon the table, and the frame put over it, which keeps it tight: when the paper drys, it will be so contracted as to leave it quite smooth upon the table. To keep the frame also fast upon the table, four pieces of brass are fastened to the frame, marked m m m m, which goes through four holes through the frame, and again fastened with four pins, that go through holes made in the four pieces of brass, which keeps the frame fast upon the table: the index is chamfered off on one side like a Gunter's scale. In the lower part of one sight is a vertical or upright slit about an inch and a half in length, and in the other opposite is a wide opening, where a hair, or piece of silk thread, is fixed exactly vertical in the centre of the wide opening, to cut the object when you look through the slit next the eye. In the opposite sight, the slit is made on the uppermost part of the slit, and the wide opening in the undermost part of the sight, and the vertical hair placed exactly in the centre; so that the aperture on one sight is at the lower part in one sight, and *vice versa* at the slit. In general, a few scales, of different sizes, are engraved upon the upper side of the index; any of which you choose you may plot the survey by, as every distance must be laid off by scale and compasses on the spot. The legs of the plain table should be a convenient height to support the table, and made so as to move out and in, which allows the table to be planted high or low to the height wanted. I shall now give one general rule how it ought to be placed at each place it is set up at.

To use the plain table. I. Place the table as nearly horizontal as you can guess, by moving the legs out or in to the height you want it, and turn the table round by the socket, upon the top of the three legs, till the north end of the needle points over the *fleur de lis*, in the compass box. The long way of the table will be always north and south, the short way always east and west; and before an observation is taken, screw the instrument fast with the screw in the socket to the cone at the top of the legs, which should have a strong ferrule put upon it, made of brass at least one sixth of an inch thick, with a groove cut out a little for the screw to go into, which will keep the table from slipping off the ferrule, when it is removed from one station to another.

Plate IV. (Fig. 6.)

Place the table as before directed, and observe that the needle settles over the *fleur de lis;* then screw it fast at A, where you begin; lay the chamfered edge of the index upon the station at A, and look through the sight, and find out the pole placed in E and the hair in the sight to coincide, and draw the line A E with a black lead pencil or the point of the compasses, and lay off the distance from any scale you have fixed upon, which suppose 510 from A to E; you then lift the index, and lay the chamfered edge of the index upon the point A, and take a bearing to B, which you will know when you see the hair in the sight and the pole placed in B to coincide; then draw the line A B, and lay off the distance from the same scale from A to B, which is 1040; you then remove the table from A, and plant it at B; loose the screw e a little that holds the table fast to the legs, and lay the thin edge of the index upon the last line you drew upon the paper, which is the line A B, and take a back sight to A; the longer the lines are drawn the better, as you can lay the index with more exactness upon a long line than a short one. Hold the index fast after it is laid exact upon the line B A, and move the table round till you see the hair in the index and the pole in A to coincide; then screw it fast as before with the screw e, and turn the index; then lay the thin edge of it over the point at B, and when you see the hair in the telescope and a pole placed in C to coincide, draw the bearing, and lay off the distance with the scale and compasses from B to C, which is 720 at every station a bearing or angle is taken at. Before drawing the line, observe that the index has not moved from the line it was laid upon. When you take a back sight while turning the table, if it should lay it upon the line again, look to the back pole, and turn the table till you see the hair and the pole to coincide exactly; then screw the table fast, and lay the cham-

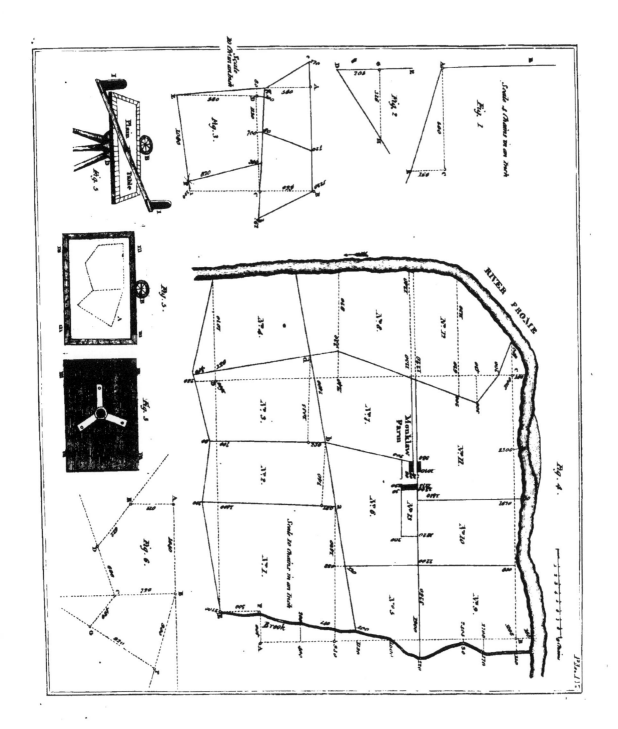

fered or thin edge of the index on the point c; next, move the index till you see, through the sight, the cross hair and the pole in D to coincide; lay off the distance C to D, which is 600, from the same scale the rest of the work is plotted by; again, plant the table up at D, and loose the screw in the socket e a little, and lay the thin edge of the index on the line C D, and take a back sight to C; here screw it fast; next take a bearing from D to E: if it answers, and also the distance to 612, which is the length from D to E, you are certain of having made no error either in measuring the distances, or in taking the angles.

The next thing to be done is to plant the instrument up in B, and lay the edge of the index on the line B A; then turn the table round till you see, through the index, the pole placed in A and the vertical hair in the sight to coincide; screw it fast by the screw in the socket, and the table will be in the same position it was in when it was planted in B as before; you can also know by the needle if it settles over the *fleur de lis*, which it will always do if there are no metallic substances to attract it.

Then lay the thin edge of the index on the point at B, and take a bearing to F, and lay off the distance, which is 900, from B to F; then plant the instrument in F, and lay the thin edge of the index upon the line F B, and turn the table round till you see the pole in B and the hair in the sight to coincide; then screw it fast, and lay the index upon the point at F, and take a bearing to G; then lay off the distance 920 from F to G; again, plant the instrument at G, and lay the thin edge upon the line G F; then take a back sight to F, by turning the table round till you see the hair and the pole in F to coincide; then screw it fast, and lay the thin edge of the index to the point G, and take a bearing to C; measure the distance from G to C, which is 480: if the angle and distance agrees it is what is generally termed an exact closing. From what has been now explained, it is presumed the method of taking the bearings and placing the table up at the different stations will be easily comprehended; great care, however, must be taken to place the table as nearly level as possible, and the centre of the legs immediately above the holes the poles were placed in at each station. The plain table, by using it in the manner above, has an advantage that no other surveying instrument has.　If an error has been committed in taking either a bearing or a wrong distance from the scale, the work will not meet.　A good method to correct an error is to leave a pole or mark of any kind at any of your stations; by applying the thin edge of the index to that mark and the station you stand at, and looking through the sights to it, the needle will° settle over the *fleur de lis* in the compass box, if no error has been committed.　If an error has been made, the needle will settle over some other of the degrees in the compass box, which should be corrected before you go farther.

Plate V.　(*Fig.* 1.)

Is an enclosure where all the angles are seen from the point C which can be measured, and a plan made of the same without moving the table from the spot where it is placed.　Suppose the angles D E F G H are all seen from the point C; place the table up at C as horizontal as you can, loose the screw a little that is in the socket at e, and turn the table round upon the head of the legs that support it, till the needle in the compass box settles over the *fleur de lis*; then screw the table fast to the head of the legs, and lay the thin edge of the index at the point C; then look through the sight or slit next your eye, till the vertical hair in the sight opposite is in a line with the angle D; measure the distance to D, which is 490; take that distance from the scale, suppose half an inch to a chain, and lay it off upon the bearing, and make a mark at D with a black lead pencil; then lay the thin edge of the index on the point C, and look through the sight next the eye, till the hair in the other sight is seen to be in a line with the angle E, and order your assistants to measure from E to C, which is 780; next, lay that distance off upon the bearing line at E, and make a mark; then lay the index upon the point C, and look through the sight next the eye, till the hair in the other sight coincides with the angle at F; draw that bearing, and measure the distance to F, which is 440; lay off that distance from the scale, and make a mark at F; then lay the edge of the index upon the point C, and look through the sight in the index till you see the hair and the angle G to coincide; then cause your assistants to measure from G to C, which distance is 550; lay that distance off upon the line, and make a mark at G; then lay the index upon C, and look through the sight till you see the hair in the other sight and the angle at H to coincide; draw in the bearing, and measure to H, which is 530; lay off that distance, and make a mark at H; lastly, draw in the fences from D to E, E to F, F to G, G to H, H to D, and D to E, which will give a plan of the enclosure; then ink in the fences, and rub out all the bearing lines with Indian rubber.

Plate V. (*Fig. 2.*)

Represents an enclosure of nine sides, to which four angles are taken at the point A, and five at B; also a line measured from A to B, a plan may be made on the spot.

First plant the table at the station A, and set it as level as possible, which you can nearly guess; when the needle traverses with freedom in the compass box, turn the table gently round till the needle settles over the *fleur de lis*; then take bearings from the station A (as directed *Plate V. Fig.* 1.) to E F G and H; measure the distances to those points, and lay them off from a scale, suppose from A to E 870, A to F 600, A to G 690, and from A to H 360.

These distances being all laid off, draw in the fence from E to F, F to G, and from G to H; then take a bearing to B, and lay off the distance 770; then plant the table at the station B, and take a back sight to A; after laying the thin edge of the index upon the line A B, look through the sight next the eye till you see the vertical hair in the opposite sight on the index to coincide with the pole left in A; here screw the table fast, and draw lines from the point B to the angles I K L M and N, and measure all the distances, and lay each distance off from the same scale as those laid off from the point A to their respective angles, *viz.* 180 from B to I, 601 from B to K, 650 from B to L, 850 from B to M, and 470 to N; lastly, draw in the fence from H I, I K, K L, L M, M N, and N E, which will give a true representation of the enclosure of nine sides, which should be drawn in with ink, and the pencil lines rubbed out.

Plate V. (*Fig.* 3.)

Represents a garden with a fish-pond in the middle of it. To survey this, plant the table up at A, and adjust it as before mentioned, and take a bearing to B, and lay the thin edge of the index to the point A, and look through the sight till you see the hair in the opposite sight and the pole in B to coincide; measure the distance from A to B, which is 110, and lay it off from the scale you choose to adopt, and also an offset of 50 to the pond, another of 20 on the right, and another on the left of 10 to the edge of the walk; which also lay off. Before moving the table, take a bearing to D; in measuring that line, opposite 100 you have an offset of 18 to the pond, and another to the edge of the walk of 13, and the distance to D is 200; all of which lay off upon the plan, and draw in with a black lead pencil part of the pond, and also the walk from B to D. Before removing the table take a bearing to E; then plant the instrument up at D, and take a back sight to A; then take a bearing from D to C, and another up the walk to H, and measure the line D C, which is 140, which distance lay off, and also an offset of 15 to the pond, and another offset of 15 to the edge of the walk taken at 70 in measuring the line D C; then plant the instrument at C, and take a back sight to D, and screw the instrument fast, and take a bearing up the walk to G, and another to B; in measuring that line at 100, an offset was taken of 10 to the pond, and another of 20 to the edge of the walk; prick off these distances, and also the distance from C to B, which is 200; then draw in the pond, and also the walk round it; you then go to A, and measure up the walk from A to E, which is 280, and the breadth of the walk 26; prick off these distances upon the plan, and draw in the walk from A to E; then place the instrument at E, and take a back sight to A; screw the table fast, and take a bearing to H and another to F; measure the distance to H, which is 630, and take an offset to the front garden wall, which is 60, and 40 to the garden wall on the right. In measuring that line, you was opposite a walk at 310 fronting the hot house; lay off these distances, and also the length and breadth of the hot house, which is 100 by 40; then draw in upon the plan the wall from E to H, also the hot house, and the walk on that side of the garden, which is 26 wide; then measure from E to F, which is 446, and an offset to the garden-wall at E, which is 40, and another offset of 40 at F; prick off these distances on the plan, and draw in the garden-wall from E to F, and also the walk, which is 26 wide; remove the instrument to F, and take a back sight to E; here screw it fast, and take a bearing down the walk from F to B; if it answers it is right, if it disagrees it must be rectified before any more is done, by going back till you find out the error. Next, take a bearing from F to G, and measure the distance, which is 630, and take an offset of 40 at F, and another of 40 at G, and draw in the garden-wall from one offset to the other, and also the walk 26 wide; then plant the instrument up at G, and take a back sight to F; then screw the table fast, and take a bearing to where the pole stood in C; if it answers, there is no occasion for measuring from G to C. Next, take a bearing to where the pole stood in H, and measure to H, which is 447; if the bearing and distance answers, the garden-wall may now be drawn in, and also the walks 26 wide, from the offset at G of 60 to the offset at H of 60, which finishes the plan; which should be inked in, and the black lead lines rubbed out. For want of room on the copper, I have been under the necessity of using small scales; but it is presumed, that, being merely for explanation, they will be understood equally well. It will not be improper to remark, that the larger the scale the work is plotted from (particularly when the figure is complex), it renders the less confusion in the multiplicity of lines; it also admits of the figure (however complicated) being protracted with facility; besides, there is another advantage; very minute parts of a plan may be represented on the large scale, which the small one would not admit of. For making out a drawing of a garden, See *Plate 35*.

Plate V. (*Fig.* 4.)

Represents a very crooked lake, which, for want of more room, is contracted to a very small scale of only ten chains to an inch. Plant the table at A, and adjust it as before, and take a bearing to B, and measure the distance 60 to the lake, and also 140 where the chain touches the edge of the water, and the distance to B 285; prick off those distances, and plant the instru-

ment up at B, and take a back sight to A, and lay off 80, the distance
that B is from the lake; then draw in the edge of the lake from the offset 60 to where the chain touched the water at 140, from thence to the
water opposite B; take a bearing to C, which should be drawn a considerable way past C, for the purpose of laying the thin edge of the index
correct upon the line; when a back sight is taken, all other bearings
should be done in the same way as is represented in *Plate* IV. *Fig.* 6. or ·
in *Plate* V. *Fig.* 5. In measuring from B to C at 200, the chain touches
the water, and the distance to C is 450, and an offset of 80 to the lake;
lay off these distances, and draw the outline of the lake from the offset at
B to where the water was touched at 200, from thence to the offset of
80; then place the table at C, and take a back sight to B; screw the table fast, and take a bearing to D; in measuring from C to D, the chain
touched the water at 280, and an offset was taken at 400 of 60, and again
was close by the lake at 500, and the distance to D is 590, and the distance from D to the lake is 60; then lay off all these distances, and draw
in the outline from the offset at C to where the water was touched at
280, to the offset 60, from thence to the mark at 500, and from thence to
the offset opposite D; then remove the instrument to D, and take a back
sight to C, and a foresight or bearing to E; in measuring from D to E,
touches the lake at 200, and the distance to E is 500, and an offset to E
to the lake is 80; lay off these distances, and draw in the outline of the
lake from the offset opposite D, to where the chain was nearest the lake,
from thence to the offset of 80; shift the table to E, and take a back sight
to D, and a fore sight to F, the chain touches the lake at 220, and the
distance to F is 400; lay off these distances, and draw in the outline
from the offset E to 220, from thence to the offset of 60, opposite F; then
plant the table at F, and take a back sight to E, and a bearing or fore
sight to G; in measuring that line, the chain was near the lake at 220,
and the whole distance to G is 430, and an offset of 90 to the lake; draw
in the outline of the water to the offset of 90; remove the table to G,
take a back sight to F, and a fore sight to H; in measuring the line from
G to H, touched the lake at 170, and the whole distance to H is 400, and
an offset taken from H to the lake is 50; lay off these distances, and draw

1

in the outline of the lake from the offset 90 to 170 ; from thence to the offset of 50, opposite H ; then place the table at H, and take a back sight to G, and take a bearing to I. Observe if the needle settles over the *fleur de lis* ; if it does, you may measure the line from H to I ; if it should not settle exactly over the *fleur de lis,* you must go back and find out the error, which you will soon accomplish by taking a few observations back. In measuring the line H I, the chain touched the lake at 130, nd the distance from H to I is 300, where an offset of 70 was taken to the lake ; draw in the outline from the offset taken at H to 130, from thence to the offset of 70 ; plant the instrument up at I, and take a back sight to H and a fore sight to K, which is 450, where an offset was taken of 80 ; lay off these distances, and draw in the outline of the lake from the offset opposite I to the offset opposite K ; the instrument is then placed at K, and a back sight to I, and a fore sight to L : in measuring that line, the chain touched the lake at 200, and the distance from K to L is 510 ; lay these distances upon the plan, also the offset of 100 to the lake, and draw in the outline of the water from the offset opposite K to 200, from thence to the offset of 100 ; then plant the instrument at L, and take a back sight to K, and a fore sight or bearing to M : in measuring that line, the chain was close upon the lake at 200, and the whole distance to M is 530, and an offset taken from M to the lake is 65 ; these distances being laid down, draw in the outline of the lake from the offset of 65, opposite L, to 200, and from thence to the offset of 65 opposite M ; next, plant the table at M, and take a back sight to L, and a fore sight to N ; in measuring that line, the chain touches the edge of the lake at 430, and the length of the line to N is 660, and an offset to the lake is 70 ; lay off these distances, and draw in the outline of the lake from the offset of 65, opposite M, to 200, where the chain touched the water, from thence to the offset of 70, opposite N. Again, take the instrument to N, and take a back sight to M and a fore sight or bearing to O : in measuring that line, the chain touches the lake at 230, and the length of the line to O is 460, where an offset is taken of 80 to the water ; lay off all these distances on the plan, and draw in the outline of the lake from the offset of 70, opposite N, to 230, where the chain touches the water to the offset of 80, opposite O ; then with the instrument at O take a back sight to N and a fore sight to P : in measuring that line, the chain touches the lake at 200, at 280 an offset is taken to the lake of 80, and the whole distance to P is 510, where an offset of 40 is taken to the lake ; lay off these distances, and draw in the outline of the lake from the offset of 80, opposite N, to where it touches the water at 200, from thence to the offset of 80, taken at 230, and also to the offset of 40, opposite P ; then plant the table at P, and take a back sight to O and a fore one to A, where the survey began. In measuring that line, the chain was close by the lake at 330, and the whole distance from P to A is 410. If the bearing from P to A and the distance agrees, you may rest satisfied no error has been made. Lastly, draw in the outline of the lake from the offset of 40 opposite P to where the chain touches the edge of the lake to the offset taken at A, which will finish the plain table plan of the lake.

Now, if the angle and distance had not met in A at the last station, it is evident that some mistake had been made ; in that case, it shews the absolute necessity of leaving marks at each station. It is in general done with three small stones laid about the holes the poles stand in ; and when stones are not at hand, some surveyors get a few wooden stakes made, and stick one in each hole where they had a station, and others carry a spade, and make a mark. The best way of correcting the error (should one have been committed) is to measure back, and set up the table as before till it is found out. If the error has been made in taking a bearing, the needle will point it out ; as, in that case, it will not settle over the *fleur de lis* in the compass box ; and if a mistake has occurred in measuring a distance, it will not agree with the extent laid off upon the plain table sheet.

Plate V. (Fig. 5.)

To survey a road, &c. with the plain table. The Plate represents a serpentine road or gravel walk, and supposed to be in the midst of a plantation, from No. 1. to No. 10. ; also from No. 10. to No. 17. a crooked river. Plant the table at No. 1. and having adjusted it, begin near the edge of the paper, and first draw a bearing to a pole placed in 2. (with a black lead pencil), which line should be a considerable length, in order to place the index exact upon the bearing when a back sight is taken ; measure from No. 1. to 2. which is 530 links, which take from any convenient scale. Before proceeding further, I must remark, that to enumerate every distance and offset that is necessary to be taken in this survey, would only render the business very complex ; but by omitting such a multiplicity of figures as the explanation would require, it will appear very plain. However, I will refer the pupil to the method used in the explanation, *Plate* IV. *Fig.* 6. *p.* 40. To proceed, plant the table to No. 2. and take a back sight to No. 1. ; then take a fore sight or bearing to No. 3. ; measure those distances, which lay off upon the plan, and also at what distance the chain reached when it was nearest the edge of the road ; then remove the table to No. 3. and take a back sight to No. 2. and a fore sight to No. 4. ; lay off that distance, and also the distance to where the chain was nearest the edge of the road, also the breadth of the road ; then set up the table at No. 4. and take a back sight to No. 3. and a fore sight to No. 5. ; lay the distance off, and likewise the distance to where the chain was nearest the edge of the road ; again, go to No. 5. and take a back sight to No. 4. and a fore sight to No. 6. and lay down that distance, together with the distance the chain was at nearest the road ; then go to No. 6. and take a back sight to No. 5. and a fore sight to No 7. ; lay off that distance on the plan, also the distance the chain was at when nearest the edge of the road ; then go to No. 7. and take a back sight to No. 6, and a fore sight to No. 8. ; measure the distance, and lay it off, also where the chain reached when nearest the road ; next, go to No. 8. and take a back sight to No. 7. and a fore sight to No. 9. ; measure that distance, which lay off upon the plan and the distance the chain was at when nearest the edge of the road ; examine the needle ; if it settles over the *fleur de lis* it is a proof of your having taken all the bearings right : again, lastly, go to No. 9. and take a back sight to No. 8. and a fore sight to No. 10. and lay down the distance, and also the extent to where the chain touched the edge of the road, which will finish the survey of the serpentine road. You should now draw in the road from all the different distances that were laid down, and you will have a representation of all the bendings and windings of the road through the wood.

How to survey the river. Place the table at No. 10. and take a back sight to No. 9. and a fore one to No. 11.; from No. 10. take also a bearing to a tree on the opposite side of the river; measure to No. 11. and lay off the distance with an offset at No. 10. and mark when the chain was at the edge of the river, noting the distance from No. 11. to the river; these distances being all marked, sketch in the river from the offset at 10. to that at 11. and the river 120 links wide; then go to No. 11. and take a back sight to No. 10. and a fore sight to No. 12.; measure that line, and lay off the distance, also the distance where the chain touched the river and the offset to the river at No. 12.; then draw in the river from the offset at No. 11. to where the chain touched the river, from thence to the offset taken at No. 12.; at No. 11. taking a bearing to the tree that was seen from No. 10. where these lines intersect, gives the distance to the tree; take also a bearing from No. 11. to another tree; then go to No. 12. and take a back sight to No. 11. and a bearing to the tree that you observed from No. 11. the intersection is the distance to that tree; next, take a bearing at No. 12. to No. 13. In measuring that line, mark where the chain touches the edge of the water, also where an offset is taken, and the length of that offset, also the whole distance to No. 13. You may now sketch in that side of the river from the offset at No. 12. to the offset taken between No. 12. and 13. Note, in measuring up one side of a river, many objects may be seen, such as a large stone, a bush, or any other mark. If you take a bearing from one station to each of the objects on the opposite side of the river, they may all be intersected by taking bearings from other stations. These intersections give the exact width of the river, which draw in upon the plan from one intersection to another. Again, go to No. 13. and take a bearing and distance to a, also take a bearing from No. 13. to 14. and from 14. to the river, in a line with the last tree that was intersected, also some offsets; then draw in the river from the offset taken upon the line between 12. and 13. from thence the one taken on the right hand near the river on the line between 13. and 14. from thence to the mark opposite the tree, and thence to No. 14. and from No. 14. to the point made upon the offset that was taken to the left hand from the line between No. 13. and 15. thence to a, and also from a to No. 13.; take next a bearing from No. 13. to 15. and measure the line to 15. and an offset to the river; lay off these distances, and draw in the river from No. 13. to the offset at the river at No. 15.; again, with the instrument at No. 15. take a back sight to No. 13. and a fore sight to No. 16. In measuring that line, note where the chain touches the edge of the river, and also the distance to No. 16. and an offset; lay off these, and draw in the river from No. 15. to where the chain touches the edge of the river; from thence to the offset taken at No. 16.: go to No. 16. and take a back sight to No. 15. and a bearing to No. 17. In measuring that line, mark where the chain touches the river, also the distance where offsets were taken, and the distance to No. 17. and all the offsets between No. 16. and 17; next, draw that side of the river from the offset at No. 16. to where the line touches the river; from thence from one offset to another to No. 17. In measuring the different stations, care must be taken to intersect as many objects at the edge of the river on the opposite side as you can conveniently take, for the purpose of ascertaining its breadth, and drawing it upon the plan; the distance from one intersection to another, is the width. In taking a survey, such as *Plate* V. *Fig.* 5. the surveyor should observe the needle frequently, to see that the north end of it settles over the *fleur de lis*, which (as I have before observed) it will do if the bearings and distances have been all right taken, and provided there is no attractive substance near. The reason of taking a back sight at every station is merely to prevent any mistake that the needle would cause, if it was influenced by attraction. If a land-measurer could trust to his needle, the plain table might be only placed at every alternate station. When all is planned upon the plain table sheet it ought to be inked in, and the multiplicity of black lead lines that are drawn rubbed out.

Plate V. (*Fig.* 6.)

Represents a small town, surveyed and planned upon the spot with the plain table.—This is performed much quicker than by any other method yet known, even with the most costly instruments, as it spares the trouble of protracting and laying off distances and bearings in the house, which a surveyor is constrained to do, if he uses either a circumferenter, sextant, or theodolite ; and although it takes longer time in the field, yet very little time in the house is necessary, as a land measurer has only to ink in the plan drawn upon the table on the spot.

To take the survey (and plan) of a town. (See *Plate* V. (*Fig.* 6.) This is tedious, and requires great care, patience, and attention. It will be proper to observe, that the table must be set up at every spot where bearings are to be taken, to the angles and corners of houses, &c. which are represented by dotted lines ; each of which is measured, as well as the station lines : For example, on the line A D, the table was erected sixteen different times before the observations were finished on that street, and measurements taken, not only to the corners of houses, but also to all the projections, and the distances all pricked off upon the spot (with the scale and compasses). This I have inserted, merely to give an idea of the labour to be expected in taking the survey of a barony or domain, most baronies having a village belonging to them.

Suppose then the measurement is to begin at A, take bearings to a pole placed at C ; then along the street to one at D, and another to B. In measuring from A to B, lay off the distance to the corner of the house; also the length and breadth, which is taken with the offset staff or a tape; then lay off the whole distance to B, and leave a mark ; return to A, and measure to C. In measuring that line, mark the distance to the corner of the house, also the length, and take the breadth ; also lay off the distance from A to another house, where a garden wall goes off, and also the length and breadth of that house, and the distance to C; all of which distances being laid down, draw in the houses and the garden walls. In measuring the line A D, at every place the table is erected lay off the distance, and lay the chamfered edge of the index upon the bearing line A D, and turn the table round till the cross hair, and the pole placed in D coincide, and *vice versa*; let the index remain, and turn yourself to the other sight, and take a back sight to A. If the hair and the pole left in A coincides, you are certain that the table is exactly on the line betwixt A and D. At every station observe that the back and fore poles are in a line with A and D. Should this not be the case, move the table till you perceive they are so : Take

5

bearings from all the stations to the corners of houses, and lay off the distance to where it is placed from A; then measure the length of all the short distances to the corner of the houses, and lay these distances down upon the plan; then draw in (with a black lead pencil) the front line of each house, as you proceed from one place to another. In many places you can determine the breadth of the houses taken, particularly to those that project, which should be laid down upon the plan and by measuring, taking the bearings and laying off the distances from each station, also those distances taken with the tape, upon the plan, to all the corners of houses on both sides of the street, which will enable you to draw in the whole length of the street from A to D; then set up the table at D, and take a back sight to A; screw the table fast, and take a bearing to F and another to E. Observe to set up the table opposite where angles are taken, and the distance laid off from D to every station; also all the short distances to the divisions of houses must be pricked off from the scale, and drawn upon the plan till you measure to E; which distance being laid down, leave a mark; then plant the table at E, and take a back sight to D, and a fore sight or bearing to C. In measuring that line, mark the distance to the corner house of the street, and also where the first garden wall goes off, and take bearings, and lay off all the distances upon the plan; erect the instrument at the corner of each garden, and lay off the breadth of each as you proceed; take a bearing along the garden walls, and prick off every distance upon the plan and the bearings, which is soon done by placing the instrument opposite to each; next, take a back sight to E, or a fore sight to C, and lay off the whole distance from E to C. If the distance meets in a point at C, it is a proof that the measure is right; then draw in all the gardens (and if necessary distinguish each by inserting the occupier's name); and if any omission has been made, it must be rectified afterwards; again, return to D, and measure the line D F; set up the instrument wherever you see it necessary, marking the distance from D to where it stands, and take offsets to all the different houses, and lay off the distances upon the plan the whole way to F as you go on; which will give the length of each house both on the right and left; then draw in upon the plan the fronts of the houses on both sides of the street, distinguishing each house by-making a short line betwixt it and the next, till the breadth of the houses is ascertained: Again, with the table at F take a back sight to D and a bearing to H, also one to G. In measuring from F to G mark the distance to the corner of the house, also the breadth, and take a bearing along that side next the gardens, which ascertains the width of the houses on that side; then go to G, and take a back sight to F and a fore sight to E. In measuring to E lay off every distance from G, where the gardens go off, and take bearings by looking through the sights of the index along each of them as you proceed to E. Observe to let the chain always lie stretched on the ground, that you may count the odd links as well as the chains, where each bearing is taken, and lay off all the distances as you go on to E; which lay down upon the plan, and the distance to E. If it agrees, what is done so far is right. Return to F, and measure to H, and lay off the distance; Set up the table at H, and take a back sight to F and a fore sight to I. In measuring to I, lay off the breadth of each garden or yard as you proceed, and take bearings of each as before directed; then go to I, and take a back sight to H and a fore sight down a narrow lane; measure the length and breadth of the lane; return to I, and take a bearing to B. In measuring that line, take a bearing along the yards, and also offsets where they occur, and note the breadth of each yard or garden till you come to another lane, which should be measured as far as the street and the length and breadth of the houses. Proceed all the way to B, and be particular in pricking off all the offsets (the gardens being very irregular on this side), and lay off the distance from I to B. If it answers, it is right. Ink in the plan upon the table as carefully as you can. If any thing is omitted, such as the breadth of houses, &c. you must return, and measure them, and lay off the distances, and insert them on the plan. When all the outline is done, rub out all the black lead lines, and write in the name of every proprietor or occupier in every yard or garden. Observe, that the dotted lines that are inserted in the sketch are merely to show where bearings were taken and distances measured.

Plate V. (*Fig.* 7.)

Represents three enclosures, containing three plantations, a moss, a bog,

3

and a pond, measured and planned with the plain table.—The table was set up at A as level as possible ; and being adjusted, a bearing was taken to the far corner of the plantation, the distance to which is 500 links ; lay that distance off upon the plan ; another bearing was taken to H, and a distance measured of 1010, and an offset of 10 ; on the right at H a line was drawn from the corner of the plantation to the offset of 10 at H ; another bearing was taken from A to B. In measuring that line, an offset was taken of 170 at 350, to the angle in the plantation, which lay off, and the distance to B 780 ; then draw the fence from A to 170, from thence to B. The table was then taken to B, and a back sight taken to A ; also a bearing, with a distance of 160, taken to the low corner of the plantation, and a line drawn from the upper corner to the under corner ; which finishes the plantation : a bearing was taken from B to C. In measuring that line, an offset was taken of 130 at 1130 to the corner of a round planting, and the distance from B to C 1300. The fence is drawn in from B to the offset of 130 ; from thence round to C. The instrument was then taken to C, and a back sight taken to B, and a bearing to H close by the hedge. In measuring from C to H, a moss goes off at 200, and the distance to H is 560. Draw in the fence ; which finishes the first enclosure. Again, a bearing was taken from C to D. In measuring that line, an offset was taken of 130 at 120, to the corner of a round plantation ; and the distance from C to D is 1600 : draw the fence from C to the offset of 130 round, and from thence to D. The table was then set up at D, and a back sight taken to C, and a fore sight to E, and another bearing to G. In measuring the line D G, a planting goes off from the fence at 170 and at 500 : the chain is opposite the far side of the planting, and the distance to G is 950 : draw in the fence from D to G. In measuring from D to E, an offset is taken of 130 to an angle in the fence at 260, and at 380 the chain touches the angle of the planting. Lay off that distance, and draw that line of the planting in from the mark where it went off on the line D G ; erect the table at the end of the plantation, by laying the index upon the line D E, and looking through the sight till you see the pole in E and the hair to coincide, and take a bearing along the plantation, and lay off the distance, which is 400 ; then draw in the line of the planting to the other mark, where it went off on the line D G, and it is finished.   Again, return back, and continue to measure the line D E, where an offset was taken of 150 at 990 and at 1180, another on the right hand to a bog of 200, and the chain touched the edge of the bog at 1330 ; and the length of the line from D to E, where there is an offset of 40, is 1580 : draw in the fence from D to the offset of 130 ; from thence to the offset of 150 ; thence to the offset of 40 at E ; set up the table at E, and take a back sight to D, and a fore sight to F.   In measuring that line, take a bearing to the bog, and lay off the distance 100 ; set up the instrument at 490, and take a bearing ; then lay off the distance 210 ; take another bearing to the same bog, and lay off the distance, which is 200.   You may now draw part of the bog in from where you took the first offset to it on the line D E ; from thence to where the chain was nearest to it, from thence to 100, 210, and 200 : an offset of 190 was taken to the angle in the fence, where the instrument was placed at 490 ; an offset was taken of 130 at 720, and the whole length of the line E F 900 : draw in the fence from the offset of 40 at E to the angle at 190 ; from thence to F ; then plant the instrument at F, and take a back sight to E and a fore sight to G.   In measuring that line, an offset was taken of 130 at 200, and another of 200 at 320.   Draw in the bog to where these offsets are pricked off on the plain table sheet ; from thence to the first offset that was taken to it on the line D E, and the bog is finished.   Continue measuring the line to G, which is 1098. Plant the instrument in G, and take a back sight to F ; then lay the index upon the line G D : if it answer, you are certain of having performed the work right.   Take a bearing to H.   In measuring that line an offset of 160, at 330, and at 1450, you enter upon the moss, and the whole distance from G to H is 1970 ; draw in the fence from F to the offset of 160 to the offset at 10 at H, which closes the outline of the enclosures ; then return to the mark left on the line G H at 1450, where the instrument is set up, and a bearing taken to a pole placed at the corner of the moss, and a distance laid off upon the plan to the corner of 310 ; measure from thence to the fence C H, and lay off the distance, which is 450, to the point : this finishes the moss.   The next thing to be done is to go to the old mark D, and plant the instrument, by laying the chamfered edge of the index upon

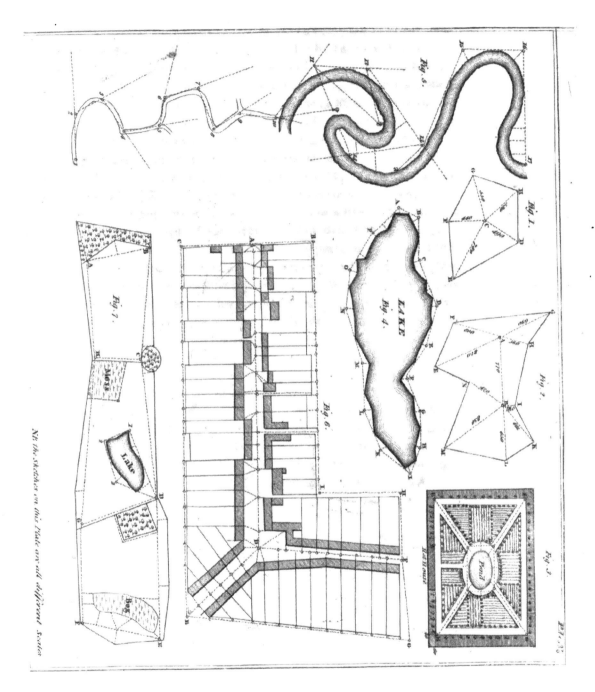

Fig. 5.

Fig. 1.

Fig. 2.

LAKE
Fig. 4.

Fig. 6.

Fig. 7.

Lake

Bog

Moss

Pond

Fig. 3.

Nb. the Sketches on this Plate are all different Scales

Pl. 1. 3.

the line G D, and take a bearing to No. 1. In measuring that line, take an offset of 190 to the lake at 220, at 450 touched the lake; another was taken of 40 at 690; and the whole distance from D to No. 1. is 850; those distances being all laid off, draw in part of the lake from the offset 190 to where the chain touched the water, from thence to the offset of 40, and thence to No. 1.; plant the table at No. 1. and take a back sight to D, and take a fore sight to No. 2. measure the distance from No. 1. to No. 2. which is 330, and an offset of 20; draw in the outline of the lake from No. 1. to 2.; then go to No. 2. and take a back sight to No. 1. and a fore sight to No. 3. at 200. In measuring that line, the chain was contiguous to the lake, and the distance to No. 3. is 530, and an offset to the water from No. 3. is 100; draw in the lake from the offset of 20 to where the chain was contiguous to the water; from thence to the offset of 100, opposite No. 3. Place the table at No. 3. and take a back sight to No. 2 and a fore sight to D. In measuring that line, the chain touches the water at 270, and the distance to D 500; lastly, draw in the lake from the offset of 100 to where the chain touched the water at the first offset taken from D to No. 1. which will finish the survey of the three enclosures.

What has been said in this and the preceding pages, with a careful inspection of the sketches in *Plate* V. is presumed sufficient to explain the common use of the plain table. I have now to point out the inconveniences, or rather defects, pertaining to this instrument, for in fact no instrument yet invented possesses all the requisite advantages for surveying and plotting, some being advantageous in one point, while counterbalanced by inconveniences (more or less) on the other. In the first place, the plain table can only be used in fair weather; and as every thing is laid down and plotted on the spot, it takes a considerably longer time in the field than any other instrument; yet, on the other hand, it gives much less labour in the house. Although the weather should be fair, yet the paper expands in a damp day; and if made use of when damp, the distances (being all laid off upon the spot) will become a little too short when the paper shrinks to its natural size; besides, the plain table is not a fit instrument for taking the measurement of an extensive estate in the common way of using it, particularly as the work runs very soon off the paper

H

that is put upon the table, which will require shifting three or four times
in a day. If the scale is large, by joining so many plain table sheets together, it becomes very difficult to get the plan of a large estate laid down
correct; yet it is my opinion, that in dry weather, for surveying a small
farm, or a pleasure ground, which include a variety of serpentine walks,
shrubberies, ponds, curved plantations, or irregular fences, it is preferable
to any other instrument.

Hitherto I have only described in what way it is commonly made use of
by land-surveyors in the field, and drawing the rough plan upon the spot.

Many surveyors create objections to it, because they cannot determine
horizontal distances by it; but this can easily be remedied, by carrying a
small quadrant, and taking the altitude or declivity, or with the chain.
as particularly described in *Page 25. Plate* II. *Fig.* 15.

Plate VI.

Represents the survey of the Common of Hassendean, containing upwards
of 300 acres, surveyed with the plain table, but in a very different manner
from that commonly practised by land-measurers.—The method I am about
to explain removes many of the objections that some have to it, and in-
creases its value even to those who are apt to condemn it. It obviates
particularly the inconvenience of shifting the paper, and commencing
upon new sheets: it also does away the great objections they have to the paper swelling and shrinking again to its natural size when it dries. In this
manner of surveying with the plain table which I am to describe, a field-
book is kept, the distances are all inserted in it, then protracted and laid
off upon one, two, or more sheets of drawing paper joined together; and
it may be plotted from any scale you choose to adopt in the house.

Fix upon any part of the paper near the centre of the table and make
a mark thus ⊙, to represent the centre, or the last letter or reference when
a back sight is taken; or it answers for the letter or reference when a
fore sight or bearing is taken. With a pair of compasses draw a circle
round the centre as large as the paper on the table will admit, which will
be about four times larger in diameter than the one represented on the
plate, and the plan will be equally large in proportion. This circle you

may call your *protractor*, which has a much larger radius than the brass protractors that are commonly used.

Begin at any part of the common you choose with your measurement, suppose at A. Plant the plain table there, as level as you can guess, and turn it round upon its axis till the north end of the magnetic needle settles over the *fleur de lis* in the compass box ; then screw it fast to the legs with the screw in the socket e, and take a bearing to No. 1. by laying the chamfered edge of the index close to the centre, and look through the slit in the sight next the eye till you see the hair in the opposite sight and the pole placed in No. 1. to coincide ; then draw the bearing, and where the chamfered edge of the index crosses the arch of the circle mark 1. ; measure the line from A to 1. and also the offsets, and insert them in the field-book, or an eye-draught, whichever you choose to keep ; then plant the instrument at 1. and lay the edge of the index at the mark 1. made across the circle and the centre, and take a back sight to A which is the centre ; then take a fore sight to 2. and measure from 1. to 2. and mark where the bearing crosses the circle at 2. and insert the distances in the field-book and the offsets, and where they were taken at ; then plant the table in 2. and take a back sight to 1. by laying the chamfered edge of the index upon the mark 2. made on the arch of the circle and the centre ; then take a fore sight to No. 3. and examine the needle if it settles over the *fleur de lis* : if it does, it is a proof that you have done right so far as 2 ; then mark where the bearing crosses the arch, and write 3. ; measure the distance from 2. to 3. and insert the distance and the offsets to the river in the field-book, and where they were taken at ; then place the instrument at No. 3. and lay the index upon the mark made on the arch at No. 3. and the centre, and take a back sight to 2. ; screw the instrument fast, and take a fore sight from the centre to the pole placed in 4. ; then mark where that bearing crosses the arch 4. ; then measure the distance, and insert in the field-book that distance, and also the offsets to the river, and where they were taken at ; then plant the instrument at 4. and lay the index at the mark made on the arch 4. and the centre, and take a back sight to 3. ; then lay the index upon the centre, and take a bearing or fore sight to No. 5. ; measure that distance, and all the intermediate ones, inserting them in the field-book ; then set up the instrument at 5. and take a back sight to 4.; screw the table fast, and take a bearing to A, which mark on the arch, and measure to A, and enter the distance in the field-book, and write Closes at A. If the needle settles over the *fleur de lis*, after taking a back sight from A to 5. it is a proof that the angles are all right taken.

FIELD-BOOK OF HASSENDEAN COMMON,

Beginning at the top of the Column.

	Offsets.	Distances.	Offsets.	
		A	70	Rivulet.
		1500	80	Rivulet.
		1940		Crosses Rivulet.
Rivulet,	200	2300		
Rivulet,	230	3096		
Crosses,		3940		Rivulet.
		4800	200	Rivulet.
End of line,		5500	50	River.
		1st.	50	River.
		840	70	River.
		1932	40	End of line.
		2d.		
		480	140	River.
		930	190	Do.
		1380	150	Do.
		1833	60	Do.
		3d.		
		710	280	River.
		1435	250	Do.
		2040	40	End of line.
		4th.		
		709	190	River.
		1095		Touches river.
		1830	200	River.
		2300	210	Do.
		2660	150	
		3400		Touches river.
		4340	190	River.
		5250	10	End of line.
	Closes.	5th. 5195	at A	

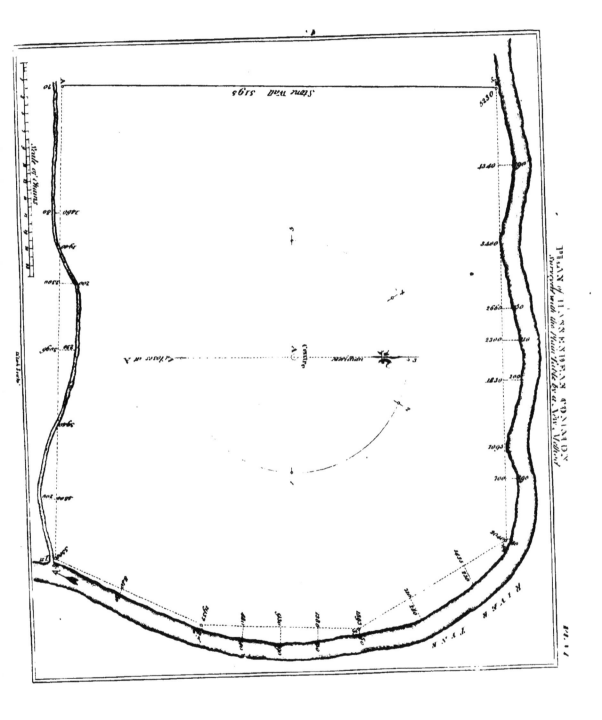

PLAN of HASSENDEAN COMMON
Surveyed with the Plain Table by a Six Wheeled

Scale of Yards

Stone Wall 5195

Meridian

Centre

A

Close on A

RIVER TEAN

Pl. II

To protract and make out a plan of the Common of Hassendean. Remove the paper from the plain table on which the circle is described, and lay it upon a sheet of large drawing paper; then with a fine point prick off all the marks made upon the circumference of the circle, also its centre; number each point, beginning at A, thus, 1. 2. 3. 4. 5. A; then with a parallel ruler, or the T square and its companion (See *Plate* VIII. *Fig.* 5. Also how it is used in the farms of Tipperty and Bonnyton, *Plates* X. and XIII.). If you begin at A, near the south west corner, on the drawing paper lay the T square upon the centre ⊙, and the prick at 1. and slide the square, by the help of its companion, parallel to where you begin at A, and draw the bearing from A to No. 1. and from any scale of equal parts, suppose four chains to an inch; then lay off the distance 5500 links from the scale, and also all the offsets, and the distance from A, and where they were taken at, which you take from the field-book; next, lay the edge of the ruler on the prick at No. 2. and the centre, and slide the ruler down, by the help of its companion to 1. and draw the bearing 2. and lay off the distance 1932, and the offset of 70, taken at 840, also the offsets taken at the stations; then lay the edge of the T square on the centre, and the prick made at No. 3. and move it parallel, by the help of its companion, to No. 2. and draw the bearing from 2. to 3. and lay off the distance from the scale, which is 1833, and all the intermediate offsets to the river inserted in the *field-book*; then place the T square upon the centre, and the prick made at 4. and move it parallel as before to 3. and with a fine pointed pencil draw the bearing from No. 3. to No. 4. lay off the distance 2040 to 4. and all the intermediate offsets to the river: again, lay the T square upon the prick made at No. 5. and the centre, and move it as formerly to 4. and draw the bearing from No. 4. to No. 5.; and from the scale lay off the distance 5230, and all the intermediate distances and offsets inserted in the field-book; then lay the T square upon A and the centre, and move it parallel to No. 5. and draw the bearing from No. 5. to A. If it agrees, you are certain the angles have been right laid off. Lay off the distance 5195. If that answers, you have made an exact closing. Now with a black lead pencil draw in from the offset at 70 where you began to the offset 80; from thence to where you cross the rivulet; thence to 200; and so on from offset to offset, till you have gone all round;

then with a pen and Indian ink draw in the whole of the boundary, and also the river Tyne about two chains wide, and it is completed.

Plate VII.

Represents a farm called *Harestanes,* and also the field-book, surveyed with the plain table.—This is performed in the same manner as Hassendean Common (*Plate* VI).; but is much more intricate, being all inclosed, and consists of upwards of 150 acres ; and if measured in the common way, the paper would require to be shifted six or eight times; to lay it down upon a scale of two chains to an inch, which is a scale small enough for enclosed lands. In order to give the learner a better idea, I have made a rough protraction in the Plate, taken from the field-book ; which I have been under the necessity of doing upon a small scale for want of room upon the copper, and is intended merely to show that a very extensive piece of land may be measured without shifting the paper, and the whole afterwards protracted upon any scale. To proceed, then, set the table up at A as level as you can, adjusting it as before ; and having previously described a circle as large as the plain table sheet will admit of, take a bearing to a pole placed in B, by laying the index over the centre and mark B, where the chamfered edge crosses the arch of the circle ; measure to B, and insert the distance as well as the offsets in the field-book ; then plant the table at B, and lay the chamfered edge of the index upon the centre and the mark made upon the arch at B, and take a back sight to A ; then take bearings to C and D, and mark where the thin edge of the index crosses the arch, noting C and D ; measure these distances and the offsets ; then erect the table at station D, and lay the index upon the centre and the mark on the arch at D, and take a back sight to B, and a bearing from the centre to the station E, noting E ; where the edge of the index crosses the arch measure to E ; plant up the table, and lay the edge of the index upon the centre and the mark upon the arch at E, and take a back sight to D, (observing, every time that a back sight is taken that the instrument is screwed fast) ; then lay the index upon the centre, and take a bearing to F ; and where the index crosses the arch mark F ; measure that distance, which enter in the field-book, and the offsets, &c. ; then plant the table at F, and lay the index upon the mark at F on the arch and the centre, and take a back sight to E: again, lay the edge of the index upon the centre, and take a bearing to G; and where the index crosses the arch mark G; measure to G, noting the offsets; then with the table at G take a back sight to F, by laying the index upon the mark on the arch and the centre; then take a bearing to H, and where the index crosses the arch mark H; measure to H, and plant up the table at H, and lay the edge of the index upon the mark H and the centre, and take a back sight to G; take a bearing to I, and where the edge of the index crosses the arch mark I; measure from H to I, and then set up the table at I, and lay the index upon the mark at I on the arch and the centre, and take a back sight to H; then take a bearing to K, and where the index crosses the arch mark K; measure from I to K, then plant up the table at K, and lay the index upon the mark on the arch at K and the centre, and take a back sight to I; then lay the index upon the centre, and take a bearing to L, and where the index crosses the arch mark L; measure to L, and enter all the distances, offsets, &c. carefully in the field-book wherever they are taken; then set up the table in L, and take a back sight to K, also a bearing to A, where the survey was begun; measure from L to A, and mark where the index crosses the arch, and write Closes at A; insert the distance, offset, &c.

Return to L, and take a bearing from the centre to M, and where the index crosses the arch mark M; measure to M, and set up the table, and lay the index upon the mark on the arch at M and the centre, and take a back sight to L; then lay the index upon M, and take a bearing to I, and mark where the index crosses the arch, and write Meets at I; measure to I, and insert the distance in the field-book; then take a bearing from M to C, and where the index crosses the arch write Closes at C; measure to C, and enter the distance in the field-book; plant the instrument in C, and take a back sight to M; then lay the index upon the centre, and take a bearing to N, and where the index crosses the arch mark N; measure that distance, which enter in the field-book; plant the table up at N, and take a back sight to C, by laying the index upon the mark made on the arch at N and the centre; then take a bearing from the centre to D, and another bearing to F, also one past the houses to O; mark all these bearings where they cross the arch, and mark D F O; measure the distances, and insert them in the field-book; then plant the table at O, and take a back sight to N, and lay the index upon the centre and the mark made at O on the arch, and take a bearing to I, and write Meets at I, where the index crosses the arch; take another bearing from the centre to G, and where the index crosses the arch write Meets at G; measure the distances, and insert them in the field-book, also the offsets, and where they were taken at; then take a bearing opposite 10 30 upon the line N O, along the north side of Harestanes garden-wall, which lay off from the centre; and where it crosses the arch, mark P, and measure the distances about the houses. The chief matter is to be well acquainted with laying off the bearings on the spot. Care must be taken, when the index is placed over the centre in taking a back sight, that you perceive the station the table was last at; and when you take a bearing or fore sight, it is from the station you are standing at; and if any error has been made, the needle is an excellent check, as it will always settle (if a good one) over the *fleur de lis*.

I must observe, that in taking a survey in this manner with the plain table, it is easily adjusted, and very little time lost in taking the back sight and the bearing to another station; it has also this advantage over other instruments, that you have no degrees and minutes to insert in the field-book, they being expressed on the circumference of the circle by a short line drawn across the arch upon the spot; and if the chamfered edge of the index is laid exactly over the point in the centre, and a line drawn across the arch with a fine pencil close to the chamfered edge of the index, it is equally correct as a protractor, and is much larger than the protractors are commonly made. Although the one represented on the protracted sketch appears small, it, as well as the sketch itself, is owing to the smallness of the scale that the sketch is plotted by, which is only seven chains to an inch, and the diameter of the circle, upon a plain table at least, thirteen inches and a half, which, as before mentioned, is a much larger radius than the common size of protractors. It is well known to surveyors, that the larger the protractors are, the work will in proportion be the more exact.

PLATE I.

Field Book of Harestones Farm

Offsets	Distances	Offsets			Distances	Offsets	
							Bratten or Yard
					740		Dike
40					440		East Side
					200		Farm Fence North Side
					200		
					40		Meets at G
K		C Riser			1680		
575	C Riser	230	298		940		Gate House N. Side
530	850 Riser	230 Morklove	200		620		
327	330 Riser		150		40		Gate House
75	40 Riser	Meadow					
750	C Riser	Cross Hedge			1077		Cross at A
537	63 Riser	Cross Hedge			1030	O	in a Road to a Gate
240	240 Riser 330 to 450 eight cm						
175	495 Riser				1045	15	Corner Garden
		I Meadow			940	15	Mews
I 13	1045	235 Cross Hedge			805	15	House of Harestones
13	1045	40 Riser			750	15	Court Yard
H	1700	11 Riser				N	
	1647	13 Riser			1480		along a Road
	1400	150 Riser			1210		
	1465	200 Riser			965	13.5	Cross at F
	740	310 Riser			6222	13.5	
	620					N	Cross at D
G	1484	140 Rivulet			17.50		in a Road
	1073	140 Rivulet				N	
	672	6 Road					Road
	40	Cross Hedge			1575	20	
F	1282	140 Rivulet			1505	40	Which a road has
	764	140 Rivulet			1050		with its other corner
	482	30 Rivulet			512		
	340	150 Rivulet				C	
	30	Cross Hedge			830		Cross at C
E	1338	F			30	M	
	1170	90 Rivulet				N	
	834	150 Rivulet			1425		Cross at I
	40	13			814	10	
D	1000	to E			40	110	
	575	in a Road				M	
	30				1465		
B	888	13			645		crosse Hedge
A	1320	40 C			40		
	90					L	
13	A	40 at			123.5		Cross at A
10	Begins here				1835		
					1125		
					600	K	Continuation

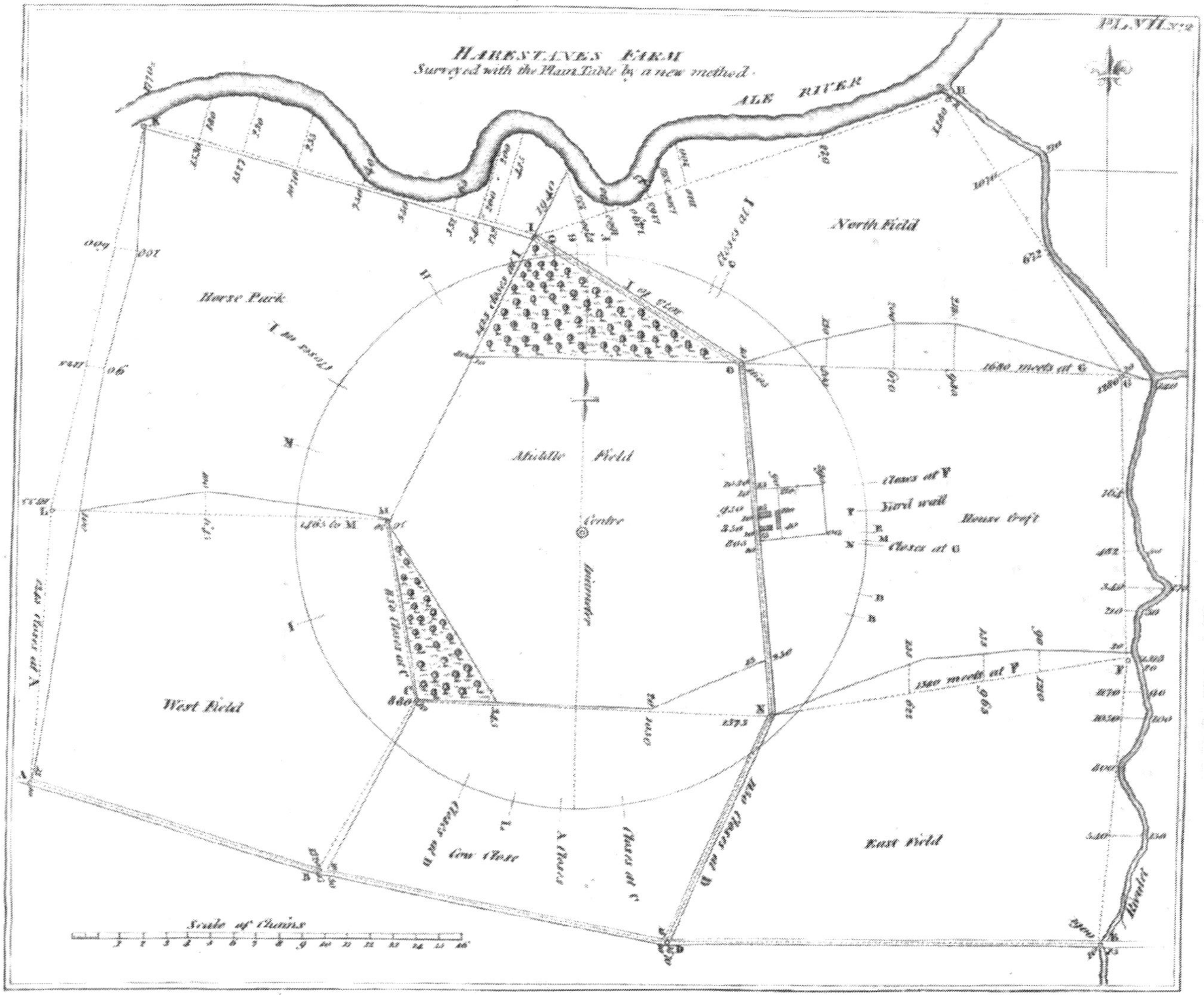

Pl. VII. N°2
Harestanes Farm
Surveyed with the Plain Table by a new method.
Ale River
North Field
Horse Park
Middle Field
Centre
Diameter
House Croft
Yard wall
Closes at Y
Closes at G
1680 meets at G
1340 meets at Y
West Field
East Field
Cow Close
A Closes
Closes at C
Closes at D
Closes at I
Scale of Chains

To protract the rough plan from the field-book. Take the sheet of paper off the table, and lay it upon a large sheet of drawing paper; prick through the centre, and also through every mark upon the arch, and insert the letters with a black lead pencil upon the paper, and make a mark thus ⊙ to represent the centre; adopt any scale you choose, suppose two chains in an inch, which will require a very large sheet to hold the plan of the farm of Harestanes. If it had been surveyed in the common method, and laid down upon that scale, the paper would require to be shifted six or seven times, and then to join them altogether, which is very troublesome to do correctly; whereas, by this method, every thing is protracted from one centre, and on one sheet of paper.

Having begun the survey at A, fix upon any part of the paper to begin at, and mark ⊙ A on the west side near the bottom of the paper; then find out the prick B; lay the T square upon the centre and B, and slide it parallel to A, which is the point fixed upon to begin at, and draw a line with a pencil; then from the scale lay off the distance, which is marked in the field-book 1320, and also the offsets taken to each side of the road, which ascertains its breadth; then lay the square upon the centre and C, and run it parallel to B; and from the scale lay off 880, which is the distance from B to C; then lay the square upon the centre and the mark at D on the arch, and move it parallel to B, and draw the bearing to D, and lay off the distance from the same scale, which is 1570, also the offsets to each side of the road: again, lay the square upon the mark on the arch at E and the centre, and slide it down to D, and draw the bearing to E; lay off the distance from D to E, which is 1900, and also the offsets taken on each side of the road; then lay the square upon the mark upon the arch at F and the centre, and slide it parallel to E, and draw the bearing to F; lay the distance off from E to F, which is 1818, and all the intermediate distances and offsets to the rivulet marked in the field-book; then lay the square upon the mark at G and the centre, and slide it parallel to F, and draw the bearing from F to G; lay off the distance, which is 1280, and all the intermediate distances and offsets to the rivulet; then place the square upon the mark at H and the centre, and slide it parallel to G, and draw the bearing to H, and lay off the distance from G to H, which is 1480; also the intermediate

I

distances and offsets to the rivulet to H; then lay the square upon the mark
I and the centre, and slide it parallel to H, and draw the bearing to I;
lay off the distance, which is 1940, and all the intermediate distances and
offsets marked in the field-book to the river; then lay the square upon
the mark at K and the centre, and slide it to I, and draw the bearing
from I to K; lay off that distance 1770, and all the intermediate distances, offsets, &c. to the river, and draw it in about 100 links wide:
again, lay the square upon the mark at L and the centre, and move it parallel to K, and draw the bearing from K to L; lay off the distance with
the scale from K to L, which is 1885, and all the intermediate distances,
offsets, &c. to the boundary; next, place the square upon L, and the mark
where it closes at A, and move it parallel to L, and draw the bearing to
where the survey was begun at A. If it joins, you may rest satisfied that
you have not only measured the distances right, but the bearings also, particularly if the distance from L to A answer, which is 1245. Then lay
the square upon the mark at M and the centre, and move it to L, and
draw the bearing from L to M; lay off that distance, which is 1465, and
the offset to the fence; then lay the square upon I and the centre, and
slide the square parallel to M, and draw the bearing from M to I. If the
bearing and distance, which is 1425, answers, you are certain it is right.
Again, place the square upon the mark where you close at C and the centre, and move it parallel to M, and draw the bearing from M to C, laying
off the distance, which is 880; then lay the square upon the mark at N
and the centre, and slide it parallel to C, and draw the bearing from C to
N; lay off the distance, which is 1575, and also the intermediate distances and offsets; next, lay the square upon the mark where a meeting is
made at D and the centre, and move it parallel by the help of its companion to N, and draw the bearing to D. If the distance, which is 1150,
and the bearing answer, you are certain that no error has been committed.
Then lay the square where a meeting is made at F and the centre, and
move it parallel to N, and lay off the bearing. If it and the distance, 1580,
answers, it is right; lay off also the offsets as marked in the field-book.
Again, lay the square upon the mark where a meeting is made at I and
the centre, and move the square to O, and draw in the bearing to I. If

the distance answers to 1075, you may rest satisfied it is right. Then lay the T square upon the mark made upon the arch where it closes at G and the centre, and move it parallel to O, and draw in the bearing to G. If it answers, and the distance to 1680, it makes an exact closing. Next, lay the square upon the mark at P and the centre, and move it parallel to the north west corner of the garden wall, and lay off the distances of the length and breadth of the garden, also the length and breadth of the houses, as marked in the field-book; draw in the whole, first with a black lead pencil from offset to offset, as before directed on other surveys; then ink it carefully in with Indian ink, rub out all the black lead lines and marks, and the protraction is finished.

Many more examples might be given in the surveying estates, &c. with the plain table by this method; but it being merely a repetition, I shall now only take notice, that if a large survey, such as the common of Hassendean and the farm of Harestanes, can be surveyed with it in a damp day, although the paper should expand, a few inclosures can be equally well done with it by describing a circle upon the sheet of paper fixed upon the table, and the bearings marked upon the arch by letters or references, the same as is done upon Harestanes; which can be protracted at home upon any scale you choose to adopt.

ART. IV. OF THE SEXTANT.

Plate VIII. (Fig. 7.)

Represents a (snuff box) sextant as made by Mr Troughton, which I have found very useful in taking an angle with great exactness in the field: it is so nicely divided, every degree and minute can be read upon it (with the assistance of a magnifying glass B), and is so convenient it may be carried in the pocket, being only two inches and a half in diameter, and only about two inches deep. It is a great improvement on the cross staff; for by setting the index to 90 degrees, it gives an exact perpendicular, by reflecting a mark or pole to an angle of 90 degrees to a bend or angle of a fence, where a perpendicular is required; it also an-

I 2

swers the same purpose as an optical square used in military observations
for taking right angles in the field. The sextant is of essential use in
trigonometrical observations, as any angle can be taken with it either vertical or horizontal. To take an observation with it in the field, set the
index to o, and look through a small hole on the side of the box at D;
hold the sextant in the left hand, and turn the pinion E with the right
hand towards the left, and it will cause the index to move towards the
right, at same time looking through the hole at D to a pole, or any other
mark you want, to know the angle where you stand to another pole or
mark : the reflecting glass in the box carries one pole to the other; and
when they coincide exactly, one over the other, the index points out the
degrees and minutes, which is read with the help of the magnifying glass
B. If the angle should be larger than a right angle, it can be taken at
two observations ; and by adding together the degrees each makes, gives
the angle required. If a third pole is set up at any distance nearly opposite where the observer stands, and the index set to o, look through the
hole at D, and the reflecting glass will carry the first pole to the pole placed nearly opposite ; mark the number of degrees and minutes cut by the
index ; again, set the index at o, and look through the hole at D, and by
turning the pinion as before, the reflecting glass will carry the pole opposite to the other pole ; and when the one pole is seen exactly over the
other, the index will point out the degrees and minutes ; which, added to
the former observation, gives the angle required ; and it may either be
plotted by a protractor or a line of cords. This little instrument is very
useful in taking small surveys, and supersedes the necessity of taking larger
instruments to the field.

Plate II. (Fig. 4.)

Shews the method of constructing a line of chords, which may be laid
down upon any scale you please (the larger it is so much the better).
Raise a perpendicular upon the line A C at A to B, of the same length of
A C ; put one foot of the compasses in the point A, and with the other
describe an arch from B to C, and divide that quadrant into nine equal
parts ; then draw a line from B to C, which is to be divided into a line of

cords; and is done in the following manner: by putting one foot of the compasses in the point C, and with an extent to the first division on the quadrant, describe an arch from it to the line of cords; also describe an arch from the second division on the quadrant from the same point C to the line of cords; in like manner, do the same with all the other divisions, which will divide the line in nine parts, which will be all unequal : each of these large divisions should be again divided into tens, as represented on the Figure.

Plate II. (*Fig. 5.*)

To lay off any angle by the line of cords. Let the angle A B D, 28 degrees, be laid off with a pair of compasses; set one foot in the point C, and extend the other to 60 on the line of cords; with that extent put one foot in B, and describe the arch A D; then with one foot in C on the line of cords extend the other foot to 28 degrees on the line of chords, and with that extent put one foot in A, and the other foot will extend to D; lastly, draw a line from the point B through the mark made on the arch A D, which gives the required angle A B C.

Let an angle of 124 degrees be laid off from A on the line B A; take 60 degrees as before between the points of the compasses, and describe the arch B C from the point A. First, take off 90 degrees from the line of cords, and lay it off from the point B upon the arch B C, which mark; then take 34 degrees from the line of cords, and put one foot of the compasses in the mark at 90 degrees, and the other foot will extend to a mark upon the arch at C; draw the line A C, which will form the angle B A C, containing 124 degrees (being the sum of 90 and 34).

Plate VIII. (*Fig. 12.*)

Is a triangular field A B C, where the short fence can only be got at, having deep quarries and other impediments, otherwise it would have been more certain, if the other fences could have been got at, to have measured both, or even one of them. A pole being placed at C, another at B, 20 links from the fence on both sides, in the inside of the inclosure, you stand at A; measure the offsets to the fence on each side, which is 20 links, which insert in an eye-sketch; then look through the little hole D in the sextant to the pole at B, and turn the pinion with the right hand till you see the pole B and the pole C exactly over one another in the reflecting glass; then look what degrees and minutes is cut by the index, which is 76 degrees 30 minutes; you then measure the distance from A to B, which is 408 links; then set the index to 0, and stand at B, and look through the hole to the pole in C; turn the pinion round as before till the pole at C is seen through the reflecting glass immediately above the pole that was left at A, and note the degrees and minutes cut by the index, which is 78 degrees 30 minutes, and insert the angle in the field-book.

The inclosure may be plotted by drawing a line at pleasure, and laying off 408, the distance from A to B, from any scale you choose to adopt; then take 60 degrees from a line of cords, and put one foot of the compasses in A, and sweep an arch with that extent; then take off 76 degrees 30 minutes from the line of cords, and with that extent put one foot of the compasses on the line you drew at pleasure, and make a mark with the other foot on the arch, and draw the line A C through the point on the arch; then with the extent of 60 degrees, taken from the line of cords, put one foot of the compasses in B, and describe an arch with the other foot, and take 78 degrees 30 minutes from the line of cords, and lay that extent off upon the arch from the line A B, and make a mark with the point of the compasses; draw a line through that mark from the point B, and the intersection of the line A C at E ascertains the distance, which is 939, and is known by applying the length of the intersected line to the scale from A to C, as well as from B to C. The angles might have been equally well laid off with a protractor of large radius. The next thing to be done is to lay off the offsets, which is 20 each way from A, and 20 each way from B; lay a ruler upon the point of intersection C and the offset at A, and draw that fence; then lay a ruler upon the point made at the offsets at B and A, and draw in the short fence; then lay the ruler upon the point of intersection at C and the prick at the offset made at B; draw in that fence, and it is finished. Note, the most correct method of ascertaining the distance of so acute an angle as B C A is to calculate it by logarithms.

5

Plate VIII. (*Fig.* 18.)

Is a method of taking the survey of an enclosure in a much quicker way than any that has hitherto been taken notice of, and is done as follows: let the square enclosure *Fig.* 18. be laid down by measuring only the diagonal and the angles taken with the sextant. Suppose the diagonal is 1267 links, place up poles (with red flags upon them, that they may be more conspicuous) at B C and D; look from A to D through the little hole at D on the sextant, and carry the pole at D till you see it coincide exactly in the magnifying glass in the box immediately above the pole in C; insert that angle, which is 84 degrees, in the field-book; then look through the hole, after having put the index to o, and turn the pinion round till you see the pole in C and the pole in B to coincide, and set that angle down in the field-book, which is 67 degrees; then go to C, and look through the hole to the pole at B; turn the pinion round till you see it and the pole left in A to coincide exactly (the one appearing immediately as it were above the other in the reflecting glass); then set down in your field-book the angle, which is 84 degrees; set the index to o, and look through the hole in the side of the box as before, and turn the pinion round till you see the pole in A and the pole in D to coincide so as the one appears immediately above the other; lastly, insert that angle, which is 53 degrees.

To make out a plan of the inclosure, draw a line at pleasure with a black lead pencil to represent the diagonal, and lay off the distance, which is 1267, from any scale you choose (the figure is laid down by a scale of one fourth of an inch to a chain); but to be very correct, you should use one much larger; then with a protractor, or the line of cords, lay off the angle C A B, which is 67 degrees, and draw a line from A through the point made in B; then lay off the angle A C B, 84 degrees, and draw the line from C through the prick or point made upon the line C B, the intersection is the distance to B; then lay off the angle C A D, 84 degrees, from A, and draw in the line A D; also lay off the angle A C D 53 degrees, and draw the line C D; and where these lines intersect, ascertains the distance from C to D, as well as from A to D; then lay off the offsets 30 and 15 from A, and draw in the fences, and it is done.

ART. V.   OF PROTRACTORS AND PARALLEL RULERS.

Plate VIII.   (*Fig.* 1.)

Represents a protractor, made small upon the plate for want of room, wherewith as many angles or bearings may be pricked off as you choose to lay off at a time with one of larger dimensions.—A is the centre, made of a piece of glass with a scratch drawn across it at right angles, on purpose that the centre may be seen through the glass when laid exactly upon the stations; B B is a moveable index and a nonius scale: it is the kind of protractors that is acknowledged the best by those that use it, and most accurate in practice: the outer circle on the limb is generally made about seven or eight inches in diameter, and is either divided into 360 degrees, or into twice 180 degrees (which is by far the best way of dividing it for a practical surveyor); each degree is subdivided by a nonius scale into five minutes (or less if it is required), which, with the index, is moved round the glass centre, and the limb and nonius points out the degrees and minutes; at C, near the end of the index, is fixed a very fine steel point to prick off the angles or bearings; at the extremity of the index the brass is filed to a sharp point in a direct line with the centre of the glass on the protractor, on purpose that the centre, when laid upon the station point and the point at the end of the index, may coincide; when the protractor is laid upon the meridian, which is a line drawn upon the protracting paper, one end representing south the other north; when the protractor is fixed as above, prick off as many bearings or angles at a time as you choose; during the time you are turning the index round with one hand, with the other hand hold the protractor fast to the paper, to prevent its shifting. This protractor is allowed to be more expeditious in laying off bearings than those that are made finer, with a rack and pinion to move the index; but a practical surveyor in general prefers a semicircular one, upwards of a foot in diameter, with each degree divided into quarters, which answers the same purpose, and can be made at one fourth of the expense, besides being more expeditious: when its centre is once laid upon the station, and

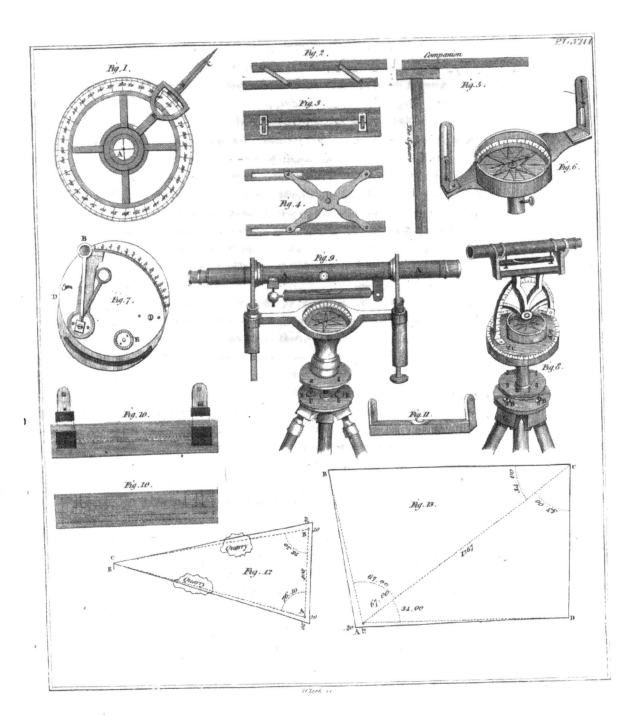

Pl. XVII.

Fig. 1.

Fig. 2.

Companion.

Fig. 5.

Fig. 3.

Fig. 6.

Fig. 4.

Fig. 7.

Fig. 9.

Fig. 8.

Fig. 10.

Fig. 11.

Fig. 10.

Fig. 13.

Fig. 12.

Quarry

Quarry

the chamfered edge laid exactly on the meridian line, which should be kept steady and firm to the paper by a weight laid upon it, with the point of a pair of compasses, a protracting pin, or a fine needle, prick off the bearings, counting each of the four small divisions that each degree is divided into fifteen minutes, which you can again divide with your eye into five minutes, or less if you choose. A land-surveyor need be at no loss although he should have no brass protractor, as he can make a semicircular one of large dimensions with a pair of compasses as large as the protracting paper will hold; fix upon any part of the paper you choose for a centre, which mark thus ⊙. As it will often have to be resorted to when you have to protract your bearings, the larger you make the protractor the better. For the easier understanding it, I have laid one down on the farm of Bonnyton, *Plate* XIII whereon the angles on that farm were all protracted; which, although done upon a small scale, you may suppose to be upon a sheet of large drawing paper at least six times the diameter of the one on *Plate* XIII. Some surveyors reckon this troublesome, and without doubt it is to make the first; but I shall only observe here, that after one has been made, you may make as many more as you please with very little trouble, by only laying the one you have made upon four, five, or six sheets of paper, and pricking off every degree with a very fine needle or protracting pin, as you will observe is done by short lines on the farm of Bonnyton, *Plate* XIII. In place of those short strokes, you have only to prick through every sheet of paper with a needle or protracting pin, which always remains visible. The only trouble that now remains is to mark the figures, representing the degrees, with a black lead pencil, which are rubbed out when the survey is protracted, similar to those that are marked on the farm of Bonnyton; so that when one is made, you may make as many more as you please, or think you will want, by the additional trouble of numbering every fifth degree, as is done on the Plate. A protractor of this kind can never shift like those that are made on brass, which the sometimes do in the hands of very careful land-measurers. If you want to be very nice, I have inserted a small scale, marked A. Supposing each degree upon your protractor to be three times larger than the degrees upon the farm of Bonnyton, you can easily make one similar upon

K

any blank corner on your paper the size of the degrees on your protractor, and divide one degree into six equal parts, which is equal to 10 minutes each division : if you choose to take the minutes, you may do it within 5 minutes with a pair of compasses applied to that scale ; for example, you want to lay off 11 deg. 25 min. set one foot of the compasses in 10 deg. marked on the protractor, and let the other foot extend 2 divisions and a half past 11, which will be 11 deg. 25 min. ; or if you wanted to lay off 90 deg. 40 min. you can with the compasses take off 4 more than 90, which is equal to 40 min. If you find it troublesome to take off with the compasses four of these small divisions on the scale A, you can put one foot in 10, and let the other foot extend 4 divisions past 11 ; then apply that extent to the protractor, and put one foot in 89, and the other foot will extend 40 minutes past 90, which mark, and draw the bearing from the centre through the mark. (A practical surveyor can guess upon the protractor the minutes very near, without applying the compasses to the scale A). Not to enlarge, I shall only say that I give the preference to a protractor of large dimensions of a surveyor's own making to any other, and that all who have used them have uniformly approved of them. In making use of one, you have no numbers nor bearings to mark, where the bearings are pricked off with other protractors, nor the bearing, or a number referring to the bearing, to set down upon the protracting paper with a black lead pencil, as every five degrees are marked upon it, and the bearing you may want to lay off is instantly found out on the paper protractor ; the odd degrees can be easily traced with the eye ; for example, you want to lay off 38 degrees, find out 35, and reckon 3 degrees more, which is 38 degrees ; if the bearing should be 38 degrees 30 minutes, count off 38 as above, and guess the half of another degree. Your protractor being of large dimensions, you can guess within 5 minutes, which is as near as most protractors made of brass can lay them off, although ever so finely divided with an index and nonius ; the breadth of the mark that is made with the point that is placed at the end of the index of those protractors covers more than 5 min. By laying a parallel ruler or the T square, which will be afterwards described, upon the centre, and the angle or bearing you want to lay down, and by moving it parallel to any station you want to lay that bearing off from, and draw a

fine from the station, and the distance laid off upon that line by the plotting scale, or from a scale of equal parts, and a pair of compasses; you
then look for the next bearing that is on the field-book, and find that bearing on the paper protractor, and lay the edge of the ruler upon the centre,
and the degree and minute, and move it parallel to the station that was
last laid off, and draw that bearing, and prick off the next distance. If
you have ten or 20 bearings and distances, they are all laid off in the same
manner.

It will be proper to observe here, that one line drawn parallel to another has the same bearing from the meridian, whether drawn from the
centre of the paper or any other part of it; so that if a parallel ruler or
the T square is laid upon the centre, and the degrees and minutes upon
the edge of the semicircle where a bearing was taken to a pole or any
other mark from the centre, and if the parallel ruler or T square is moved
parallel to any station you have to lay off the bearing from, it is the same
bearing as if laid off from the centre, corresponding to the degrees and minutes on the protractor.

Plate IX.

Represents a square protractor, with the outline of the farm of Broad
Meadows drawn upon it, which was protracted by it on a small scale of
10 chains in an inch; but you may suppose it to be on a large sheet of
drawing paper, or at the edge of a drawing board. If you will be at the
trouble of making it, one will serve for numbers of plans, and will save the
time of drawing protractors on paper, which some surveyors object to on
account of the trouble of making them; but, in my opinion, any trouble
they give is but trifling. It is well known to most of them, that the radius of a circle is the sixth part of the circumference; and if a line is
drawn through the centre, and cuts the circle in halves, then with the radius between the compasses divide the circle in 6 parts, each of those divisions being 60 degrees; again, divide each of these divisions by 6, which
is soon done by taking, as near as you can guess, a short distance between
the compasses, and run along the arch from one division to another till it
is divided into 6 equal parts. This divides the circle into 36 equal parts,

each division being 10 degrees; then divide each of those divisions into 5 degrees, or taking one half, which divides the circle into 72 parts; lastly, divide each of the 72 divisions into 5, and the circle will be divided into 360 equal parts, called degrees; then mark every 5, 10, 15, 20. degrees, till you have gone all round from the right to the left; also mark 180. Begin again, and write 5 after 180, and so on as the other semicircle, 10, 15, 20, 25, to 180. If you choose to divide the whole circle into 360 degrees, in place of beginning anew at 180, write 185, 190, 195, 200, till you have gone all round; when this is finished, you may make as many more as you please, as explained in *Page* 74.

I have now to point out what way a square protractor is made after you have made a round one upon paper of large dimensions. Get a drawing board, made at least 30 inches by 3 feet, and paste a slip of white paper round the edges of it, or, what is better, a piece of white wood about half an inch broad, sunk into the drawing board, on each side of it near the edge, and draw two lines on each side as on the plate; if it is done on paper, draw the line with a drawing pen; but if done on wood, use a sharp point, which will leave a scratch or impression on the wood; then take one of the paper protractors, and lay its centre upon the centre of the drawing board, and let the diameter be laid parallel with the sides of the board; when thus laid, fasten the paper to the board with drawing pins or wax, so as it will not shift; then apply a rule or straight edge to the centre and the divisions on the paper protractor, and where the straight edge crosses the square at the edge of the board make a scratch with the steel point; do the same at every division till you have gone all round; when that is done, mark every 5th degree as directed above. When you have any thing to protract, lay a sheet of paper upon the drawing board, and fix it upon the board with drawing pins, wafers, or wax. The centre of the white paper is easily found out by applying the straight edge to the meridian, and drawing a line with the point of the compasses close to the edge of the ruler; do the same, by crossing the meridian line at right angles by laying the straight edge upon 90 degrees; and 90 degrees, if divided into twice 180, but if divided into 360, let the straight edge be laid to 90 on the east side and 270 on the west side, and draw a, line close to the edge of the straight edge; and when that line bisects the meridian line, it fixes the centre upon the plotting paper, which should be marked thus ⊙.

Parallel lines to a land-measurer, &c. occur so often in plotting, it is no wonder that so many different kinds of parallel rulers have been invented to expedite and facilitate his work. Many ingenious improvements have been made, and to give an account of each would be unnecessary; let it suffice to describe first the simple parallel ruler.

Plate VIII. (Fig. 2.)

Represents a parallel ruler, acting on the principal of the vertical angles, they being equal in every situation of the ruler.—It consists of two straight rules, which are so connected together as to keep in a parallel position by two equal and parallel bars, which move very freely on rivetted pins, by which they are fastened to the rules.

Plate VIII. (Fig. 3.)

Is a rolling parallel ruler, so called from the easy manner in which it runs, being supported by two wheels, which are connected together by an axis: the wheels are made the same size, and their rolling surfaces being parallel with the axis, when they are rolled backwards and forwards, the axis and rulers move in a direction parallel to one another; the wheels project a little on the underside of the rule, and are chamfered and grooved to prevent them from sliding. In using it, the finger should be placed nearly in the middle, that the one wheel may keep pace with the other. The wheels should only touch the paper when the ruler is moving, and the surface of the drawing paper should be smooth and flat upon a table or drawing board.

Plate VIII. (Fig. 4.)

Is what is known by the name of a *cross bar parallel ruler*, and is made of two straight rules joined by two brass bars, which cross each other on a centre. One end of each bar moves upon a centre in each, the other moves in a groove as one rule recedes from the other. This, as well as the simple parallel ruler, is used in the same way as most other parallel rulers.

I will only farther observe, that when working with them, you should press the edge of the lower rule tight with one hand, and with the other move the ruler up or down till it coincides with the given point, through which a line is to be drawn.

Plate VIII. (*Fig. 5.*)

Is a well known square, amongst architects called a *T square*; which undoubtedly answers the purpose of a parallel ruler to a land-surveyor, with the addition of a piece of loose wood about sixteen inches in length, an inch and a half broad, and half an inch thick, smoothly plained and made straight to let the head of the T square run easily along it, and is called the T square's companion. The T square requisite for a land-surveyor should be at least 2, or 2 feet and a half in length, and the head of it 6 or 8 inches, fixed exactly at right angles. By mere accident the T square and its companion was found to answer much better than any of the above described parallel rulers, or any others yet invented for the use of land-surveyors, in facilitating their protractions; and not one surveyor that I am acquainted with has ever used any other parallel ruler since they made a trial of it; and all of them allow, that it is not only the most exact, but the most expeditious : and I may venture to say, that all other land-measurers who survey with a theodolite, after having once made a trial of it, will give it the preference to all other rulers that they ever used, both for expedition as well as facility and cheapness.

Art. VI. Of the Circumferenter.

Plate VIII. (*Fig. 6.*)

Represents a circumferenter, which is a compass box with two plain sights, like those on the plain table index (see *Plate* IV. *Fig. 5.*), and a magnetic needle, which points out the bearings. The one sight is placed over the *fleur de lis*, or north point, and the other is placed exactly opposite over the south point.

To take an angle or bearing with it, set it up upon the legs which support it, as level as you can, which you will easily know by the needle's traversing freely in the compass box. If you look through the sight that is over the north point, the south end of the needle will point out the bearing when it settles. The divisions in the box are numbered in the compass box the contrary way you look, east being put where west should be, and *vice versa*. This is the reason of the south end of the needle pointing out the bearing. It is best to get it divided into 180 degrees, and either end of the needle will point out the bearing. In this way the protractor is divided the contrary way that the needle goes; therefore the degrees in the compass box are divided in the opposite way of the protractor. Some surveyors that use this instrument have it divided into four ninetys, and reckon so many degrees from the north to the east, and so on from east to south, and from south to west, and from west round to.north. Whatever way it is divided, the protractor must be divided the contrary way to the degrees in the compass box, otherwise the work will not protract; in short, those that use this instrument divided into 360 degrees, must protract their work by a protractor diametrically opposite the degrees in the compass box. By taking bearings with the circumferenter, every thing is trusted to the needle; and the method of protracting and laying off the bearings is done in the same way as in the farm of Tipperty. It is needless to give here a particular description. Since the great improvements that have been made on theodolites, this instrument, as well as the semicircle, is gone very much out of repute in Britain; but no instrument has yet been invented equal to it for taking surveys through woods and uncleared grounds, such as in America; and it is still very much used in that country, particularly where it is intricate. It is found by experience, that the circumferenter, when placed at every other station, by taking a back sight and then a fore sight, providing the degrees in the compass box be divided into twice 180 degrees, is not only the most correct method, but the most expeditious to survey with. It is also used in coal pits and mines in taking bearings, which are protracted in the same way as particularly described on the farm of Tipperty, *Plate* X. Much more might be said of this instrument; but this will be deferred to the surveying of land with the theodolite. The way colliers use this instrument below ground is by planting it at the bottom of the pit, and taking a bearing, suppose in a zigzag mine, and measuring the distance to a candle, which is placed as

far along the mine as the candle can be seen, and the distance and the bearing inserted in a book.   The instrument is planted up immediately above
the mark where the candle stood, and the candle again placed as far as it
can be seen through the sights, and another bearing and a distance measured, which should be also marked in the book.   In this manner you go
on to as many different stations as the mine is in length, setting down
every distance and bearing to the end of the mine.   The same operation is
repeated above ground as was done below.   Plant the instrument as near
the pit as you can get it placed, and order your assistant to go forward
with a pole; in the mean time, set the needle to the same bearing it was
at below ground in the bottom, to the first candle that was placed in the
mine, screw the circumferenter fast with the screw that fixes it upon
the legs, and look through the sights to your assistant; if he is not
right, cause him move to the right or left till you see him exactly on the
line, and sign to him to place up his pole, which is in a line with the same
bearing that was taken below ground on the first line; then examine your
book, and measure the same distance above ground you measured below,
in a line to your assistant, and place the instrument up at the end of the
line; then order your assistant to go forward while you place the needle
exactly over the second bearing you took below ground, and sign to him
to place his pole; when he is seen exact on the line, you look your book
for the length of the next line, and measure the length above ground;
go on in this manner till you have taken the same bearings and the same
distances above ground as you measured below, which determines the spot
for digging a new pit to reach a certain vein of coal.

An experienced land-measurer, in place of using the circumferenter,
would take all his bearings with a theodolite, and protract and lay down
all the zigzag angles and distances carefully that were taken below ground
upon a plan, and draw a line upon the plan from the pit mouth to the end
of the mine; he would then apply the protractor, and lay it upon the plan
in the same way it lay when he laid down the zigzag angles, and see how
many degrees and minutes the line cuts upon the edge of the protractor:
he then goes to the pit mouth, and sets his theodolite in the same position
it was below ground, and then puts the index to the same degrees and minutes as were cut upon the protractor, and orders one of his assistants to

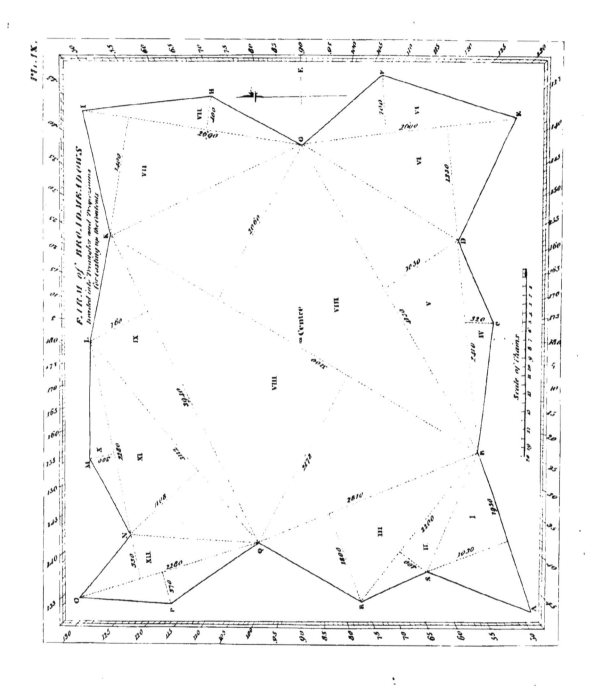

PLAN of BROAD-MEADOWS

Divided into Triangles and Projections
for casting up the contents

go forward and place a pole, by directing him to the right or left till he is seen through the telescope or sights. The surveyor then measures the length of the line upon his plan with a pair of compasses, and applies them to the same scale he protracted the bearings, by which he ascertains the distance to be measured from the pit mouth in a line towards the pole, which determines the place for digging a new pit by measuring one line only.

Plate $\frac{IX}{VIII}$. (Fig. 6.)

Is the outline of the farm of *Broad Meadows*, which was surveyed with the circumferenter, and each bearing taken with the needle by its pointing to the degrees marked in the compass box, and protracted by a square protractor, which is engraved round the plan of the farm of Broad Meadows, and which is divided into triangles and trapeziums, to give a learner an idea how it and other grounds are commonly divided before the area is obtained. (See the calculation in Areas).

The field-book of Broad Meadows was kept as follows:

Bearings.				Distances.
Deg.	Min.			Links.
70	30	Easterly	from A to B	1930
96	24	Do	from B to C	1460
65	30	Do	from C to D	1000
115	00	Do	from D to E	1520
10	30	Northerly	from E to F	1620
140	0	Do	from F to G	1240
27	0	Do	from G to H	1218
174	0	Do	from H to I	1550
76	50	Westerly	from I to K	1450
101	0	Do	from K to L	1212
90	30	Do	from L to M	1326
60	0	Do	from M to N	1000
131	0	Do	from N to O	915
5	30	Southerly	from O to P	1000
146	15	Do	from P to Q	1250
28	0	Do	from Q to R	1380
156	30	Do	from R to S	860
20	25	Do	from S to A	1300, which makes a Close.

N. B. *In surveying with the circumferenter, every bearing or angle is entrusted to the magnetic needle.*

L

ART. VII.   OF THE THEODOLITE.

Plate VIII. (*Fig.* 8.)

Is the representation of a theodolite, which is now the most common instrument that is made use of by experienced practical surveyors, and has many advantages over all other surveying instruments, particularly for taking the surveys of large estates.   To say any thing here of the invention would be superfluous, as most mathematical instrument makers claim of having made improvements upon it.

Mr Sisson was the first person that made any great improvements.   His first theodolites were made with plain sights, like those on the circumferenter; two of which were fixed, one over the north point, and the other over the south point.   There were also two moveable sights that went round the centre, which pointed out the degrees and minutes upon the limb, with an index and nonius for reading the minutes.   Mr Sisson afterwards made his theodolites with a telescope, and divided the limb into twice 180 degrees each half circle, which made it answer a semicircle as well as a theodolite.   Messrs Adams, Jones, Ramsden, Cary, Troughton, and Bennet, lay claim to having made great improvements; and indeed, it may be safely allowed, that the united abilities of those gentlemen have brought the theodolite to a state of the highest perfection.   Since the invention of Mr Ramsden's dividing machine, instead of dividing the limb into twice 180 deg. they now divide it into 360 deg. and many of them have two telescopes; one of which is always in a line with the north and south division on the limb, and the other is moveable with a rack and pinion, which moves round the limb, and points out the degrees and minutes by a fine graduate nonius. These fine divisions, where every minute can be ascertained, is no doubt very correct in taking an observation that is to be calculated by logarithms; but to a practical surveyor, a theodolite that tells within five minutes, which is as near as he can protract his bearings, answers the purpose equally well, and most practical surveyors prefer Mr Sisson's method of dividing the limb of the theodolite into twice 180 degrees.   To my knowledge, numbers of surveyors get their theodolites altered, although made by the first makers, to make the figures correspond to Mr Sisson's method; that is to say, into twice 180 degrees in place of 360, and take the under telescope off, which they make no use of. The best size for common use is about four inches and a half and five inches in diameter, with a telescope and two spirit levels fixed to it at right angles, with a quadrant divided on one side into degrees, and the other side divided so as to point the number of links to be allowed for each chain's length in ascending or descending a hill. To bring the length of the chain to the horizontal distance, great care is required, before a theodolite is used, that it is properly adjusted, and to observe if the cross hairs in the telescope be exactly in the centre of the tube, and that the level be exact. If a theodolite is used with plain sights, observe particularly if the vertical hairs in the aperture be exactly in the middle of the opening, and also if it is tight.

To use a theodolite, place it as firm as you can on the ground where you intend to begin, and also as level as possible, by moving the legs out and in till within the limits of the level screws: you may then level it exactly by the help of the four screws B B between the brass plates, which is fixed to the head of the legs; you then loosen the screw a little that holds the theodolite fast to the brass plates at the head of the legs, which screw is not seen in the figure. With both hands turn the theodolite round upon its axis, till the north end of the needle settles over the *fleur de lis* or letter N in the compass box, and observe that the vernier or nonius is exactly over 180 on the limb if it is divided twice into that number; if the theodolite is placed over 360, bring the letter N in the compass box, or the eye-glass and nonius, to 360, and the south end of the needle will point out the same degree as the nonius does on the limb, if the degrees in the compass box be divided the contrary way that they are divided on the limb. The screw that holds the instrument fast to the brass plates on the head of the legs is sometimes placed below the brass plates, and is not seen; on other instruments it is fixed in the socket C. This screw must be made very fast when the theodolite is placed, so as the needle in the box and the limb is set to correspond; and before an observation can be taken, the screw C must be loosened or unlocked a little, which holds the tele-

scope and quadrant fast to the limb, so as the pinion D may turn the telescope easily round with the thumb and fore finger, till you observe the pole
placed in the second station to coincide exactly with the cross hairs in the
telescope; then apply your thumb and finger to the screw C, which clamps
the telescope and quadrant fast to the limb; insert the bearing to the
pole in the second station, and measure the distance. If the theodolite has no pinion, recourse must be had to turn the telescope or plain
sights gently round with the hand, and then fix it fast with the screw
C, and mark the bearing, that is to say, the number of degrees and
minutes pointed out by the nonius on the limb; then plant the theodolite at the second station as before directed. The centre of it should
be exactly placed over the hole where the pole stood. Unlock the
screw a little that holds the instrument fast to the legs, and turn the theodolite round till you see through the telescope the pole left at the first
station : here screw it fast again, and unlock the other screw C a little, which holds the telescope and quadrant fast to the limb, and turn
the pinion round to the third station, and mark down the degrees and minutes of that bearing. If the magnetic needle cuts the same degree in the
compass box that it does on the limb, it is a proof that no error is made,
and that the needle has not been attracted, which it sometimes does 10 or
12 degrees ; but this you can allow for in circumstances where the needle
is influenced by attraction. Notwithstanding, in such cases, little dependence can be placed on the needle, yet it is of great use, as it affords an
excellent check. If it should be found wrong at one station, it will come
right again at another ; and if it has nothing to attract it, the degrees in
the compass box will coincide with the degrees on the limb of the theodolite, if no error has been made. What is said, I trust, will be sufficient
for a pupil to understand the manner he is to use his theodolite at each
station.

There is another method much practised by a number of land surveyors,
by setting the needle and limb of the theodolite to correspond with the
north point, and the eye-glass being brought to 360 on the limb, and the
north end of the magnetic needle to be made to settle over the south point
in the compass. Turn the pinion round till you see a pole placed in

station second, and insert the bearing in the field-book, and set down the degrees and minutes cut by the index on the limb; measure the distance from station first to station second; then plant the instrument as before at station second, by placing the north in the compass box to correspond to 360 degrees on the limb, and turn the instrument round till the south end of the needle plays over the north point in the compass box. Here screw the theodolite fast, and loosen the screw D a little that holds the instrument fast to the limb, and turn the pinion till you see the cross hairs and the pole placed in station third; set down the bearing cut by the index on the limb, and measure to the third station. If you have taken all the bearings right, the south end of the needle will correspond with the limb and nonius. Go on in this manner till you have finished the survey. By this method of measuring, every angle depends on the needle alone, and is liable to error, although the bearings are set down from the limb and index; as the needle, being set at every station over the south point in the compass box, if there is any thing to attract it, the bearing will be false. The above is supposed to be taken with a theodolite divided into 360 degrees, and the degrees in the compass box divided into the same number, but the reverse way.

Many land-measurers, who trust to the magnetic needle, have their theodolites divided into twice 180 degrees, which is preferable, as I have before observed, to dividing it into 360 degrees all round; for this particular reason, if you set up the theodolite, and turn it round upon its axis till the north end of the needle settles over 180 degrees, the south end of the needle will be over the opposite 180 degrees; so that whenever a bearing is taken, both the fore sight and back sight will cut the same degree and minute on the limb. To use the theodolite in this manner, plant it only every other station; leave a pole at station 1st, and measure the distance to station 2d, which distance mark on an eye-draught or field-book; then plant the instrument at station 2d, and turn the instrument round till the north end of the needle settles over 180 deg. in the compass box, and observe that the index is exactly at 180 on the limb; here screw the instrument fast to the legs, and unlock the screw C a little, and take a back sight to station 1st, by turning the telescope round with the pinion till you see through it the cross hairs and the pole left in station 1st to coincide : observe what degree and minute is cut by the index on the limb, which mark either on an eye-draught or a field-book, whichever you choose ; then turn the telescope round by the pinion till you see the pole in station 3d and the cross hairs in the telescope to coincide exactly, and observe the degrees and minutes cut by the index on the limb, which insert on your eye-sketch ; measure the distance from station 2d to station 3d, and also to station 4th, where the instrument is again planted ; set the index to 180 degrees, and also the needle to 180 ; here screw it fast, and take a back sight to station 3d, by turning the pinion till you see the pole and the cross hairs in the telescope to coincide : observe the degrees and minutes cut upon the limb by the index ; then turn the pinion round till you see the pole placed in station 5th ; and when the cross hairs and it coincide, mark the degrees and minutes in your eye-sketch : go on in this manner from station to station till you have finished your survey, by placing the instrument up at every other station. This is a very quick method of working with the theodolite ; but at every other station the needle is liable to be attracted, particularly if the country is mountainous and rocky. In many parts of England you may work with great safety, without the least apprehension of danger of the needle being attracted, unless you are near a gate with iron hinges, or a blacksmith's smithy, where I have observed the needle very much influenced by attraction.

Plate X. (Fig. 1.)

Is a field-sketch or draught of the farm of *Tipperty*, surveyed with a theodolite, and divided into 180 degrees from north to south, and into 180 degrees from south to north, by setting the magnetic needle at every station over the *fleur de lis*, and taking the bearings or angles from the meridian.

1st, A bearing was taken from A to a pole placed at B in the road of 120 deg. 36 min. In measuring that line, an offset was taken of 15 links to the right, and another of 20 to the left ; at 1540 an offset of 15 on the right to the corner of a yard, and another of 15 on the left ; the whole distance from A to B is 2180, from which an offset of 20 on the left and 10 on the right, to the corner of the yard ; another bearing was taken from

B to C of 115 degrees 30 minutes; the distance to C is 905, a bearing was taken from C to a pole placed at D, of 51 degrees; crossed the hedge at 20; at 400 an offset on the left of 300, at 700 an offset of 400, and at 1000 another of 500, both on the left; and at 1400, which is the whole distance from C to D, an offset of 10 to the fence or boundary; a bearing was taken from D to E of 95 degrees. In measuring that line, an offset was taken of 24 at 500, and the whole distance to E is 750, where an offset of 20 to the boundary of Mr Williamson's property; a bearing was taken of 102 deg. 40 min. from E to a pole placed in F. In measuring that line, crossed a hedge into the cow-field at 5 links; at 600 an offset was taken of 120 on the left to an angle in the fence; and the whole distance from E to F is 1380, where an offset of 15 is taken to Mr Williamson's boundary. A bearing was taken from F to a pole placed in A, where the survey was begun of 13 degrees 24 minutes. In measuring that line, an offset of 180 was taken at 1000 on the left to an angle in the hedge; and the whole distance is 2050 to A. Began again at B, where a bearing was taken to a pole placed in G of 15 degrees 40 minutes. In measuring that line, was close by the end of the house of Tipperty; and the whole distance from B to G is 380. A bearing was taken from G to a pole placed in H of 129 degrees. In measuring that line, was close by the end of Tipperty house at 26, which ascertains the breadth of the house at 130; close by the corner of the barn at 166, close by the other corner, and the length of the house is 100; and the whole distance from G to H 429. A bearing was taken from H to a pole placed in E of 28 degrees, and the distance measured to E of 1240, which finishes the house enclosure; another bearing of 129 was taken from H to I, and the distance to I is 900; a bearing was taken from I of 13 degrees to the corner of the yard, where an offset was taken to the corner on the line A B at 1540; the distance from I to that corner 260 links, which finishes the cowpark.

Began again at A, where a bearing was taken of 35 degrees 36 minutes to a pole placed in K. In measuring that line, crossed the fence at 20, and at 400 an offset was taken of 100 on the left to the boundary of Mr Williamson's property; and the whole distance from A to K 640, where there is an offset of 10. A bearing was taken at K to a pole placed in L of 95 degrees. In measuring that line, an offset of 230 at 1400; and the whole distance from K to L 2280. A bearing of 28 deg. 30 min. from L to a pole placed in B at 1590; crossed the fence to the road; and the whole distance from L to B 1610; which finishes the horse-park. Again, an offset of 20 at L to the fence on the left, and a bearing from L to M of 159 deg. In measuring that line, an offset of 350 at 600, and another of 10 at 1490; which is the length of the line L M. Lastly, a bearing of 44 deg. 30 min. was taken from M to C, and the distance to C is 655; which finishes the survey.

Plate X. (Fig. 2.)

Is the protracted plan of the farm of Tipperty, which is laid down upon a scale of 7 chains in an inch. The plotting of which is done in the following manner: Being provided with a large sheet of plotting paper, at least 90 inches by two feet, first draw a meridian line, to represent the magnetic north and south on any part of that line; near the centre make a mark ⊙, which is called the centre. The protractor used for this plan was a semicircular one about six inches in diameter, and was divided into 180 degrees, which answered to the divisions of the theodolite, and which is by far the best way of dividing a theodolite, as every time it is turned round with the pinion, either end of the magnetic needle will cut the same degree in the compass box that the limb and nonius points out on the instrument, if no error has been made in taking a bearing.

Lay the protractor upon the meridian, and the centre of it upon the mark ⊙ made on the paper; then prick off 190 deg. 36 min. and mark B, 115 deg. 30 min. C, 51 deg. D, 95 deg. E, 102 deg. 40 min. F, 23 deg. 24 min. 15 deg. 40 min. G, 129 deg. H, 28 deg. 30 min. E, 129 deg. L, 13 deg. 35. deg. 36 min. K, 95 deg. L, 28 deg. 30 min. B, 159 deg. M, 44 deg. 30 min. C. The above bearings being all pricked off from the protractor with a protracting pin, or a fine needle, with a black lead pencil either write in the figures which denotes each bearing, or the letter of reference where the prick is made, it does not matter which you insert on the plotting paper, but let them be as near the point as possible. When all is done, take up the protractor, and with a parallel ruler, or the T square and its companion,

S

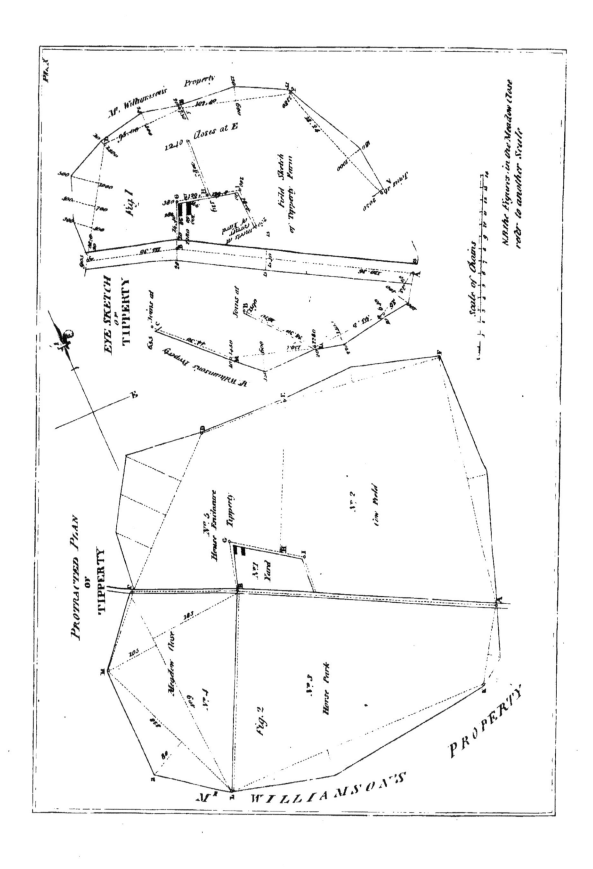

Pl. XI.

† The mark thus † shews the Bearing inclines to the Right of the last Bearing

‡ This mark shews the Bearing inclines to the Left of the last Bearing

Field Book of Hard Acre Farm

Field Book of Tipperty Farm

(see *Plate* VIII. *Fig.* 5.), lay the edge of the T square on the centre ⊙, and the prick made at 120 deg. 36 min.; then lay the companion close to the head of the T square, and slide the T square parallel to that part of the plotting paper where you begin at A, and draw that bearing with a sharp pointed black lead pencil, or the point of the compasses, and upon that line lay off the distance from A to B 2180 links from the scale you think most convenient to adopt, either with a feather-edged scale (see *Plate* II. *Fig.* 22.), or with the compasses from a scale of equal parts, and mark each station ⊙ round the prick or point made with the protracting pin or the point of the compasses; then lay the T square as before upon the centre, and its edge over the prick made at 115 deg. 30 min. and lay its companion close to the head of the T square, and slide it parallel to the mark made at B, and with a black lead pencil draw the bearing B C, and lay off the distance from the scale 905, and mark it exactly on the black lead line or bearing from B to C; then lay the edge of the square upon 51 deg. 30 min. and the centre, and slide the T square parallel to the point made at C, and draw in that bearing, and prick off the distance 1400 to D; then lay the edge of the T square upon the prick made at 95 deg. and the centre, and lay the companion close to the head of the T square, holding the companion fast to the paper while you are sliding the T square parallel to the prick made at D; then draw the bearing from D to E; then lay off the distance to E 750; again, lay the edge of the square upon the prick made at 102 deg. 40 min. and the centre, and slide it parallel to the mark made at E; draw in that bearing, and lay down the distance to F, 1380; then lay the square upon the mark made at 13 deg. 24 min. and the centre, and draw in that bearing, and lay off the distance 2050 to A. If it closes at A, where the survey was begun, it is right. Next, lay the T square upon the centre and the mark made at 15 deg. 40 min. and slide it parallel to B, and draw in that bearing, and lay off the distance 380 to G; then lay the edge of the square upon the prick made at 129 deg. and move it parallel to G; draw in that bearing, and lay off the distance to H 429; then lay the edge of the square upon the mark made at 28 deg. and the centre, and slide it parallel to H; then draw in that bearing, and lay off the distance 1240 to E. If the bearing and distance answers, you may

M

rest satisfied that you have not only taken the angles (or bearings) right, but measured the distances correctly. Then lay the edge of the T square on the mark made at 129 deg. and the centre, and slide the square parallel to H; draw in that bearing, and lay off the distance 200 to I; then look for the next mark made at 18 deg. and lay the square upon that mark and the centre, and move it parallel to I, and draw the bearing to the corner of the yard, where an offset was taken on the line A B of 15 at 1540. If it and the distance 260 answers, that part of the farm is finished that lies on the north side of the road. Again, lay the edge of the T square upon the prick made at 85 deg. 36 min. and the centre, and slide it to A; then draw in that bearing, and lay off 640 to K; then lay the edge of the square upon the mark at 95 deg. and the centre, and slide it parallel to K, and draw in that bearing with a sharp pointed pencil; then lay off the distance 2280 to L; then with the T square upon the mark made at 28 deg. 80 min. and the centre slide it parallel to L, and draw that bearing, and lay off the distance 1610 to B. If it closes right, both the bearing and distance will meet in a point. Next, lay the T square at the mark at 159 deg. and the centre, and slide it parallel to L, and draw in that bearing, and lay off the distance 1450 to M. Lastly, lay the edge of the T square upon the mark at 44 deg. 30 min. and the centre, and slide it parallel with the help of its companion, which must always be held fast with one hand while the T square is moving parallel to M; draw in the bearing from M to C, and lay off the distance, which is 655. If both the bearings and distance answer, it is a proof that no mistake has been made.

Then lay off all the offsets wherever they were taken, which are inserted both in a field-book *Plate* XI. of this survey, and in the eye-sketch, *Plate* X. *Fig.* 1. The manner of laying down the offsets is particularly described in *Plate* II. *Fig.* 14.

The above method of surveying with the theodolite is more or less liable to error, as the whole depends on the needle, which is very apt to be attracted. In some parts of the country, as some hidden magnetic power is frequently met with, and particularly in a rocky country, I have known it in a very short distance vary from 8 to 10 degrees.

Plate XII.

Shews another method of surveying with the theodolite, which many land-measurers practise in preference to any other, as no dependence is left to the needle farther than to form an idea where to draw a meridian line to fix a compass in some blank corner of the plan. The method I am to mention removes the objections which are apt to arise from the needle's variability. In this method, every angle is supposed to be read off on the limb of the instrument; and in this manner the farm of Bonnyton is surveyed. First, plant the theodolite at A near Bonny Bridge, and set the index to 360 or 180 (according as your instrument is divided) on the limb, and look through the telescope to a pole placed in B; then turn the telescope round by the pinion till you see the other pole placed in C; mark the degrees and minutes cut by the index on the limb on an eye-sketch, which is 75 deg. In measuring the line to B, insert all the offsets to the road, noting its breadth, also the distance where each offset was taken at, and the whole distance from A to B, which is 900 links. In measuring the distance from A to C, which is 560, enter in your field-book all the intermediate offsets to the river, and where they were taken at; then plant the theodolite immediately above the hole where the pole stood at station C, and set the index to 360 on the limb; loosen the screw a little that holds the instrument fast to the brass plates fixed upon the legs, and take a back sight to A and a fore sight to D and E, and set down the angle cut by the index on the limb, which is 132 deg. 30 min.; measure the line first to D 395, and then to E 300; then plant the instrument at E, and set the index to 360 on the limb, and look through the sight till you see the pole in C and the cross hairs in the telescope to coincide; then screw the instrument fast, and turn the telescope round by the pinion till the cross hairs and the pole in B coincide; then look what degrees and minutes are cut by the index on the limb, which is 72 deg. In measuring to B, an offset was taken of 105 at 450, and the whole distance to B 870. Again, plant the theodolite at B, unlock the screw a little that holds the theodolite to the legs, and put the index to 360 on the limb, and look back to E; screw the instrument fast, and take an angle to A, which is 80 deg. 30

M 2

min. which insert on your eye-sketch. You may prove upon the spot if you have taken all the angles right, by adding them together; and if the sum amounts to 360, you are certain no error has been made in taking the angles; you then return to D, and set the index to 360 on the limb, and plant the instrument, and turn it round till you see the cross hairs in the telescope and the pole left in E to coincide. Here screw it fast, and turn the telescope round till you see the pole placed in F; set down that angle, which is 88 deg. 30 min. which enter in your eye-sketch, including all the offsets, and where they were taken at to the river, and the distance to F, which is 630; set the instrument up at F, and place the index at 360, and turn the instrument round till you see the pole in D, and screw it fast, and turn the telescope round till you see the pole placed in G, and mark the angle, which is 71 deg. and the distance to G 778; then plant the instrument in G, and set the index to 360 on the limb, and turn the theodolite round till you see through the telescope the pole in F, and screw it fast, and take an angle, by turning the telescope round till you see the pole placed in E; mark the angle on your eye-sketch, which is 59 deg. and also the distance from G to E, which is 572, and also the offsets, and where they were taken at in measuring that line. Again, plant the theodolite at E, and put the index to 360, and take a back sight to G; then turn the pinion round till you see through the telescope the pole placed in D; mark that angle, which is 141 deg. 30 min. You may again prove the angles by adding them up; if the sum amounts to 360, you are certain of having made no error.

Again, plant the instrument at G, and put the index to 360, and turn the theodolite round till you see the pole in E, and screw it fast; then turn the telescope round with the pinion till you observe the pole placed at H, insert the angle on your sketch, which is 130 deg. 20 min. and the distance from G to H, which is 550; also the offsets to the river; then go to H, set the index to 360, and turn it round till you see the back pole at G; there screw it fast, and turn the telescope round with the pinion till you see the pole at I: note the angle, which is 86 deg. 20 min. also the distance from H to I, 760, likewise the offsets taken to the river. Next plant the theodolite at I, put the index to 360, then turn the theodolite

round till you see the back pole at H ; then turn the telescope till you see the
pole placed in E ; mark the angle on your sketch, which is 78 deg. 20 min.
also the distance from I to E, 928 ; then with the instrument at E, turn
it round till you see the pole placed in I ; then turn the telescope till you
perceive the pole placed in G ; mark that angle 70 deg.; return to I, and plant
the instrument as it was before, and turn the telescope round with the pinion till you see the pole in K ; insert the angle in your sketch, which is
106 deg. 40 min. and also the distance to the pole at K, 420, and an offset to the river at O, which is 128 ; then plant the instrument at K ; placing the index to 360, take a back sight to I, and turn the telescope round
till you see a pole placed in L ; mark the angle, which is 78 deg. and the
distance from K to L, 420 ; next plant the instrument in L, and put the
index to 360, and take a back sight to K ; then turn the telescope round
till you see the pole placed in M ; mark that outward angle, which is 90
deg. 22 min. and the distance to M, which is 460, also all the offsets and
small distances about the houses of Bonnyton ; then set the instrument at
M, adjust it as before till you see the pole placed in the old mark at B,
and mark the angle 95 deg. 6 min. in your sketch, also the distance to B,
which is 430 ; then plant the instrument at B, look back to M, and turn
the telescope round till you see the pole placed in the old mark in E ; insert that angle in your eye-sketch, which is 99 deg. 30 min.; then return
to M, and take a back sight to L, and turn the telescope round till you see
a pole placed in N ; mark that angle in your sketch, which is 85 deg. 32
min. and also the distance from M to N, which is 550, likewise all the offsets and measurements mark on the sketch near the houses of Bonnyton.
Again, plant the instrument at N ; it being directed, look back to M, and
turn the telescope till you see the pole placed in the mark that was left at
O ; insert the angle, which is 92 deg. 30 min. also the distance from N to
O, which is 365, which closes the survey.

Lastly, plant the instrument at O, and put the index to 360 as before ;
take a back sight to N, and turn the telescope round with the pinion till
you see a pole placed in L, which is in a line with the mark left at K ;
mark the angle in the field-sketch, which is 91 deg.; 30 min. all the angles,
distances, and offsets, and where they were taken at, being carefully marked

in the field on the spot in the field-sketches or a field-book. I shall only recommend to those who use a theodolite in a survey taken in the above method, to be very attentive, wherever it is set up, to place it as nearly level as possible with the levelling screws, and to erect it over the hole where the poles or station staffs stood. Although a practical surveyor is seldom so nice as to the levelling, imagining it sufficiently correct when he sees the needle get free play in the box, (and, in practical surveying, this is near enough in general for taking horizontal angles', yet in taking angles of elevation or depression from the horizon, the instrument must be levelled to a great nicety. At every station where the theodolite is placed, when the index is put at 360, or if divided twice into 180 deg. on the limb, the screw that holds it fast, which is commonly placed between the legs below the brass plates, must be unscrewed a little, to let the head of the instrument run easily round upon its axis: with both hands turn it round till you see the cross hairs in the centre and the pole that was left at the back station to coincide exactly; then screw it fast; you then loosen the screw marked C a little, (see theodolite *Plate* VIII. *Fig.* 8.) which holds the telescope and quadrant fast to the limb, which gives the pinion D liberty to turn the telescope round to the next pole you intend to take an angle to; and when that pole is seen to coincide with the cross hairs, screw the telescope and quadrant fast with the screw C to the limb, and then mark what angle is cut by the index on the limb. This must be particularly observed at every station. To take the survey of an estate in the manner above described, is more certain than trusting to the needle, but is more tedious, not only in taking the survey but in laying off the angles *.

I shall now point out the mode of plotting or laying off the observations contained in the sketch of the west enclosure of the farm of Bonnyton. To give an explanation of each of the enclosures throughout the whole farm, would be extremely tedious, and contain frequent repetitions: a pupil comprehending the protraction of one enclosure, can perform the whole

---

* Many practical surveyors, who use a theodolite in the above manner, are not at the trouble of taking more than two or three angles in measuring an enclosure, but make use of the chain to finish the other lines, which saves them some time in the field; but it is not so satisfactory, as they cannot prove their angles in the way mentioned in *Page* 92.

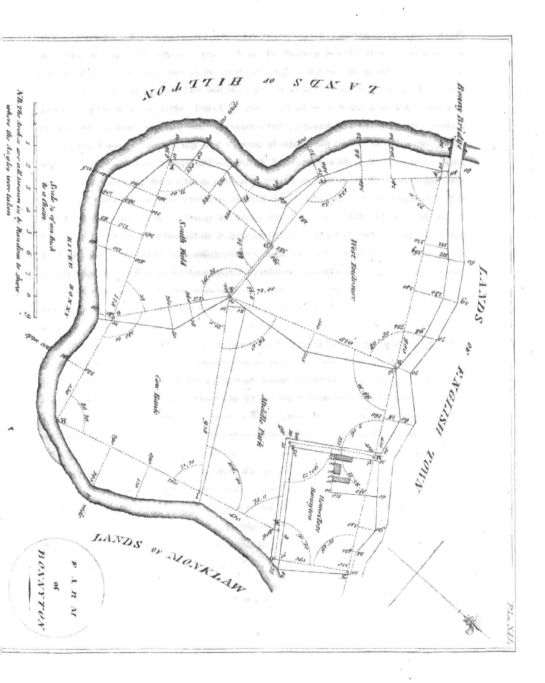

LANDS of HILTON

Bonny Bridge

LANDS of ENGLISH TOUR

LANDS of MONKLAW

PLAN
OF
FARM

West Enclosure

South Field

Gar Bank

Middle Park

Plantation

Scale by a feet
to a Chain

RIVER TEVIOT

1 2 3 4 5 6 7 8 9

N.B. The Arches are all drawn in from Random to shew
where the Angles were taken

Pl. o. XLio

with facility ; and an inspection of the sketch will give him a very good
idea of it. The best protractor for this purpose is a whole circle divided
into 360 deg. Draw an obscure line at pleasure, to represent the line A
B, and lay off the distance from A to B, which is 900 links ; then apply
the protractor to the line A B, lay its centre upon the point A, and 360
on the line B ; prick off the angle 75 ; then lay a straight edge or ruler
upon the point A and the point at 75, and draw a long line with a black
lead pencil ; then lay off the distance 560 to C, and make a mark round
the point thus ⊙ ; then lay the centre of the protractor upon that point
and 360 on the line C A, and prick off the angle 132 deg. 30 min. ; then
apply the ruler to the point C and the prick, and draw a long line, and lay
off 395 to D, and 300 more to E, and make a mark at E ; then lay the protractor upon the line E D C, and the centre on the point E, and prick off
the angle, which is 72 deg. which should meet in B ; lay off also the distance
from E to B 870. If the distance answers, you may then lay off the offsets, by
applying the feather-edged scale to the line A B, and prick off all the distances where offsets were taken at 330, 369, 540, 784 ; then 122 from 330 to the
road ; then 122 and 60 across the road from 369, the offset 150 to the road,
and 59 more across it from 540 ; then 98 and 70 more across the road from
784, and from B 70 across the road ; you then draw in the road from one
mark to another ; then prick off 40 to the road from A, and 60 more for
the width ; then draw in the road to those offsets ; from A an offset was
taken of 35 to the fence, and 50 more to the water at 240, on the line A C
and opposite it an offset of 100 to a fence, and 50 more to the water ; draw
in the fence, and also the river from the bridge, and prick off 20 to the
fence, 70 more to the water at C, and 100 wide ; draw in the fence, and
also Bonny river ; then lay off the distance from C to D, which is 395, also
the offset of 60 opposite 182, and mark where the hedge was crossed at
382 ; then draw in the fence from C to the offset at 60, from thence to
where the hedge was crossed ; next, draw in the fence from D to where
it was crossed at 12 from D ; lastly, lay off the offset of 105 opposite 450 ;
then draw in the fence from E to 105, and from thence to an offset of 20
at B, which finishes the west field : the other enclosures are all laid down
in the same way. Observe particularly, when you lay off an angle with

3

the protractor, that the centre of the protractor is exactly laid upon the mark at the station, and that 360 and 180 is exact upon the line, which should be produced a considerable way past both stations, on purpose to have more scope for the protractor.

Plate XIII.

Is a plan of the same farm of Bonnyton, surveyed with the theodolite in a very different and more expeditious manner than the method described in *Plate* XII. as every bearing is observed and reckoned by the index and limb, and no regard paid to the magnetic needle, farther than being a check to know if any error has been made in shifting the instrument from one station to another, which it is apt to do if not made fast with the screws. The best theodolite for this purpose is one divided into twice 180 degrees, that is to say, from north to south one way, and from south to north the other, and the degrees in the compass box numbered the reverse way from those on the limb of the theodolite; and if the magnetic needle is a good one, and there be no attraction, both ends of it will always correspond with the deg. shewn by the index on the limb. As theodolites are expensive, should the only one you have be divided into 360 deg. in place of into twice 180 deg. the bearings can be taken with it equally well; the needle in the compass box will correspond with the deg. on the limb every other station. To know, however, if the needle and limb coincide exactly at each station, subtract 180 : if the angle should be more than that number, then the remainder will be the degree cut by the north end of the needle; and if you use a semicircular protractor, you must do the same. *Example.* If the degree cut on the limb by the index be 195, subtract 180 from it, the remainder is 15 deg.; and when you protract the survey, you can lay off 15 deg.; or if you subtract 180 while in the field, you can there insert 15 deg. on your eye-draught or field-book, whichever you choose to keep : for my part, I give the preference to an eye-sketch; for when you are protracting and laying down your surveys, you have a much better idea of what you are doing, as at once you see whether the angles bear to the right hand or the left from the last protracted line.

To avoid repetition, I will give one general rule how the theodolite

SKETCH of BONNYTOON

Pl. XIII.

Scale of Chains

N.B. The Scale is supposed Part of a Particular Nature larger than the one on the Plan.

PLATE XIII.

Field Book for the Farm of Bonnington begun at A

ought to be used at every station. Fix upon any part of the grounds for your first station, and set the theodolite as level as you can, first, by means of the legs and the levelling screws; then set the index exactly over 180 on the limb, and unlock the screw a little that holds the instrument fast to the legs, and take both hands and turn the head round till the north end of the needle settles over the south point in the compass box. Here screw the instrument fast to the brass plates, then loosen the screw C a little that holds the telescope and quadrant fast to the limb; then turn the telescope round with the pinion D, which on some theodolites is made to project out from the outer edge of the limb (see *Plate* VIII. *Fig.* 8.), till you see the pole placed in the 2d. station and the cross hairs in the telescope to coincide; then make it fast with the screw C, which will keep it from shifting in carrying it from one station to another, and set down the bearing cut by the index on the limb. The same operation must be performed at each place the theodolite is planted at, except setting the needle in the compass box, which is only done the first time to ascertain the bearing. In this method of surveying every angle is taken from the meridian. This keep in mind; then plant the instrument at A in the west enclosure near Bonny bridge, and take a bearing to B, which is 62° 30', and the distance to B is 900; which mark on an eye-draught or field-book, with all the intermediate distances on that line; that is to say, not only the offsets, but the distance must be marked where they were taken at, which insert either in an eye-sketch or a field-book (see *Plates* XIII. and XIV.): then return to A, and take a bearing to C 138°; then screw the telescope and quadrant fast to the limb, and measure to C, which is 560; which insert on your eye-draught or field-book, also all the intermediate distances and offsets to the river. Again, plant the instrument at C, and unlock the screw a little that holds the head of the theodolite fast, and turn the theodolite round till you see the pole placed in A and the hairs in the telescope to coincide (this is called taking a back sight); then screw it fast, loosen the screw C a little, and turn the telescope round with the pinion D till you see the pole placed in D and E, which are in a line; mark the bearing, which is 89°, also the distance to D 395, and from D to E 300, and where the offset was taken of 60 at 182, and where the hedge was crossed at 382 near D; all of which being entered on your sketch, set up the instrument in E, and take a back sight to C and a fore sight or bearing to B, which is 162° 48′, and the distance to B is 870; which mark on your eye-sketch or field-book, also the offset of 105 at 450, and mark Meets at B, which will keep you in remembrance that you made a close at B.

You then return to the mark left at D; erect the instrument, and put the index to 89° on the limb, and take a back sight to E, which is the same bearing as was before observed; then turn the telescope to F, and make it fast with the screw C, and mark the bearing, which is 177° 36′, and the distance from D to F is 630; which mark in the sketch or field-book, likewise all the intermediate distances taken to the river. Again, plant the instrument at F, and take a back sight to the pole left in D; then turn the telescope about till you see a pole placed at G; insert the bearing 68° 48′, also the distance to G 778, and all the intermediate distances on that line; then plant the instrument at G, and take a back sight to F, and turn the telescope round to E, and mark the bearing 127° 12′, and also the distance 572, and all the intermediate distances and offsets taken on that line, to prove if the angles have been all right observed. Plant the instrument in E, and take a back sight to G; then turn the telescope round till you see the pole placed at the old mark D. If the bearing is 89°, it is the same as it was before, which makes you certain that no error has been made in taking the angles. Return to G, and put the index to 127° 12′, and take a back sight to E, and turn the telescope about with the pinion till you see the pole placed in H; mark the bearing 77° 24′, also the distance 550 to H, and the offsets taken to the river. Plant the instrument in H, and take a back sight to G, and turn the telescope about to I; insert the bearing 164° 44′ on your eye-sketch or field-book, also the distance from H to I 760, likewise the intermediate distances and the offsets to the river; next plant the instrument in I, and take a back sight to H, and turn the telescope about till you see the pole placed in E, and insert the bearing 57° 12′, and also the distance 928 to E, and also the offsets, and mark Closes at E; then take a bearing to K 164° 44′, and mark also the distance from I to K 420; then plant the instrument in K, and take a back sight to I ; turn the telescope round, and take a bearing to O; mark the bearing 57° 30′, and the distance to O 128°; both of which enter in the eye-sketch or field-book ; then take a bearing from K to L 57° 30′, also the distance 420 from K to L, and the short distances and offsets about the houses of Bonnyton ; then go to L, and take a back sight to K, and a bearing to M, which is 147° 6′, and the distance from L to M 400. Plant the instrument in M, and take a back sight to L, and turn the telescope about till you see a pole placed in B. If it answers to 62° 30′, and the distance 430 from M to B, it is right. Then turn the telescope round with the pinion from M to N, and mark the bearing 62° 30′ on the eye-sketch or field-book, and also the distance from M to N 550, and all the intermediate distances and offsets about the houses of Bonnyton. Lastly, go to station N, and turn the telescope about till you see the pole placed in the old mark at O, and mark the bearing 147° 30′, and the distance from N to O, which is 366 ; the angle and distance being noted down, write Closes at O; then plant the instrument in O, and take a back observation to N, and turn the telescope about till you see a pole placed in L. If the bearing answers to 57° 30′, which it will do if no error has been made, you may be certain your survey will close, if no mistake has been made in measuring the distances with the chain : if an error has been made, the protracting will not close; which will oblige the surveyor to go out to the field again to find out where the mistake has been made.

I have no doubt but some land-measurers, who have uniformly used the theodolite by setting the index and limb to 360°, and taking the angles in the field at each corner of the fences, will not allow this method to be so good as that which they have been particularly accustomed to; but I can with safety inform them, that a land-surveyor can, by the method just described, take the bearings with equal expedition in the fields, and can (by using a T square or parallel ruler) protract them from one centre in half the time usually taken by using a protractor or line of chords.

To protract the observations from the field-book on the farm of Bonnyton, I will refer the learner to the same method as particularly described in laying off the meridian and distances in the farm of Tipperty, *Plate* X. by protracting all the angles from one centre, and using a parallel ruler or the T square; which undoubtedly is the best parallel ruler that was ever made use of by a land-measurer for expediting his protractions, either from a field-book or eye-draught, which should be kept as regular as possible, something in the manner of the field-sketch of Tipperty *Plate* X. or of Hardacres *Plate* XV. The sketches must be made much larger than those used on the Plates. A land-measurer need not be particular as to the proportion of either length, breadth, or size of his sketches in the field; but only to make them so as he may have room upon his paper to insert all his figures, fences, boundaries, &c. and may use as many pages on his book as he chooses, but to be sure to mark where he leaves off on one page, and where he begins upon another. If the surveyor prefers keeping a field-book, specimens are shewn in *Plates* X. XV. and XVI. In writing a field-book out of doors, it cannot be expected to be kept very clean and regular; only observe to make your figures as regular and legible as possible, and to mark every thing minutely down, in such a manner as you can clearly understand it. At night, protract what has been measured during the day; and if an error has been made, it must be rectified the first thing that is done in the morning in the fields.

The only difference in protracting the above farm of Bonnyton from the method used in Tipperty farm is, that the latter was laid off with a brass semicircular protractor, and the former laid down by a semicircular one, supposed to be drawn upon a large sheet of paper, at least three times the diameter of the one engraved upon *Plate* XIII. In the farm of Tipperty, every angle has to be pricked off with a protracting pin, and has to be properly numbered or figured; whereas by a protractor drawn upon your plotting paper, you have only to look for the degrees you want, which are instantly found out, they being regularly marked round the arch. I shall here give a short description of laying off the bearings and distances of the principal lines that were measured on the farm of Bonnyton; and the bearings laid off with a protractor I shall suppose drawn upon paper of large dimensions.

1st. Lay the T square upon the centre ⊙ and 62° 30', which is the bearing from A to B; and then lay the companion to the head of the T square, and move it parallel to A; then draw in that bearing, and prick off the distance, which is 900 links to B. Again, lay the T square upon the centre ⊙ and 138°, which is the bearing from A to C; then lay the companion to the head of the T square, which hold fast with one hand till the other hand slides the T square parallel to A ; draw the bearing, and lay off upon it the distance, which is 560 links from A to C *. Again, apply the T to 89° and ⊙, and move it parallel to C ; then draw the bearing, and lay off the distance 395 to D, and 300 more to ‚E; apply the T to ⊙ and 162° 48′, and slide it parallel to E ; draw the bearing, and lay off the distance 870 to B, which makes a close. Lay the T on ⊙ and 177° 36′, and move it parallel to D ; draw in the bearing 177° 36′, and lay off the distance 630 to F ; lay the T on ⊙ and 68° 48′, and move it parallel to F, and draw in the bearing, and lay off the distance 778 to G ; lay the T upon 127° 12′ and ⊙, and slide it parallel to G ; draw in the bearing, and lay off the distance 572 to E, which makes another close. Lay the T on ⊙ and 77° 30′, and move it parallel to G, and draw in that bearing, and lay off the distance 550 to H ; lay the T upon ⊙ and 164° 44′, and move it parallel to H ; draw in that bearing, and lay off the distance 760 to I ; lay the T on 57° 12′ and ⊙, and move it parallel to I ; draw that bearing, and lay off the distance 928 to E, where it should meet ; lay the T upon 164° 44′ and ⊙, and move it parallel to I ; draw in that bearing, and lay off the distance 420 to K ; lay the T on 57° and ⊙, and move it parallel to K ; draw in that bearing both to the right and left of K, and lay off the distance 128 to ⊙ on the right, and 420 to L on the left along the road ; lay the T upon 147° 6′ and ⊙, and draw it parallel to L ; draw in that bearing, and lay off the distance 400 to M ; lay the T upon 62° 30′ and ⊙, and move it parallel to M, and draw in that bearing both ways from M ; lay off the distance 430 to B and 550 to N ; lay the T upon 147° 30′ and ⊙, and slide it parallel to N ; draw in the bearing and lay off the distance 366 to O, where it should meet if no error has been made. The laying down the offsets, and where they were taken, is done in the same manner as those described in *Plate* II. *Fig.* 14. *Page* 19.

Plate XV. (*Fig.* 1.)

Represents the field-sketch of the farm of *Hardacres.*—The survey was

* To shorten the description, ⊙ stands for centre, T is the T square and companion ; which will avoid repeating those words at full length

begun near the bridge of Allan with the chain, and a theodolite divided into twice 180°, which, as I have observed before, is the best way of dividing the limb of that instrument, as the needle and the limb will always coincide when there is nothing to attract it from its natural polarity. Enough has been, I hope, already said, to describe the method practised in measuring, taking bearings, offsets, &c. &c. This being the case, it would only be a repetition of what has been done in the farms of Tipperty, Bonnyton, &c. The first line measured, and a bearing taken, was from Allan bridge-end down the river, and all the necessary offsets taken to the river to a mark left at B at 1450; returned again to the bridge-end, and took a bearing up the river to a mark left at C, distance 1200; returned again to the bridge-end, and took a bearing up the road. In measuring that line, made a mark at 800, where an offset was taken on the left of 26, and another on the right of 30, where a hedge went off to the right and another went off on the left; both of which were straight, and continued the line to a pole placed at D; and the whole distance is 1569, as may be seen both in the field-book *Plate* XI. and the eye or field-sketch *Plate* XV. *Fig.* 1. The instrument was planted at D, and a back sight taken to a pole left at A at the bridge-end, and a bearing taken on the right of 21° 20′ to a pole at E, and the distance to it is 1380, where the instrument was again planted, and a back sight taken to the pole left at the cross roads, and a fore sight of 97° taken to B to a pole placed in the old mark made at the river. In measuring that line, crossed the straight hedge at 610; and the whole distance is 1390, which is marked in the eye-sketch as well as in the field-book *Plate* XI. Returned back to the cross roads at 1569, where the instrument was erected, and the index put to 102° 6′, on the limb which is the former bearing from the bridge-end; the telescope was then turned round with the pinion, and a bearing of 120° taken up the road. In measuring that line, mark the distance to Hardacres' houses, and also to the cross hedge; also insert the whole distance to F 1500, where the theodolite was again planted, and a back sight taken to the last station, and a bearing to the right of 30°. In measuring that line, insert all the offsets to the boundaries in the eye-sketch, as well as in the field-book, and the whole length of the line 1290 to G, from which a back sight was taken to a pole left in the road

3

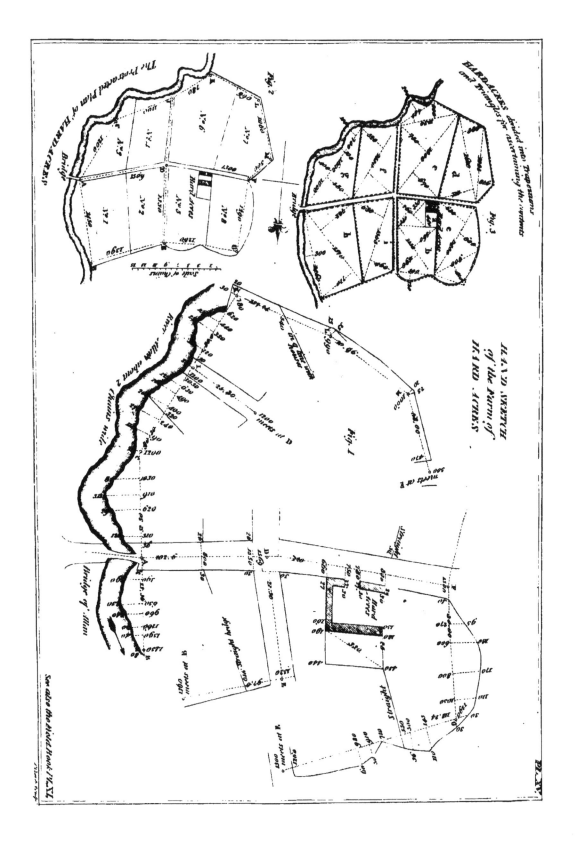

at F, and a bearing of 113° 24′ taken to the old mark in the road at E. In measuring that line, crossed a straight hedge in a line with the houses of Hardacres at 550, which had a bearing of 25°, and the whole distance was 1300 to E, where another close was made. Returned to C to the mark at 1200 at the side of the river Allan, where, after placing the index to 52° 30′ on the limb, took a back sight to a pole placed where the survey was begun at A, and turned the telescope round by the pinion, and took a bearing of 90° 30′ to I, to a pole at the end of the cross road. In measuring that line, crossed the straight hedge to the houses at 320; the whole length of the line is 1100 to I, where the instrument was set up, and a back sight taken to a pole at the last station, and a bearing taken to a pole on the right of 25° 30′, along the road to a pole which was set up at the old mark at D, and insert the distances in the sketch, and also the whole distance to the middle of the cross roads, which is 1200, which made another joining. Returned again to I, and setting the index to 25° 30′ on the limb, which is the former bearing to the cross roads, took a bearing to a pole of 80° to K, and measured the distance 780, and the offsets to the river. The instrument was again planted, and a back sight taken to the pole left in I. In measuring that line, crossed a straight hedge, which runs in a line towards the houses at 540, and the whole distance to the pole 990, where a back sight was taken to the last station, and a fore sight of 10° 6′ to a pole at M; the distance to which is 1060. The instrument was again placed at M, and a back sight taken to a pole left at 990, and a bearing of 68° and a distance measured of 500 to a pole placed in the old mark at the head of the road at F, which makes another close or joining. Returned to the houses, which were all measured, and also the yards, as may be seen by the sketch, which finished the survey.

I shall now again refer the learner to the method of protracting used in laying down the angles and distances in the farm of Tipperty, *Plate* X. or the farm of Bonnyton, where the bearings were all laid off by a large protractor drawn upon paper, (see *Plate* XIII.) and he may either lay off his parallels with the T square or a parallel ruler, and lay off his distances either with the scale and compasses or a feather-edged scale, as it suits conveniency.   If he prefers keeping a field-book to an eye-draught, see *Plate* XI.

Plate XV. (*Fig.* 2.)

Is the farm of Hardacres protracted from a small scale, on purpose to give the learner an idea how one part bears from another   On it I have only inserted the principal lines that were measured, which are dotted, and the length of each station. To have put in all the bearings and offsets upon so small a scale would have made it confused and unintelligible. The pupil may make a plan upon a large scale for improvement, either from the eye-sketch *Fig.* 1. or field-book *Plate* XI.

Plate XVI.

Is a sketch of the farm of *Dundaff*, where all the measured lines are represented by dots, also the offsets, and where taken at; likewise the bearings, and is protracted from a scale of four chains in an inch, and is partly measured within the grounds and partly without, and the bearings taken with a theodolite divided into 360°, and made use of in the same manner as described in the farms of Bonnyton *Plate* XIII. and the farm of Hardacres *Plate* XV. By setting the north end of the needle over 180° degrees in the compass, and the index over 360° on the limb of the theodolite; by this way of beginning the survey, the needle corresponds with the limb of the index only every other station; whereas in the above-mentioned farms of Bonnyton and Hardacres, both ends of the needle always correspond with the limb, if no error is made, and no hidden magnetic powers to attract it. The only difference is, that in taking a bearing one way, I shall suppose 90°, in looking forward to a station, and when you go up to that station, and take a back sight to the pole left at the last station, the bearing is 270, whereas, when the limb of a theodolite is divided into twice 180, the fore sight and the back sight is always the same, which requires only a semicircular protractor to prick off the bearings, but the other requires a whole circle, which must be divided into 360°. Should you not make use of it in taking a fore sight, and then a back sight, it must be used in the same way as described in *Plate* XII. farm of Bonnyton, with the addi-

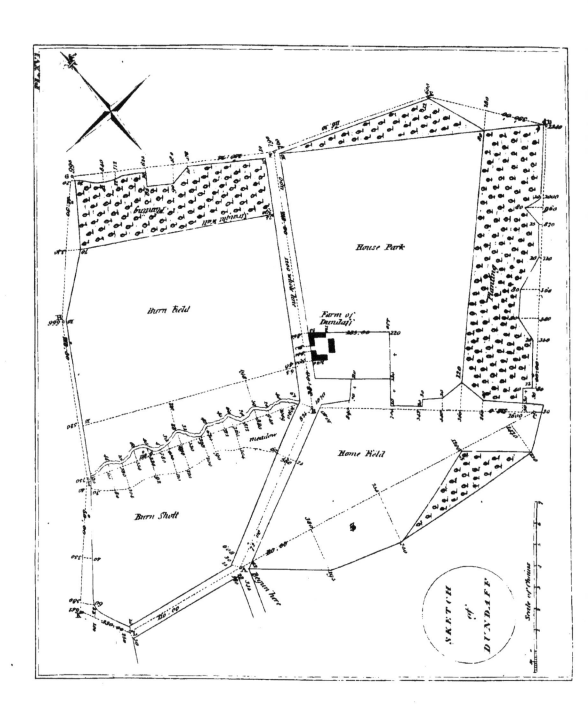

PLAN I

House Park

Farm of
Dunlaff

Home Field

Burn Shott

meadow

SKETCH
of
DUNDAFF

Scale of Chains

FIELD BOOK of PINSLEY

tional trouble of putting the index to 360 on the limb every station to take the back sight, which is very tedious to protract, as the protractor must be removed from one station to another, to lay off every angle that has been taken at the different stations.   Although this method of surveying is practised by four-fifths of the land-measurers in the united kingdom, it is neither so quick in the field, nor so soon protracted, as fixing the screw C on the theodolite, *Plate* VIII. at every bearing that is taken, and remains fixed till you go to another station and take the back sight : indeed some land-measurers that make use of two telescopes, the one below the limb, and the other above the quadrant, may be as quick in the field, the under telescope being always fixed under 360, and the upper one that is above the quadrant is moved round the limb by the rack and pinion.   A theodolite of this description is called *the new improved theodolite ;* but few practical surveyors make use of the under telescope ; besides, in surveying with it, when you come to lay off the angles, the protractor must be removed from one station to another, as described of *Plate* XII. farm of Bonnyton, as I have taken notice of above, which is extremely tedious.   But for preferring one method of surveying and protracting to another, I am aware of exposing myself to censure ; for well do I know, that every surveyor is partial to his own method of working, both in the fields and in the house, It is not uncommon for a land-measurer who has been accustomed to measure with the chain alone, to condemn all other instruments whatever ; but this may be owing to their being ignorant of the use of any other. What I have principally been attempting is, to describe the *different* methods of using the theodolite in the field, pointing out the various methods of protracting the observations, keeping the field-book, and taking eye-sketches in the field, that a learner may adopt whichever method he is partial to.

Plate XVII.

Is the field-book of *Dundaff.*—The survey of Dundaff was begun at A, and a bearing of 72° and a distance measured of 824 to B ; returned to A, where a bearing of 110° was taken to a pole placed in C.   In measuring that line, all the intermediate distances were inserted, which are marked on the sketch, and the distance 1600 to C, where the instrument was again planted, and a back sight taken to A : the screw was loosened a little, and the telescope turned round by the pinion to B, and the bearing 318°, as also the distance 1070 to B, inserted in the field-book, with all the intermediate distances and offsets ; a bearing of 50° was taken, and a distance of 1340 from C to D, with all the intermediate distances. The instrument was planted at D, and a back sight taken to C, and a bearing of 330°, and a distance of 600 to E. The instrument was set up at the corner of the planting at E, and a back sight taken to D, and a bearing of 116° 30′, and a distance of 790 to F, where the instrument was again planted, and a back sight taken to E, and a bearing of 218°, also a distance of 1200 to B, which makes a close ; another bearing was taken from F of 130° 24′, and a distance of 995 to G. The instrument was set up at G, and a back sight taken to F, and a bearing of 51° 30′, and a distance of 668 to H, where the instrument was again planted, and a bearing of 218° 30′, and a distance of 750 to I ; where the instrument was again set up, and a back sight taken to H, a bearing was taken up the brook of 118° 6′, and a distance of 1090 to the corner of a hedge at the road near the houses ; another bearing was taken from I of 50° 00′, and a distance of 642 to K. The instrument was again set up at K, a back sight taken to I, a bearing of 330°, and a distance of 250 to L, where the instrument was again planted, and a bearing of 110° and a distance of 608 to A ; which makes a close. Returned to the houses, and took a bearing of 135° along the yard dike, and measured the length, breadth, &c. of the yard and houses ; which are all inserted in the field-book, as are also all the offsets and intermediate distances on each of the lines, whether in the farm or out of it.

Great care is required in protracting a farm measured in the way that Dundaff is with a theodolite divided into 360° : when a back station is taken it reverses the degrees, that is to say, the first station from A, the bearing was 110 to C, when the instrument is placed at C and a back sight taken to A ; and if another pole was put in the same line, the bearing to it would be 290. The only way that I know to rectify this is, by putting the index to the limb to coincide with 290, which is known by adding 180 to 110, or subtracting 180 from the number of degrees between that and

360, and protract the remainder. For example, in looking down, the bearing from F to B is 218, in looking up from B to F the bearing is 38°; now if 180 is subtracted from 218, the remainder is 38°, which the index should be placed at on the limb in taking a back-sight from F to B. This may be thought troublesome, which no doubt it is. I know of no other method to go regularly on, but by placing the theodolite at every station, and setting the magnetic needle over the *fleur de lis* in the compass box, and taking the bearings and angles from the meridian in the same way as described of *Plate* X. *Fig.* 1. farm of Tipperty, which was surveyed by a theodolite divided into twice 180°, and which is preferable to a theodolite that is divided into 360 to a practical surveyor; yet I must acknowledge I give the preference to a theodolite that is divided into 360° for taking a range of bearings in taking the survey of a county. To protract and lay off the angles, I refer the pupil to the same method as described of *Plate* XIII. farm of Bonnyton, *Page* 96. or *Plate* X. farm of Tipperty.

The most tedious and troublesome survey a land-surveyor generally meets with (except a large town), is taking the measurement of common fields, in some places called *Borough-acres*, and in other places *Run-rigs*. The method I have hitherto practised has been, by first measuring and taking offsets where necessary, and marking every distance, and inserting the name of every proprietor on an eye-sketch, which I make as large as I have room for, as there are a great number of short distances to set down, as may be seen on *Plate* XVIII. *Fig.* 1.

The survey was begun at A at the corner of Robert Brown's ridges, where the theodolite was properly adjusted and planted, and a bearing taken to D of 26° 48', and another to B of 155° 30'. In measuring the line from A to D, entered upon David Rennie's property at 300, upon Thomas Smellie's property at 397, upon Mrs George's at 560, upon Gabriel Peacock's at 640, upon Robert Thomas's at 1000, upon John Dice's at 1162, upon John Wilson's at 1290, and crossed John Wilson's far boundary at 1432; and the whole distance to D is 1500; which is inserted both in a field-book and an eye-sketch, also all the offsets and intermediate distances, and where they were taken at: returned to A, and measured towards B; entered upon Robert Brown's property at 793, and left it at 1400, and measured on to B 1560, where the instrument was planted. After having inserted in the field-book and eye-sketch all the intermediate distances and offsets, a back sight was taken from B to A, and a bearing of 43° taken to C. In measuring that line, inserted every proprietor's name where the chain entered their property, also the distances, in the same manner as marked on the line A D, and the whole distance 1740 to C, likewise the offsets, and where they were taken at. The instrument was again set at C, and a bearing of 142° 24′ taken to the old mark left at D, after taking a back sight to B. In measuring that line, entered upon John Wilson's property at 100, and left it at 1162, and the whole distance to D is 1900 ; which made a close. That distance, as well as the intermediate ones and the offsets, and where taken at, were entered upon the sketch, as well as the field-book kept by one of the assistants by way of a check.

Plate XVIII. (Fig. 2.)

Is the eye-draught, representing where the fields were crossed to ascertain the different breadths, which are very irregular, as may be seen by *Fig.* 3. The field was crossed, as may be observed, at six different places, at the distance of 250 links from one crossing to another, except the last, which was only at 200 : a bearing was taken of 43° at each crossing, on purpose to go parallel with the line B C, as no back sight could be got : the needle in that case was trusted to, by setting it over the north point in the compass box and the index to 180 on the limb, and turning the pinion round till the index cut 43° on the limb. One of the assistants was sent forward with a pole to John Wilson's boundary, and a sign is made to him to move to the right or to the left till he is seen through the telescope, where he sticks in the pole, which is parallel with the line B C. Began to measure across the different properties at Robert Brown's boundary, being the line b b, to the outside of John Wilson's boundary, which is 1808, and marked each property at entering upon them, and also the name of every proprietor, as was done upon the line A D. Returned again to Robert Brown's boundary, and measured the line c c, where a bearing of 43′ was taken across the properties as before on the line b b, and marked where every proprietor's land was entered upon, as also their names, and

PLATE XXVII.

Scale of Acres

Scale of chains

Scale 8 chains to an inch.

Fig. 1

Fig. 2

Fig. 3

Fig. 4

Fig. 5

Rob. Brown

David Renne

Thomas Smith

Mrs Greegs

Geo. Pollock

Robt. Thomas

Joseph Dow

John Hilson

Sketch in going round the Boundary

Contents of the Boundary

Pl. XIX.

FIELD BOOK of the Common Field

Begins at Bottom
Left hand Column

	Distances and Bearings	
Enters	1370	for Boundary
	1090	John Wilson
	1000	Jas Dixe
	902	Robt Thomas
	500	Gabriel Pedrick
	237	Mr George
	1300	Thos Smellie
		David Rennie

Returns to Robt Browns Boundary 2010 below last crossing

Enters	1360	for boundary
	1128	John Wilson
	1110	Jas Dixe
	920	Robt Thomas
	420	Gabriel Pedrick
	247	Mr George
	1300	Thos Smellie
		David Rennie

Returns to Robt Browns Boundary 2010 below last crossing

Enters	1405	for Boundary
	1128	John Wilson
	1087	Jas Dixe
	707	Robt Thomas
	325	Gabriel Pedrick
	208	Mr George
	1300	Thos Smellie
		David Rennie

Returns to Robt Browns Boundary 2010 below last crossing

Enters	1605	for Boundary
	1326	John Wilson
	1226	Jas Dixe
	822	Robt Thomas
	430	Gabriel Pedrick
	250	Mr George
	1300	Thos Smellie
		David Rennie

Returns to Robt Browns Boundary 2010 below last crossing

Enters	1907	for Boundary
	1680	John Wilson
	1590	Jas Dixe
	1175	Robt Thomas
	1012	Gabriel Pedrick
	860	Mr George
	630	Thos Smellie
	278	David Rennie
	1300	

Returns to Robt Browns Boundary 2010 below last crossing

Continuation of the Common Field

		John Wilson for Boundary
	1808	John Wilson
Begins	1570	Jas Dixe
	1477	Robt Thomas
	1355	Gabriel Pedrick
	1110	Mr George
	740	Thos Smellie
	528	David Rennie
	1300	across the Lands

Returned to Robt Browns Boundary B C
2010 below B C

Meets at D

Leaves J Wilson	58	
	33	
	63	

Enters	1740	J Wilson for Boundary
Enters	1420	John Wilson
Enters	1310	Jas Dixe
	1090	Robt Thomas
Enters	1070	Thos Pedrick
	800	Mr George
Enters	400	
Enters	400	Thomas Smellie
	400	David Rennie

	1000	Robt Brown
	1225	
	1322	
Leaves R Brown	1050	

Returns to A

Enters	1340	John Wilson for Boundary
Enters	1453	
	1035	John Wilson
	1162	Joseph Dixe
Enters	1000	Robt Thomas
	900	
	945	
Enters	1030	Gabriel Pedrick
Enters	1656	Mr George
	1558	Thomas Smellie
Enters	597	
	3000	David Rennie

The Common Field

A

the whole distance, which is 1904. Returned again to Robert Brown's boundary, and measured the line d d across to John Wilson's far boundary, which is 1605 ; returned again to Robert Brown's boundary, and measured the line e e to John Wilson's far boundary, which is 1464 ; returned again to Robert Brown's boundary, and measured the line f f, which is 1360 : lastly, went to the old mark in A, which is only 200 links from f f, and measured across to John Wilson's far boundary, which is 1322. The distances were all carefully set down on an eye-sketch, and also on a field-book, with every distance where each proprietor's land was entered upon, and also their names on each of the crossings. A land-surveyor that has had much practice, instead of returning always back to Robert Brown's boundary, after having finished one line, would measure 250 links from John Wilson's boundary across to that of Robert Brown's, after taking the bearing 43° across the properties ; and so on alternately, by measuring across one way and returning the other. But this method is not so distinct as the way described above, although it would save a great deal of time in the field. It is not material whether you cross the properties at 100, 200, or 250 links ; but it is absolutely necessary that you know the distance of one crossing from another.

Plate XVIII. (*Fig. 3.*)

Is the protracted plan of the common-field, laid down upon a small scale. The lines that were measured are represented by dots ; each angle is inserted, and the whole length from one station to another ; but on account of the smallness of the scale, being only eight chains to an inch, there is not sufficient room for inserting all the intermediate distances of each person's property, nor the offsets, or where they were taken at : however, it is apprehended it will give the learner an idea of plotting, either from a field-book or eye-sketch of the ground.

In plotting this field, draw a line at pleasure to represent a meridian, and lay a protractor upon that line : first prick off the centre ⊙, and also the bearings 26° 48', 155° 30', 43°, and 142° 24' ; then apply the T square, or a parallel ruler, to the centre and the prick made at 26° 48', and slide it parallel to any part of the paper you intend to begin at, and with the compasses take off the distance 1500 from a large scale, and lay it off from A to D; then lay the T square upon 155° 30', and the centre ⊙, and move it parallel to A; draw that bearing, and lay off the distance 1560 to B; then lay the T upon ⊙ and 43°, and draw the bearing from B, and lay off the distance 1740 to C; then apply the T to the ⊙ and 142° 24'; draw in that bearing from C, and lay off the distance 1900, where it ought to close; which it will do if the angles have been all right taken, and the distances measured correct. Again, lay off all the intermediate distances and offsets round the field, draw in the boundary from one offset to another; and when you lay off the cross lines, lay down the bearing 43°, which will always be parallel with the bearing laid down from B to C, and prick off every intermediate distance from Robert Brown's boundary to John Wilson's far boundary, which was measured across the field, and make marks with the point of the compasses where you crossed every property; do the same upon all the other lines that were measured across the field; then draw in with a black lead pencil from one mark to another, humouring the natural bends of the curve of each property which are very crooked, which ink in without loss of time, and insert each proprietor's name upon his ridges.

Plate XIX.

Is the Field-book of the common-field, run-rigs, or burrow-acres.

Plate XX.   (*Fig.* 1.)

Is an eye-sketch of a survey taken of a harbour, which is reckoned a very difficult survey, as so many objects have to be taken notice of. This survey was taken with a theodolite divided into twice 180°, which was first planted at the farther part of the east new pier, where a bearing was taken of 50, and a distance measured of 460 feet to a pole. The instrument was again set up at 460, and the theodolite turned round, by taking a back sight to the last station and a bearing to the east head of 110°, and the distance to the end of the east head was 210; another bearing was taken from 460 of 90° 30' to a pole placed at 140; the instrument was again planted at 140, and a back sight taken to the last station, and the telescope turned round to the corner of a house next the harbour, which

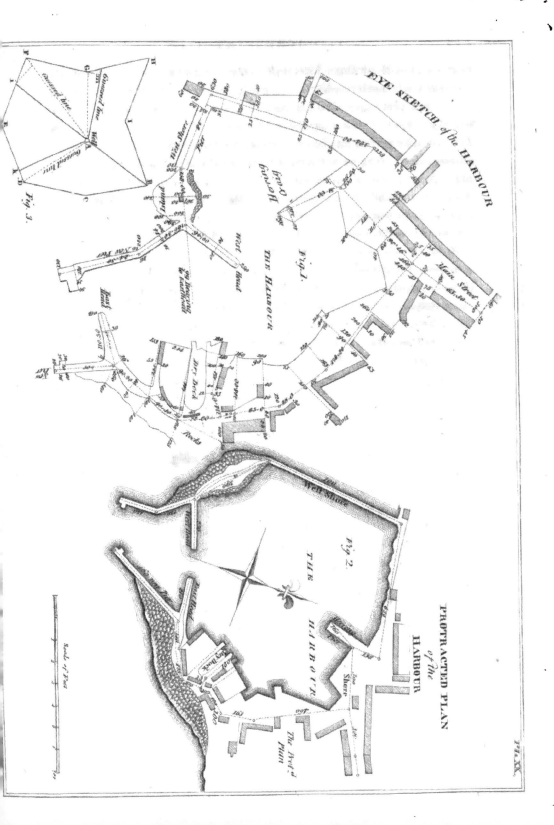

EYE SKETCH of the HARBOUR

Fig. 3.

Fig. 1.

THE HARBOUR

Fig. 2.

THE HARBOUR

PROTRACTED PLAN
of the
HARBOUR

PL. XX.

Scale of Feet

bearing is 135°, and a distance of 153; another bearing was taken from 140 of 90° 30′ to a pole placed at 125; from whence a bearing was taken of 144° along side of the dry dock, which measured 244; another bearing was also taken from 125 of 22°, and the distance measured 100 feet; a bearing was taken from 100 of 114° to a short distance of 33, and from 33 a bearing was taken of 151° to the end of a house on the north side of the dry dock, which measured 180 feet. It will be proper to observe, that many offsets were taken, and the distances set down in the sketch, which the pupil must refer to. Another bearing was taken from 100 of 22° to a short distance of 40, from whence a bearing of 148° was taken, and a distance measured of 160 feet to the harbour; another angle was taken from 40 of 65° to a pole at 120; from thence a bearing was taken of 15° to a pole placed at 163, and a bearing taken of 178° 20′ to a pole placed in 460, and offsets taken to the left to the harbour, and also to the right to the houses; at 460 a bearing of 85° 30′ to the right hand up the main street, and a distance measured of 300; another bearing to the left of 97° 36′ was taken at 460, and a distance measured of 300 to the corner of the herring pier, which measured 300; from whence a bearing was taken of 51° to the south corner of the herring pier, which measured 160 feet; another bearing was taken from 300 to a pole placed at 138; from thence a bearing was taken of 104° to a pole placed at 630. To enumerate all the different offsets, and where taken, I refer the pupil to the sketch, which will give him a better idea than lengthening the description to several pages. A bearing was taken of 28° at 630 along the west shore pier to a pole placed at 700; from whence a bearing was taken of 158 to a pole placed at 390; from thence a bearing was taken of 96° 30′ along the west head, and a distance measured of 250; another bearing was taken from 390 across the mouth of the inner harbour to the east head of 99°; also another bearing was taken from 390 to a pole of 166° 30′, and a distance measured of 220; from thence a bearing was taken to the end of the new west pier, and a distance measured of 150.

To plot the observations taken of this survey will require a considerable time, on account of the numerous distances and offsets. To give an explanation here, would merely be a repetition of what has been already fully explained of *Plate* X. farm of Tipperty, also of *Plate* XIII. farm of Bonnyton.

Plate XX. (*Fig.* 2.)

Is a small protracted plan of the harbour laid down from the rough eye-sketch, upon a scale of one fourth of an inch to 100 feet in length, inclu-ding the principal measured lines set down upon it from one station to ano-ther only, which, it is thought, will tend to give the learner an idea what he will have to do if he thinks proper to lay it down upon a larger scale.

Plate XXI. (*Fig.* 3).

Land-surveyors are frequently employed to take the survey of a road, and to ascertain the distances of such farm-houses as are near to it on each side, as well as those places that are adjacent to it. *Fig.* 3. is an eye-sketch of a road, the dimensions of which are taken in feet, and the bear-ings taken with a theodolite divided into twice 180°. The survey was be-gun at Stage-hall, where the instrument was planted, and a bearing on the right taken of 38° to Hemp-house; the next bearing is 21° 30' to Hill-head, and another bearing was taken on the left of 84° 30' to Hillton, and a bearing taken to a pole along the road of 130°, and the distance of 1500, to the pole where the theodolite was planted, and a back sight taken to a pole left at Stage-hall; a bearing of 102° taken to Hemp-house, also ano-ther to Hillhead of 83° 48',and another on the left to Hillton of 170° 30'. In protracting these bearings, where they intersect will ascertain the distance they are from the road. An angle was also taken up a bye-road of 97°, in a line with the house of Janefield, and a bearing along the road to a pole of 176° 30', and the distance of 1670 measured to the pole where the instrument was planted, and a bearing taken of 130° 24' to Hillhead, when you protract that bearing. If the intersection answers by all three bearings meeting in a point, it is a proof that no error has been made. Another bearing was taken on the right to Bogton of 168°, also one of 83° on the left to Janefield, likewise another of 88° 30' to White-kirk, and a bearing of 130° 24' along the road to a pole, and a distance of 1800 mea-sured to the pole. In measuring that line, past by the house of Tippermore on the right at 800, and a bye-road on the left at 1300.   The instrument was next erected at 1800, and a bearing of 70° 18′ on the right to Bogton, and another of 148° to Jock's Lodge, also a bearing on the left of 172° 30′ to Janefield, and another of 20° 30′ to Whitekirk, likewise another of 80° 24′ to Primrose, and a bearing along the road of 122° to a pole at 1200, where the instrument was planted, and a bearing of 84° 24′ to Jock's Lodge ; also another of 148° to Wallton, and a bearing on the left of 168° 24′ to Whitekirk, and another of 41° to Primrose, and a bearing along the road of 87°, and a distance of 1850 to the pole.   In measuring that line, past a bye-road on the right and the house of Knotting at 800 ; and at 1600 entered the village of Durham, the whole distance to the pole being 1850 in the middle of the village, where the instrument was planted, and a bearing taken on the right of 46° to Walton, another on the left to Primrose of 128° 36′, another of 185° along a straight road to Janefield, and another of 148° along the road to Wicklaw. In measuring that line, past the house of Coldhome on the left at 1000, and the house of Fairholm on the right at 2500, and left off at 4000 at Wicklaw. A pupil will observe to be very careful in protracting his distances and bearings, wherever the bearings intersect one another, as observed before. If right taken, they will be the exact distance from the road, also the precise distance from one another ; and if three or more bearings to any one place intersect in a point, it is a proof that the distances, as well as the angles, have been all right taken.   If the road was 50 or 60 miles in length it must be all done in the same way.   A surveyor ought always, if possible, to have three or even more bearings to an object, in order that he may be completely certain of the intersection.

Plate XXI. (Fig. 4.)

Is a protracted plan of the road laid down from the eye-sketch upon a scale of 200 feet in an inch, which is introduced to point out the length of the road, and how the different houses stand, and also how they are situate one from another.   It was laid down from one centre, and the bearings laid off by a paper protractor, as described in *Plate* XIII. and the bearings drawn with the T square and its companion, as particularly described of *Plates* X. and XIII. which it is needless to repeat here, as the method of

P

using the theodolite, the protractor, and T square, have been so often taken notice of in this work.   An eye-sketch for a survey of this kind is
preferable to keeping a field-book ; for to set down all the distances, bearings, and names of places, &c. in a field-book, would make it so complex,
that it would not easily be understood; besides, a sketch gives a much
better idea how to protract the road.

Plate XXXIV.   (Fig. 9.)

Represents the section of two hills that the boundary of an estate goes
over, where the hypothenuse can only be measured, which is much longer
than the level line A E.   As a convex surface cannot be laid upon a sheet
of drawing paper, the difference must be found out by reducing the hypo-
thenuses to horizontal measure, which is commonly done on the spot, if
the quadrant on the theodolite is divided, as is observed it should be in *Plate*
VIII. *Fig.* 8. description of the theodolite, page 83, which shews at once
what number of links to allow in each chain's length in ascending or descending a hill at a certain angle.   If it is not divided in that way, the
following table must be applied to when you are plotting your survey,
otherwise great mistakes will occur in calculating the adjoining lands, as it
will give the measure of them shorter upon your plan than what they really
are : for example, if you take a piece of thread, and put in pins at A, B,
C, D, and E, and apply the length to the level line A E, it will reach to
F, which is 392 links too long.   The figure being laid down upon a scale of
ten chains to an inch, this makes it evident that the line measured across the
hills must be reduced to horizontal measure, that every field on the plan
may lie in its true situation ; which they will not do if no allowance is
made ; and will not only displace the next fence, but over-run a great space
into the next field, and make it too little.

The following Table shews the number of links to deduct from each chain's length in ascending or descending a hill, or any uneven ground. to reduce the hypothenusis to a level.

If the ascent or descent of a hill be nearly as below.

Deg.	Min.	Links.	Deg.	Min.	Links.
4	00 deduct	$\frac{1}{8}$	28	55 deduct	$12\frac{1}{2}$
5	44	$\frac{1}{2}$	29	30	13
7	6	$\frac{3}{4}$	30	5	$13\frac{1}{2}$
8	10	1	30	40	14
11	30	2	31	15	$14\frac{1}{2}$
12	50	$2\frac{1}{2}$	31	45	15
14	4	3	32	20	$15\frac{1}{2}$
15	10	$3\frac{1}{2}$	32	50	16
16	15	4	32	25	$16\frac{1}{2}$
17	15	$4\frac{1}{2}$	33	55	17
18	10	5	34	25	$17\frac{1}{2}$
19	30	$5\frac{1}{2}$	34	55	18
19	55	6	35	25	$18\frac{1}{2}$
20	45	$6\frac{1}{2}$	35	55	19
21	35	7	36	25	$19\frac{1}{2}$
22	20	$7\frac{1}{2}$	36	55	20
23	5	8	37	20	$20\frac{1}{2}$
23	45	$8\frac{1}{2}$	37	50	21
24	30	9	38	15	$21\frac{1}{2}$
25	10	$9\frac{1}{2}$	38	45	22
25	50	10	39	15	$22\frac{1}{2}$
26	30	$10\frac{1}{2}$	39	40	23
27	10	11	40	5	$23\frac{1}{2}$
27	45	$11\frac{1}{2}$	40	40	$23\frac{1}{2}$
28	20	12	41	0	24

Explanation of the Table.

For example, as the length of the line A B, *Plate* XXXIV. *Fig.* 9. is 1200, and the angle of declivity is 17° 15′, shews that 4 links and a half are to be deducted from every chain, which shortens the distance 54 links; the length of the line B C is 830, and the angle of declivity is 16° 15′, shews that 4 links is to be deducted from each chain, which shortens the line 98 links; the length of the line C D is 800, and the angle of declivity 34° 55', shews by the table that 18 links is to be deducted from each chain's length, and that the distance must be shortened 144 links; the length of the line D E is 700 links, and the angle of declivity is 39° 40', which shews that 23 links must be deducted from each chain; which shortens the distance 161 links.

Plate XXI. (Fig. 1.)

Represents a large enclosure of 74 acres 49 perches, the outline of which is upon a gentle declivity, but has a very serpentine brook or rivulet running through it, with very steep banks on each side of the brook. The proprietor wished to know the difference betwixt the horizontal and the surface measure. Angles of declivity were taken on various parts of the bank, to find out the difference of the hypothenuse and level. It was found that the difference was 6.05 acres; which, when added to the amount of the enclosure by the first measure, would have made the park 80 acres 54 perches, in place of 74 acres 49 perches, as before mentioned. Those deep ravines, glens, or gullies, are frequently met with in large surveys. Great care ought to be taken by land-measurers to make the allowance for ascending or descending hills and steep banks by the table for shortening the hypothenuse lines in plotting, otherwise the lines will not meet upon paper when the distances are laid down upon the plan. For example, if you was to take the breadth of the enclosure across the middle from A to B, it would extend the line to D, which makes a difference of 170 links in width. This park is merely introduced to shew the difference betwixt horizontal and surface measure; which by some surveyors is disputed, on account that hilly ground is not so productive as level land. I certainly agree with them; but it is not a land-measurer's business to mind whether one part of the ground is more fruitful than another, but that of a valuator, who places such value as by experience he thinks the land is worth per acre; and the land-measurer's duty is to do his business correct. The additional trouble in measuring and plotting hilly ground is undoubtedly their objection for not giving the surface measure the pre-

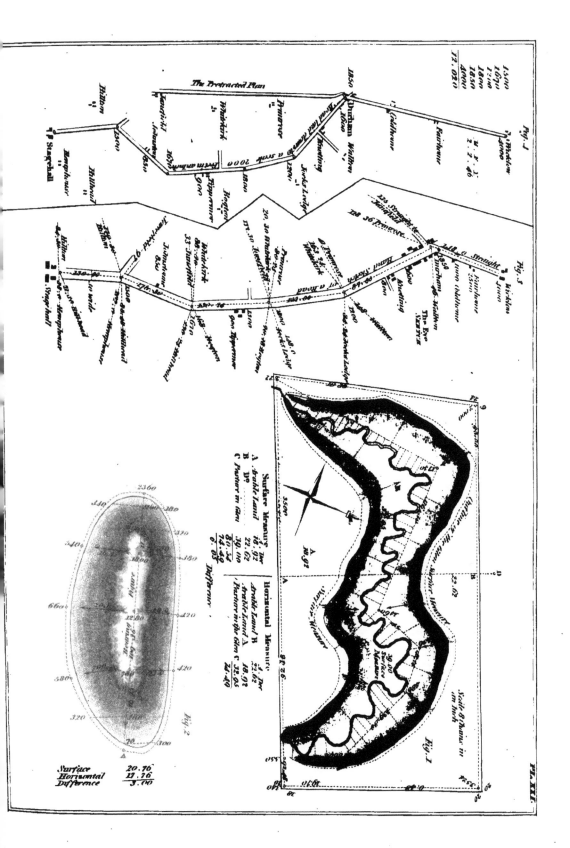

PL. XLI.

ference to that of the horizontal, which every surveyor ought to allow for in laying off the distances upon their plans, otherwise the lines will not meet, and the adjoining land will have too little measure.

Plate XXI. (*Fig. 2.*)

Represents a hill; and the difference is required between horizontal and surface measure? The surface measure is 20 acres 76 perches, and the horizontal measure only amounts to 17 acres 76 perches, which makes three acres of difference. In measuring up the hill from whence the survey was begun at A, an angle was taken up the hill of 16° 25′, and the distance to the pole is 780, which shortens the line 31 links and a half at 780; a line was measured down the hill on the right of 420, and the angle of declivity is 23°, which shortens the line 38 links; a line was also measured from the same place on the left of 580, and the angle of declivity is 20°, which shortens that line for plotting 34 links; a line was measured from 1280 on the right of 420, and the angle of declivity is 26°, which shortens that line 44 links; a line was also measured on the left from 1280 of 660, and the angle of declivity is 20°, which shortens that line 43 links; at 1800 a line was measured of 380 on the right, and the angle of declivity is 26°, which shortens that line 40 links; another distance of 540 on the left, and the angle of declivity is 16° 15′, which shortens that line 21 links: continued the line to the far side of the hill, which is 2360; deduct 1800, there remains 560, and the angle of declivity is 11° 30′, which shortens that line 11 links for plotting. *Note,* The black line round the hill is the horizontal, and the dotted line is the surface line for calculating the contents of the hill. It must be observed, if this hill had stood in the middle of a plain, and no allowance made for reducing the hypothenuse to a horizontal level, it would encroach upon the plain, and make it too little by three acres.

Plate XXII.

Is a plan of the farm of *Jamesfield*, the boundaries of which lie very flat; but there are four enclosures near the centre of the ground, which

are situate upon a hill. After having measured round the farm, and protracted the angles, and laid off the distances, they answered very exact;
but in protracting the angles, and laying off the distances across the hill
from station 1st to station 6th, in place of meeting in a point, the distance
over-stretched as far as *, which a surveyor calls a *bad closing*. A line
was then protracted across the ground from station 4th to station 9th over
the hill, which over-lapped station 9th as far as the mark *; from which it
is evident the surface measure over the hill was the cause of the protracting not meeting. The ascents and descents of the hill were then tried
to find out these errors.

The theodolite was planted at A, and set level, and an angle of acclivity taken of 20° 40′ to B, and the distance from A to B, which measured
548; the instrument was then planted at C, and an angle of declivity taken of 19° 55′, and the distance from C to D measured 575; the instrument
was then set level at E, and an angle of acclivity taken of 28° to F, and
the distance measured from E to F 417; the theodolite was then set level
at H, and an angle of declivity taken to I of 18°, and the distance measured to I 465.

By the table, the line A B being 548, and the angle of declivity 20° 40′,
shews that the line must be shortened 6 links and a half each chain, which
in the whole is 35 links, leaving the plotting line only 508, the line C D
being 575, and the angle of declivity 19° 55′, shews by the table, that 6
links must be shortened per chain, which in the whole is 35 links, and
leaves the plotting line but 540; which makes a difference of the whole
length from station 1st to station 6th of no less than 70 links. The line
E F being 417 and the angle of acclivity 28°, must be shortened 8 links
in each chain, in the whole 33 links, and leaves only 384 for plotting.
The line H I being 465, and the angle of declivity 18°, must be shortened
5 links in each chain, in the whole 23 links, and leaves but 442 links for
plotting; which makes a difference of the whole length in crossing the
hill from station 4th to station 9th of no less than 56 links.

After having made the above allowances in plotting, it turned out that
the closing came very near the truth. But the surveyor, when he calculates his survey, must be particularly careful to cast up the contents by

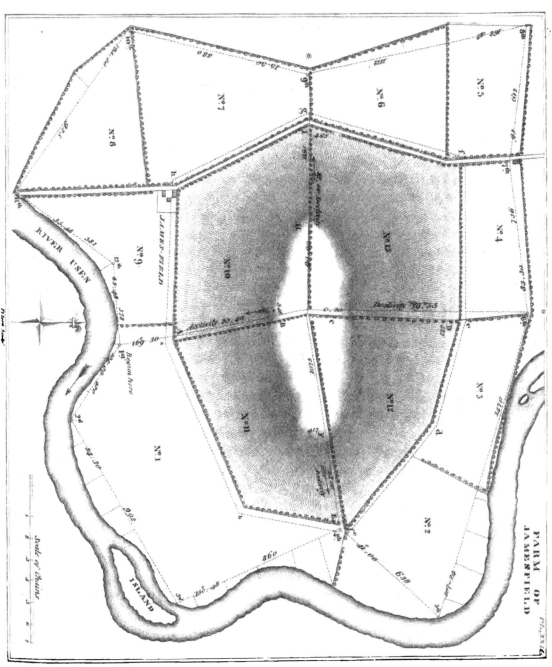

FARM OF JAMESFIELD

PLATE XXXV.

the surface measure, and not by the distance given in plotting the four enclosures on the hill, but must make his triangles and trapeziums extend to the dotted line a b c d e f g h when he casts up the contents of the four enclosures ; and he must observe, when he calculates the surrounding fields, to make his triangles and trapeziums to extend to the plotted line or hedge.

This plan is introduced principally to shew the bad effects of making no deduction in plotting, as the four enclosures on the hill, and each of the adjoining enclosures in the valley, would have been several poles too little ; which points out the necessity of making the deduction betwixt the hypothenuse and level in plotting the survey of an estate, where hills or rising grounds are met with ; otherwise it is impossible that the angles and distances will meet, and consequently the calculation will be false.

On this plan I have only inserted the length of each line in going round the farm, and also the angle that each bearing makes with the meridian. To have inserted all the intermediate distances and offsets would have made it too complicated, and not answered so well the purpose intended. The plan is laid down from a scale of four chains in an inch, and the angles laid off by a semicircular protractor, the same as represented on *Plate* XIII. farm of Bonnyton.

Having hitherto treated of taking the surveys of inclosed lands, I now come to shew the method of taking the survey of a large uninclosed farm of upwards of 190 acres, with a theodolite divided into twice 180 degrees.

Plate XXIII.

Represents the *Field-book* of Greenside Hill farms.

Plate XXIV.

Is the grazing farm of *Greenside Hill*, the survey of which was begun at A, and a bearing of 113° 30', and a distance measured of 1080 to B, to a mark at red river ; returned to A, when another bearing was taken of 92° 48', and a distance of 2060 to C. In measuring these lines, several offsets were taken to the north brook, which were entered in a field-book, and on the plan also where those offsets were taken, which are re-

presented by dotted lines, as well as the bearings from one station to another, there not being sufficient room upon so small a scale to insert
upon the plan all these short distances, and where they were taken at,
without creating confusion.   An eye-sketch is much preferable to a field-
book for a survey of this sort, as, upon it, a land-surveyor can sketch in
the hills upon the spot, and can also make his sketches so large as to allow every figure to be legibly inserted.   The theodolite was planted at C,
at the edge of a morass, and a bearing inclining a little to the right hand
of the last line A C of 94°, and a distance of 3800 to D; also all the offsets to the north brook, and where the morass was left, regularly entered
in the field-book in measuring the line; the instrument was again taken
to D, and a bearing on the left of the last line C D of 171° 30', and a distance measured of 2360 to E, and also an offset of 60 at 1300; the theodolite was planted at E, and a bearing of 153° 30', inclining a little to
the left of the last line DE, and a distance measured of 1400 to F; the
instrument was then planted at F, and a bearing inclining a little to the left
of the last line E F of 138° 46', and a distance of 1500 measured to G;
the theodolite was then placed at G, and a bearing of 107° 30', inclining
a little to the left of the last line F G, and a distance measured of 700
to H, also all the offsets to the south brook or burn; the instrument
was then placed at H, and a bearing at a very acute angle on the left
of the last line G H of 49° 30', and a distance measured of 310 to I; the
instrument was then planted at I, and a bearing of 97° 12' on the right,
and a distance measured of 1180 to K, and also all the offsets to the south
brook, and where they were taken at, and entered in the field-book; the
theodolite was taken to K, and a bearing of 72° 40' inclining to the left,
and a distance of 510 measured to L; the instrument was then planted at
L, and a bearing of 85° 30', inclining a little on the right of the last line
K L, and a distance measured of 1720 to M, also all the intermediate distances and offsets taken to the south brook entered in the field-book; the
instrument was then placed at M, and a bearing of 24° on the left down
the river, and a distance measured of 960 to N, and all the offsets to the
river, and where they were taken at, and entered in the field-book; the
instrument was planted at N, and a bearing of 140° 30' taken on the left,

FIELD BOOK of GREENSIDE HILL.

Bearings inclining to the Right thus
D° D° to the Left

	Offsets	Bearings and Distances	Offsets	
		700	10	H South Brook
		470	150	Tynehouse Lands
		260	60	
		107.30		
		1560	10	G
		136.18		
		1400		F
		153.30		
		2360	10	E
		1300	60	
		121.30	24	
		3800	208	D The north Brook
		3600	110	
		3250	90	
		3080	10	
		2920	20	
		2730	100	
		2600		
		2450		
		2270	190	Lands of Hyndlee
		2100	180	
		2020	100	
		1750		
		1580	12	
		1500	140	
		1380	20	
		1230	30	
		1150	18	
		980	180	
		800	80	
		660	180	
		380	220	
		9400		
		2060	10	C
		1800	100	·100
		1280	70	The north Brook
		1100	70	
		910	170	
		630	10	
		380	170	
		100	10	
		92.48		
	Returns to A.			
		1080		B
Water	300	880		
	280	770		
	80	700		
	2	500		
Junction of Brook	200	200		with the Water
		113.30		A

Begins here

	Offsets	Bearings and Distances	Offsets	
		800	200	T
		640		
		400	110	
		200	110	
		156.00		
		550	5	S Water
		71.00		
		380	60	R Water Edge
Crosses Brook		130		
		3600		
		725	70	Q
		570	10	
		130	230	
		115.00		
		770	10	P
		660	30	
		400		Red Water or River
		62.30		
		900	200	
		320	10	
		240	30	
		140.30		
		980	5	N
		310	90	
		400		
		60		Crosses Road
		2400	140	Edge of water and Brook foot
		1220	10	M
		1540	260	
		1400	180	
		1140	240	
		930	180	
		710		
		520	140	
		340	80	
		140	140	
		85.30		
		510	140	L
		360	10	Along the south Brook
		230	110	
		110	150	
		72.40		
		1180	80	K
		1000		
		870	60	
		600	100	
		340	10	
		280	70	
		97.12		
		310	100	I
		220	20	
		80	106	
		40.30		

	Offsets	Bearings and Distances	Offsets	
		2000		Closes at X
		7.38		
	Returns to X			
		1500		Meets at C
		62.00		
Along a Sike		1620		Y
		140.00		
	Returns to U			
		2150		Closes at D
Brook head	300	1120		
	240	880		
	80	580		
	90	380		
		280		Crosses Brook
		144.00		
		1370	18	X
		1240	90	Mid Brook
		870	90	
		600	110	
		400		
		180	70	
		137.40		Returns to W
Closes at V		1540		
		1200		Crosses Brook
		980	80	
		660		
		500	100	
		370		Crosses Brook
	70	120		
		53.30		
		720		
		600	10	W
		400		Mid Brook
		270	10	
		93.06		
		720	20	V
		480	120	
		300		
		200	60	
Heath		44.40		
		2580	10	U
		2480		Crosses Brook
	10	2380		
		2270		Crosses Brook
		2140	70	
		1980		Crosses Brook
Opposite a Sike	10	1600		
		1500		Crosses Brook
		1380	80	
		1000		
		900	100	
		570	10	
		500	70	
		220	100	Corner Yard + 200
		40		Crosses Road
Returns to Q		92.30		
		625		Closes at B
		300	40	
		280		
		62.00		T

Field Book of the Hill Farm of Greenside begins at A.

Pl. XXIV.

LANDS of PRIMROSE

Red River

North Brook

Mid Brook

South Brook

West Pasture

Dry Pasture

Morass

Hill Pasture

Mess

Heath

Scale of Chains.

PLAN
of
GREEN-SIDE
HILL

and a distance of 900 to O; the theodolite was carried to O, and a bearing of 62° 30′ sharp on the right, and a distance of 770 to P; the instrument was then planted at P, and a bearing of 115° on the left, and a distance of 725 to Q; the theodolite was then taken to Q, and a bearing on the right of 5°, and went close by the farm house, and a distance of 380 to R; the instrument was placed at R, and a bearing of 71° on the right down the river, and a distance of 550 to S; the instrument was planted at S, and a bearing of 156° on the left, and a distance of 800 to T; the instrument was set up at T, and a bearing taken down the river of 67° to the mark that was left, and the distance to B measures 625; which makes a close. All the distances and intermediate distances, with the offsets, were all regularly inserted in the field-book from M to B to the river, which the pupil is referred to. Returned to the mark near the houses at Q, where the theodolite was planted, and the index and the limb was set to 115°, which is the same bearing as before, and a back sight was taken to P, and bearing of 92° 30′, and a distance of 2580 to U, and also the intermediate distances and offsets, and where the line crossed the brook, were entered in the field-book; a bearing was then taken from U on the left of 49° 40′, and a distance of 720 to V; a bearing was taken on the right from V of 94° 6′, and a distance of 740 to W; a bearing was then taken from W to F of 53° 30′, and a distance of 1540 up the small branch of the brook; which made another close at F. Returned again to the mark at W, where a bearing was taken up the mid brook of 137° 40′, and a distance of 1370 to X; from X a bearing was taken, inclining a little to the right, of 141° to D, and a distance of 2150; which makes another closing at D. Returned to U, where a bearing was taken up a syke or small run of water of 140°, and a distance of 1620 to Y, where a bearing was taken of 62° along the side of the morass, and a distance measured of 1500 to C; which makes another joining. Then returned to the mark at V, and placed poles on the line from V to I; as the pole placed in I could not be seen from V, a bearing was taken from V of 2° 38′ to a pole placed in the same line with I, and a distance measured along the side of the dry ground and the moss of 2060 to I, but is obliged to allow 60 links for the rise of the hill, which makes another closing. It is to be observed, wherever a bearing is men-

Q

tioned to be taken, that the theodolite is exactly placed over the marks where the poles were placed, and a back sight taken to the station it was last set up at.

After a careful perusal of what has been already said, it is hoped the pupil will find no difficulty in plotting Greenside Hill farm, with a theodolite divided into twice 180°. To cast up the contents, the plan should be laid down upon a large scale, and the quantity of heath, moss, morass, wet and dry pasture, calculated separately, and the quantity of ground contained in each inserted on the plan by some of the methods, as will be particularly described in the next Section *.

* There are many land-measurers who prefer taking angles or bearings with a theodolite, and measuring round the boundary of a farm, although it should be three or four miles in circuit, and are very particular in marking, either in a field-book or on an eye-sketch, every thing remarkable near to the boundary as they measure along, leaving marks on the ground where they cross fences, brooks, roads, and also where they ascend or descend a hill, to make an allowance to bring the acclivity or declivity to the horizontal distance for plotting, as described in *Page* 83.; and they are also very particular in digging a hole with a spade, or driving in a stake, at each station the instrument was planted at, till such time as they have gone all round and made a close. When this is done, they protract the bearings or angles, and lay off the distances from any scale they choose to adopt. If no error is made, the angles and distances will meet in a point, (if great care and attention is taken). Afterwards they go to the field, and measure and finish all the other lines with the chain alone, in the same manner as described of *Plate* III. *Page* 19. farm of Longlee. Those that practise this method of surveying are very partial to it, as it saves the inconvenience of carrying the theodolite to the field, unless they meet with particular parts of the farm where angles are required to be taken, which they can perform quicker than measuring with the chain alone, it being every surveyor's chief aim to be as expeditious and accurate as possible, which can only be attained by attention and practice.

SECTION THIRD.

OF AREAS.

ART. I. TO FIND THE AREA OF REGULAR AND IRREGULAR FIGURES.

THE *Area* or *Content* of land is in general named in England and Ireland, *acres*, *roods*, and *perches*; in many parts of England the *perches* are named *poles*; in Scotland, the perches are named *falls*. Now there being 100 links in a chain, and ten chains long and one chain wide being one acre, 1000 links, which is the number of links contained in ten chains, if multiplied by 100 links, the product is 100,000 square links, which is equivalent to one acre, and is known by cutting off the five cyphers on the right hand, thus 1.00000.

Also five chains in length and two chains in breadth is one acre, and four chains long and two and a half wide is also an acre. Land-surveyors seldom write down the words chains and links when in the field; but thus, 500 for 5 chains, 200 for 2 chains. Now if 500 be multiplied by 200, the product is 100,000; and when the 5 right hand figures are cut off, there remains 1.00000 as before; which 1 is an acre: but if a distance is measured of 11 chains and 50 links, it is marked 1150; or, suppose you have measured a line 19 chains and 75 links in length, it is expressed 1975. Now if 1975 is multiplied by 1150, the product is 22.71250; by cutting off 5 figures on the right hand, there remains 22 acres on the left; the decimals .71250 are square links, which when multiplied by 4 (the number of roods in an acre) brings the decimals into roods. After cutting off 5 figures on the right, the product is 2.85000 roods; then .85000 multiplied by 40 (the number of perches, poles, or falls in a rood), the product is 34.00000, which is 34 perches; which gives in the whole 22 acres, 2 roods, and 34 perches or falls.

The calculation as under will appear plain.

$$
\begin{array}{r}
1975 \\
1150 \text{ multiplied by} \\
\hline
98750 \\
1975 \\
1975 \\
\hline
\end{array}
$$

acres 22.71250 product
           4 multiplied by

roods 2.85000
           40 multiplied by

perches 34.00000

A practical surveyor is seldom at the trouble of casting up the contents of the decimals of an acre, but cuts off the 5 figures on the right hand, and what is above 5, adds the letter A, which represents acres.

In the following examples I shall use a few algebraic notations, merely for shortening the calculations, viz. + for the sign of addition; — for the sign of subtraction; × for the sign of multiplication; ÷ for the sign of division; and = as signifying equal to.

The area or superficial content of a square is easiest found.

Suppose the square, *Plate* II. *Fig.* 6. each side of which is 800 links, what is the area? The product of 800 × 800 is 6.40000 acres; which × by 4, to bring the decimals into roods, and the remaining decimals × by 40, to bring them into perches as before directed, is = 6 acres, 1 rood, 24 perches.

Suppose the parallelogram or oblong, *Plate* II. *Fig.* 7. is 1167 long and 305 wide; then 305 × 1167, the product is 3.55935; which × 4, to bring the decimals .55935 into roods, is = 2.23740 roods; then .23740 × 40 is, = 9.49600 perches, which is = 3 acres 2 roods 9 perches and a half nearly.

It is presumed, from what has been stated above, that a pupil will be at no loss in understanding how the amount in square links is turned into acres, roods, and perches.

Example III. Plate II. (Fig. 8.)

Is a triangle, the base of which is 1125, and the perpendicular 550: the half is 275; which × 1125, the product is 3.09375 = 3 acres 15 perches. It will turn out the same measure if half the base had been multiplied by the whole of the perpendicular; half the base 562 × 550, the product is 3.09375 = 3 acres 15 perches.

All triangles are measured in the same manner, either by taking half the length of the perpendicular, and multiplying it by the length of the base, or by taking half the length of the base, and multiplying it by the perpendicular.

Example IV. Plate I. (Fig. 12.)

The right-angled triangle A B C, whose sides are 740; the square of which is 5.47600 acres, the half is 2.73800 acres, = 2 acres, 2 roods, 38 perches.

Plate I. (Fig. 21)

The trapezium, whose diagonal from A to B is 1200, and the sum of the perpendiculars are 1080; the half of which is 540 × 1200, the product is 648000 = 6 acres, 1 rood, 37 perches.

In place of measuring the two perpendiculars separately, and adding them together, and then halving the sum, a practical surveyor would lay a parallel ruler upon the diagonal A B, and move it parallel to the angle D, and draw the line D e, and take off the distance with his compasses from the angle C, by putting one point in C, and measuring to the nearest part of the dotted line D e; which will give the same distance as the sum of the two perpendiculars, by applying that extent on a scale equal to double the extent of the scale the figure is laid down by. This operation saves the trouble of adding and dividing.

Plate II. (*Fig.* 9.)

Is another trapezium, whose diagonal from A to B is 1290, and the sum of the perpendiculars is 1080, the half is 540 × 1290 = 6.96600. In this Figure an angle is supposed to be taken with the chain (see *Plate* II. *Fig.* 12. and *Page* 16.), which saves the trouble of measuring the diagonal across the enclosure: it also shews, by drawing a line parallel to the diagonal D B from A to e, and by applying the compasses to the angle C, and extending them to the nearest part of the line A e, is the sum of the two perpendiculars; which distance, if applied to a double scale, saves the trouble of adding and halving the same, as in *Plate* I. *Fig.* 21.

The area or contents of irregular fields, of whatever number of sides, are generally determined by dividing them into triangles, trapeziums, &c. and measuring them separately; and the products being added together will be the sum total or area (see *Plate* IX.). Regular circles, polygons, or ellipses, seldom occurring in practice, for the sake of the curious, I shall merely give a few examples how the areas are commonly calculated.

Plate II. (*Fig* 10.)

Is a circle, the contents of which is wanted. Various methods have been tried to get the exact contents; the common method is by multiplying half the diameter by half the circumference, which gives the area. For example, half the diameter of the above figure is 605, half the circumference is 1901; when multiplied into one another, gives 1150101 square links, which is equal to 11 acres, 2 roods.

Another method is by squaring the diameter, and multiplying the amount by .7854: the square of the diameter is 1464100, multiplied by .7854 is 1149904.14; cut off the decimals, and there remains 1149904; cut off 5 figures to the right hand, multiply the remainder by 4, and cut off 5 figures on the right; then multiply by 40, and cut off 5 figures, and there remains 84772 decimals of a pole or perch; the amount is 11 acres, 1 rood, 39 $\frac{8}{16}$, very near the first calculation.

It frequently happens that the diameter of a circle cannot be measured,

1

particularly in a round plantation, a round building, hay-cock, or fish-pond : in that case, if you can get the circumference measured, the diameter is found out thus.

Plate II. (*Fig.* 11.)

The circumference of the outmost circle is 4400, which, if multiplied by 7, is 30800, and divided by 22 is 1400. For the length of the diameter, the content is found out in the same way as described above in Figure 10th, which amounts to 15.40000, or 15 acres, 1 rood, 24 perches. The circumference of the inner circle is 2515.2, and the diameter is found as above to be 800 : square the diameter as before directed, and multiply by .7854, and cut off the four decimals, and there remains 5.02656 for the amount of the inner circle, which subtract from the outermost, which is 15.40000, which also gives the amount of the space between the circles, which is 10 acres, 1 rood, 2 perches.

Another method for finding the contents of the space betwixt the outermost and innermost circle. The diameter of the large circle is 1400, and the diameter of the little or innermost circle is 800 links; when they are added together is 2200. This sum, multiplied by 600, the difference of the diameters, is 1320000, and again multiplied by .7854, gives 1026728, or 10 acres, 1 rood, 2 perches, the same as before.

Plate IX.

Contents of the triangles and trapeziums of the farm of Broad Mea
dows, surveyed with the circumferenter.

				A. Dec.
Triangle	I.	1930 × 515	half the perpendicular............	9.93950
Do.	II.	2200 × 200	do. do.	4.40000
Do.	III.	2810 × 900	do. do.	25.29000
Do.	IV.	2410 × 160	do. do.	3.85600
Do.	V.	4130 × 525	do. do.	21.68250
Trapez.	VI.	2600 × 1015	half sum of the perpendiculars	26.39000
Do.	VII.	2690 × 900	do. do.	24.21000
Do.	VIII.	5100 × 2119	do. do.	108.06900
Triangle	IX.	3940 × 380	half of the perpendicular.......	14.97200
Do.	X.	2280 × 150	do. do.	3.42000
Do.	XI.	3112 × 554	do. do.	17.24048
Trapez.	XII.	3280 × 450	half sum of the perpendiculars	10.26000

A. R. P.

269·72948=269 2 56 ⁷⁄₇₆

Plate XVIII. (Fig. 4.)

Is a plan of the same *Common field*, as *Fig.* 3. each division of which is
divided into equal distances of 250 links wide, which is introduced merely
to point out the best method of calculating the contents of such an irregular field, which has not a straight line; the boundaries being very crooked
and curved, would require much trouble in dividing it in the common way
into trapeziums and triangles, to ascertain the areas. This plan being protracted from a scale of eight chains in an inch, four chains or half an inch
will then make a scale of acres, that is to say, when each division is 250
links, each half inch upon a scale of equal parts is one acre. The making
scales of acres will be particularly taken notice of in an after part of this
work. In the figure, there are only inserted the amount in each of the columns of George Peacock's property, merely to shew how they ought to
have been inserted in the same way in all the other properties; and by simply adding the amount of all the columns together, we have 5·972 for the

area of George's Peacock's property; and if the amount of the others had been inserted in each column as in George Peacock's, the sum of them would be the area. If the breadth of the columns is short, as in Joseph Dice's property, the amount may be ascertained by applying the compasses but once to the scale of equal parts or acres. Thus, put one foot of the compasses in the centre as near as you can guess, in the left hand column at a, on the boundary betwixt Joseph Dice and Robert Thomas, and extend the other foot to the centre of John Wilson's boundary; then with that extent put one foot of the compasses in the middle of the next column between Joseph Dice and Robert Thomas, and let the other foot next you be fixed upon the paper, which will reach into George Peacock's property in the second column; then extend the compasses from thence, over John Dice's property, to John Wilson's; then put in one foot of the compasses between Robert Thomas and Joseph Dice, and let the other foot, which is towards yourself, be fixed somewhere about the middle of the third column of George Peacock's property, and extend the other foot to John Wilson's boundary; go over the other columns in the same way. When done, apply the compasses to the scale of acres, which is 1.736; then add to it the amount of the small square, which is .132 square links, and the sum is 1.868 acres, equal to 1 acre, 3 roods, 19 perches. This small plan is merely introduced to give a pupil an idea of the quickest method of finding out the content of an irregular boundary like what the figure is, which should be laid down upon a larger scale, and the area of each property will be correctly ascertained. If the learner chooses to keep a field-book in preference to the sketches *Fig.* 1. and 2. there is one in *Plate* XIX.

Plate I. (*Fig.* 25.)

Represents a hexagon, each side of which is 520: First calculate the contents as described in *Plate* II. *Fig.* 8. for finding out the content of a triangle, by multiplying half the perpendicular by the base, and multiplying the amount of one triangle by 6, the number of sides, which gives the area. For example, the side B C is 520, the perpendicular is 450, the half is 225, × 520, is 1.17000 × 6, the number of sides, is 7.02000, = 7 acres, 3 perches.

R

When one side is only given, the area may be found out by the multiplier in the annexed Table.

No. of sides.		Multiplier.
3	Equilateral Triangle	0.433013
4	Square	1.000000
5	Pentagon	1.720477
6	Hexagon	2.598076
7	Heptagon	3.633912
8	Octagon	4.828427
9	Nonagon	6.181824
10	Decagon	7.694209
11	Undecagon	9.365644
12	Duodecagon	11.916153

Rule. Square the side of any regular polygon, and multiply the square by the multiplier in the Table.

Example. One side of the above Hexagon is 520 × 520 = 270400, × 2·598076, is 7·02519·75040 = 7 acres 4 perches.

Plate I. (*Fig.* 26.)

Is an octagon. One side is 340, and a perpendicular let fall from one of its sides to the centre is 410, the half is 205 × 340 is 69700 × 8 is 5·57600 = 5 acres 2 roods 13 perches.

Or thus, by the multiplier in the Table; the square of 340, one of the sides, is 115600 × 4·828427 is 5.58166·161200 = 5 acres 2 roods 13 perches.

Plate I. (*Fig.* 29.)

An Oval or Ellipsis. 1st, Let the longest or transverse diameter be 1740, and its shortest or conjugate diameter 1270. *Rule.* Multiply the 2 diameters into one another, and the product by ·7854. Thus 1740 × 1270 is 2209800 × ·7854 is 17.35576·9200 acres = 17 acres 1 rood 17 perches.

Plate XXV. (*Fig.* 1.)

A B C D E F is a field of six sides divided into two trapeziums, represented by dotted lines, which should be drawn with a sharp pointed black lead pencil on your plan. In finding the contents, some surveyors draw the lines with red ink, and write in the length of the diagonals and perpendiculars in the same manner as I have done ; but in general most surveyors use a black lead pencil, which is rubbed out after the work is calculated.

The calculation of *Fig.* 1. turns out as follows :

                                                        A. Dec.

The Trapezium N° 1. 1465 × 605, half sum of the perpendiculars 8·86325

    Trapezium N° 2. 1800 × 600, half do. do......................10·80000

                                                     A. R. P.

                                      Total   19·66325=19 2 26

Plate XXV. (*Fig.* 2.)

Is the same field as *Fig.* 1. but calculated in a different manner, by dividing it into one large trapezium and two triangles.

                                                    A. Dec.

The diagonal of trapezium A, 2160 × 760, half sum of the perpendiculars, is...16·41600

The base of the triangle   B, 1580 × 175, half the perpendicular, is.. 2·76500

The base of the Triangle   C,   540 × 90, half do   48600

                                                 A. R. P.

                                      19·66700=19 2 27

Plate XXV. (*Fig.* 3.)

Is the same field as *Fig.* 1. and *Fig.* 2. and is calculated by equalizing the sides, as particularly described of *Plate* XXVII. and the contents ascertained by one calculation.

                                         A. Dec.   A. R. P.

Viz. The diagonal 2186 × 900, half sum of the perpendiculars, is 19·67400 = 19   2 28

                                          B 2

Plate XXV. (*Fig. 4.*)

Is a very irregular field of ten sides, divided into one trapezium and five triangles.

			A. Dec.
The trapezium A, Diagonal 1438 × 615, half sum of the perpendiculars, is			8·84370
Triangle	B, Base	980 × 250, half the perpendicular	2·45000
Do.	C, do.	920 × 150, half do............	1·38000
Do.	D, do.	1680 × 290, half do............	4·77200
Do.	E, do.	1200 × 228, half do............	2·73600
Do.	F, do.	860 × 140, half do............	1·20400

A. R. P.
21·38570 = 21 1 21

Plate XXV. (*Fig. 5.*)

Is the same field as *Fig.* 4. divided in a different manner, *viz.* into three trapeziums and two triangles.

			A. Dec.
The trapezium G, Diagonal 1430 × 410, half sum of the perpendiculars................			5·86300
Do.	H, do.	980 × 650, half do............	6·37000
Do.	K, do.	1220 × 435, half do............	5·30700
The triangle	I, Base	820 × 150, half the perpendicular	1·23000
Do.	L do.	1040 × 250, half do............	2·60000

A. R. P.
21·37000 = 21 1 19

Plate XXV. (*Fig. 6.*)

Represents the same field as *Fig.* 4. and 5. and the contents ascertained by one calculation, by equalizing the different sides into a square. (For the equalizing of figures see *Plate* XXVII).

A. R. P.
The diagonal 2234 × 957, half sum of the perpendiculars, is 21·37938 = 21 1 20

Plate XXV.   (*Fig.* 7.)

Is a very irregular moor, having a brook or burn running round the greatest part of it.

The contents are cast up or calculated by dividing it upon the plan into a square figure, as A B C D, and casting up all the different angles and corners separately, and that part of the land falling without the square to be added, and the vacant part within the square to be deducted.

The calculation will be thus :

Amount of the square ABCD, Diagonal 3820 × 1240,

    half sum of the perpendiculars..48·36800

Amount of triangle N° 1. Base 1100 ×   70 half the

    perpendicular... ·77000

Do.   N° 2. do.   760 × 60 half do. ·45600

Do.   N° 3. do.   620 × 130 half do. ·80600

Do.   N° 4. do.   830 × 135 half do. 1·12050

                                       3.15250

                                       51.52050

             Deduct,

Amount of triangle N° 5. Base   820 × 150 half the

    perpendicular... 1·23000

Do.   Triangle N° 6. do.   1450 × 135 half do. 1·95750

Do.   .N° 7. do.   1000 × 140 half do. 1·40000

Do.   N° 8. do.   600 × 130 half do. ·78000

Do.   N° 9. do.   830 × 135 half do. 1·12050

                      Deduct ————— 6·48800

                                      A.   R.   P.

      Total amount of the moor................45·03250 = 45   0   5

Plate XXV. (*Fig.* 8.)

Is the same moor as represented in *Fig.* 7. divided into 11 triangles and one trapezium.

Triangle	N° 1.	Base	860 × 200 half the perpendicular is	1·72000
Do.	N° 2.	do.	780 × 250 half do.	1·95000
Do.	N° 3.	do.	750 × 70 half do.	·52500
Trapezium	N° 4.	Diagonal	1400 × 390 half sum of the perpendiculars	5·46000
Triangle	N° 5.	Base	1260 × 130 half the perpendicular	1·63800
Do.	N° 6.	do.	1500 × 430 half do.	6·45000
Do.	N° 7.	do.	2360 × 615 half do.	14·51400
Do.	N° 8.	do.	2360 × 335 half do.	7·90600
Do.	N° 9.	do.	1400 × 70 half do.	·98000
Do.	N° 10.	do.	1200 × 200 half do.	2·40000
Do.	N° 11.	do.	760 × 70 half do.	·53200
Do.	N° 12.	do.	640 × 150 half do.	·96000

$$\text{A. R. P.}$$
$$45·03500 = 45 \quad 0 \quad 5$$

Plate XXV. (*Fig.* 9.)

Is the same moor as *Fig.* 7. and 8. with the contents calculated in a different way from any of the above-mentioned methods, *viz.* by drawing lines round it, which forms a square E F G H, and calculated as other trapeziums by multiplying the diagonal by the half sum of the two perpendiculars; but there falls to be deducted all the land that lies betwixt the dotted lines E F and G H and the moor.

The calculation will be as under :

Diagonal			4300 × 1540 half the perpendiculars	66·22800
Triangle	a	Base	820 × 150 half its perpendicular	1·23000
Do.	c	do.	1860 × 200 half do.	3·72000
Do.	b	do.	1860 × 300 half do.	5·58000

Carried over   10·53000   66·22800

1

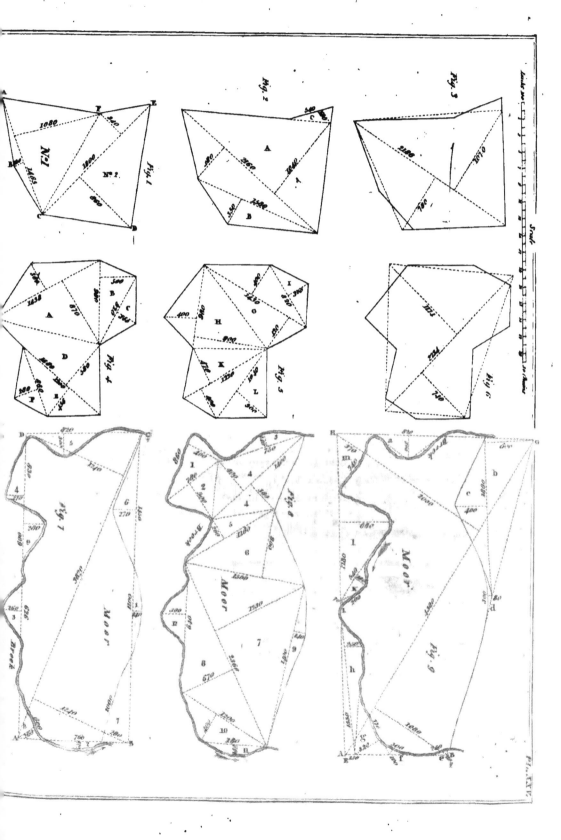

Brought forward   10·53000 66·22800

Triangle	d Base	300 ×	40 half its perpend.	·12000
Do.	e do.	250 ×	55 half do.........	·13750
Do.	f do.	300 ×	50 half do.........	·15000
Do.	g do.	770 ×	160 half do.........	1·23200

Trapezium h Diagonal 1550 × 190 half sum of the

perpendiculars.. 2.94500

Triangle   i Base   200 × 35 half the perpen-

dicular... .07000

Do.	k do.	540 ×	90 half do.........	48600
Do.	l do.	1280 ×	325 half do.........	4·16000
Do.	m do.	740 ×	185 half do.........	1·35900

Subtract ————— 21·18950

————— A. R. P.

Total   45·03850 = 45 0 6

Plate XV. (Fig. 3.)

Is a reduced plan of the farm of *Hardacres* which is calculated as under. This will give the learner an idea, how to arrange his rough draught before he inserts the contents into a finished plan.

		Diag. and Base.	Per-pendi-culars.			A.	R.	P.
a	House & Yard	440 × 190	length and breadth..............		.83600 =	0	3	14
b	Trapezium	D. 760 × 345	half sum of perpend.	2·62200				
	Do.	D. 1150 × 525	half do.............	6·04750	8·96950 =	8	3	35
	Triangle	B. 500 × 60	half the perpend...	·30000				
c	Trapezium	D. 400 × 615	half sum of perpend.	8·61000	10·50000 = 10	2	0	
	Triangle	B. 900 × 210	half the perpend...	1·89000				
d	Trapezium	D. 1610 × 545	half sum of perpend.	8·77450	10·96280 = 10	3	34	
	Triangle	B. 1385 × 158	half the perpend...	2·18830				
e	Trapezium	D. 1800 × 710	half sum of perpend.	12·78000				
	Triangle	B. 1130 × 150	half the perpend...	1·65000	14·87000 = 14	3	19	
	Do.	B. 440 × 100	half do.............	44000				
	Trapezium	D. 1510 × 540	half sum of perpend.		8·22950 =	8	0	37
g	Do.	D. 1600 × 490	half do.............	7·84000	8·54000 =	8	2	6
	Do.	D. 700 × 100	half do.............	·70000				
h	Do.	D. 1590 × 716	half do.............	11·24120	13·43120 = 13	1	29	
	Triangle	B. 1460 × 150	half the perpend...	2·19000				
	Trapezium	D. 1505 × 545	half sum of perpend..............		8·20225 =	8	0	32

84·54125 = 84 2 6

Various methods have been invented to facilitate and lessen the labour attending the calculation of the contents of land by different scales; but few deserve notice except the following.   It must be admitted that as few figures as possible ought to be used in the calculations, because, when the figures are complex, there is a greater liability to error; and no one can be certain his calculation is right without recalculating, which ought to be done in some other way from the former.   If the two do not agree, a third must be resorted to, and sometimes a fourth.   It has been observed before, that ten chains in length and one chain in breadth is one acre; when multiplied into one another is 1·00000 square links, the square root of which is 316·2277 links, for the sides of a square acre to be delineated on a plan; and *Euclid*, 47. *Prop.* 1. *Book.* 1. demonstrates, that the hypothenuse is equal to the sum of the squares of the two other sides; therefore the square of 316·2277 links is 100000 links, when doubled is 200000 links; the square root of which is 447·2137 links for the diagonal of a square acre; that distance taken from the scale the plan is protracted and plotted by, and made one of the large divisions of another scale, and very finely divided into a diagonal scale in 100 equal parts, forms a new scale for the diagonal of a square acre. The divisions, being larger than the plotting scale, in proportion as 447 exceeds 1000, this will give the area in fewer figures than the plotting scale; and in proportion as a square or parallelogram is to a triangle of the same base and altitude; consequently, if the diagonal and perpendiculars of any trapezium are measured upon a plan, or the base and perpendiculars of any triangle by this diagonal scale, and multiplied into one another, the product is the whole of the area, and saves the trouble of halving the perpendiculars.   The perpendiculars have only to be added together, and their product multiplied by the whole length of the diagonal, which shews that a fewer number of figures are used to multiply into one another (to ascertain the area) than by the plotting scale.

Plate XXVI.   (*Fig.* 1.)

Is a diagonal scale, constructed for calculating a plan plotted by a scale of 7 chains to an inch.   Suppose the meadow close in the farm of Tip-

3

perty, *Plate* X. *Fig.* 2. which is plotted from the scale just mentioned, and the calculation of enclosure No. 4. cast up by the new scale.

The Trapezium M B C L, Diagonal 409 × 288, the sum of
   the perpendiculars is..11·7792
Triangle L M a, Base 528 × 80, the whole of the perpendicular 2·6240

                A. R. P.
14·4032=14 1 24

In using this new scale, there requires only four decimals to be cut off upon the right hand, which multiply by 4 and then by 40, which converts the decimals into roods and perches in the same manner as formerly described. It will be proper to observe, that a scale of this kind is very useful to take off the diagonals and perpendiculars, to prove the calculations: but by no means will I recommend it as superior to the plotting scale the work has been laid down from, notwithstanding some land-measurers give it the preference on account of its expedition in casting up the contents in fewer figures than the scale the enclosure is plotted by.

Plate XXVI. (*Fig.* 2).

Represents a meadow, which is bounded on one side by a brook or rivulet, and on the other side by a steep bank, the lower part of which is very winding. To divide it into trapeziums and triangles, and calculate them all separately, would require more time than a practical surveyor might conveniently spare. The best and most expeditious method is to divide it into a number of equal distances, suppose each division a chain in breadth (See *Scale, Fig.* 8.); then with a pair of compasses take the length of each division as near the middle as you can guess, and apply that extent to the same scale the meadow is plotted by, and note how far it measures upon the scale ; insert the distance, which is 200, as you will perceive marked on the figure in the first column on the left hand ; do the same with every division, and set down the distance as above in each respective column ; then by a simple sum of addition the area is pointed out by cutting off three figures on the right hand ; the figures on the left are acres. If the amount of the figures in the columns had been multiplied by the breadth, which is 100 links, then five figures must have been cut off.

s

The total sum of all the lengths, when added, is 6 acres 102 decimals; but there is a small piece of .032 decimals, which is cast up by multiplying the length by the breadth; when added to 6 acres 102 decimals, it makes the whole amount 6 acres 134 decimals = 6 acres 0 roods 21 perches. After multiplying the decimals .134 by 4, and then by 40, there remains the odd 21 perches.

Plate XXVI. (*Fig.* 3.)

Represents the same meadow as *Fig.* 2. with the contents cast up by a method more expeditious, *viz.* by dividing it into equal distances of two chains each, and instead of ten chains being an acre, as *Fig.* 2. five chains is a scale of acres, as may be seen by the annexed scale, *Fig.* 9. (this as well as the other is plotted from a scale of $\frac{1}{4}$th of an inch to a chain). 1st, From the plotting scale take half an inch or two chains between the compasses, and with that extent divide the figure into equal distances; and if the last division is short, the length and breadth must be multiplied into one another, and the amount inserted in that column; then use a scale half the size of the plotting scale, and ten chains of it will be one acre; apply the compasses between the brook at g and h as near the middle of each column as you can guess, which upon the scale of acres of five chains is 440; place that number in its respective column; take off all the other squares or columns in the same way, and insert each distance in its respective column, as you will see marked on the figure; then copy all the distances, and add them up, which amounts to 6 acres 136 decimals = 6 acres 0 roods 21 perches. *Note*, If all the distances had been taken from the plotting scale, and the sum multiplied by 2, it would have given the amount, except the small column, which is added after the multiplication by 2.

Plate XXVI. (*Fig.* 4.)

Represents the same meadow as *Fig.* 2. and *Fig.* 3. in which the area is ascertained by a method still more expeditious than the former, and equally correct, by dividing it into $2\frac{1}{2}$ chains, or 250 links each column; then every four chains or one inch is a scale of acres. This is a more ready scale than that of five chains (see *Scale, Fig.* 10.). Apply the com-

1

passes, suppose from e to f, and note how much it measures upon the inch scale, which is 582; insert that distance in its respective column or square; do the same with all the other columns, and insert the distance of each in its respective column; add up all those distances, and the sum is 6 acres 125 decimals; multiply the decimals as before directed by 4, and then by 40, which is equal to 6 acres 0 roods 22 perches.

There is another method still shorter than any yet mentioned, particularly to a surveyor who can use the compasses expeditiously, by taking the extent of four, five, or six columns all at once, and applying that extent to the scale. For example (*Plate* XXVI. *Fig.* 2.), put one foot of the compasses at the side of the rivulet at a, and extend the other foot up to b, and with that extent put one foot of the compasses at the side of the brook in the next column under 240, and the other foot next you will reach to c; keep that foot in c, and extend the other foot over the meadow to the bank in the 2d column; then with the same extent put one foot of the compasses at the edge of the rivulet in the 3d column under 280, and the point of the compasses that is next you will reach to d; keep that point of the compasses in d, and extend the other to the bank in the 3d square or column; then put one foot of the compasses at the edge of the brook under 300 in the 4th column, and the foot next you will reach to e; keep that point in e, and extend the other foot to the bank in the 4th column; then put one foot of the compasses at the edge of the brook in the 5th square or column, and the foot next you will reach to f; keep that foot in f, and extend the other foot over the meadow to the bank; then apply the compasses to the scale of acres, which is 1320, which insert in the 5th column; begin again at column 6th, under 272, and proceed in the same manner till you take in the length of 6 columns, which is 1600, which insert in the 11th column; begin again at the edge of the rivulet in the 12th column under 290, and proceed on to the 18th column, and see how far the compasses extend upon the scale, which is 1860, which insert in the 18th square; begin again in the 19th column under 250, and proceed in the same way as directed in the first 5 columns to the last, which extends to 1320 on the scale of acres; add up all the numbers, including the small piece of 32 at the end, and the sum will be 6.132 = 6 acres 0 roods 21 perches.

The calculations following are all considerably shorter than if the meadow had been divided into triangles and trapeziums (which is the common method of finding out the contents). Figure 3d and 4th might have been done in the same way as Figure 2d.

The calculation of the meadow by four different methods as under.

First Method refers to Fig. 2.	First Method continued.	Second Method refers to Fig. 3.	Third Method. refers to Fig. 4.	Fourth Method refers to Fig. 2.
1. Col..... 300	Brought up......3·652	1. Col..... 440	1........... 582	5. Col..... 1320
2........... 240	15.Col .. 210	2........... 580	2........... 780	6........... 1600
3........... 280	16........... 260	3........... 572	3........... 670	6........... 1860
4........... 300	17........... 320	4........... 504	4........... 680	6........... 1320
5........... 300	18........... 340	5........... 532	5........... 702	little piece 32
6........... 272	19........... 250	6........... 584	6........... 500	———
7........... 252	20........... 180	7........... 440	7........... 770	Total 6·132
8........... 252	21........... 180	8........... 450	8........... 591	
9........... 252	22........... 240	9........... 660	9........... 600	
10........... 280	23........... 260	10........... 430	little piece 260	
11........... 294	24........... 210	11........... 410	———	
12........... 290	little piece 32	12........... 470	Total 6·155	
13........... 240	———	little piece 64		
14........... 200	Total 6·134	———		
———		Total 6·136		
3·652				

Plate XXVI.   (*Fig.* 5.)

Is a semicircle, the diameter of which is 720, and it is divided into equal distances of 100 links each column. The sum of the divisions when added, including a small segment of the circle of .026 decimals, or part of an acre, amounts to 2.084. Land-surveyors seldom meet with regular curved lines in practice; it is introduced here, merely to shew that the dividing of curved lines into equal distances may sometimes be made use of with success, for ascertaining the area. Many surveyors seldom think of calculating the contents, but by dividing the arch as near as they can guess with their eye, either into a triangle, parallelogram, or trapezium, by including a part, and excluding another, so as to compensate. By this method a person with a correct eye can attain exactness even beyond concep-

Pl. XXVI

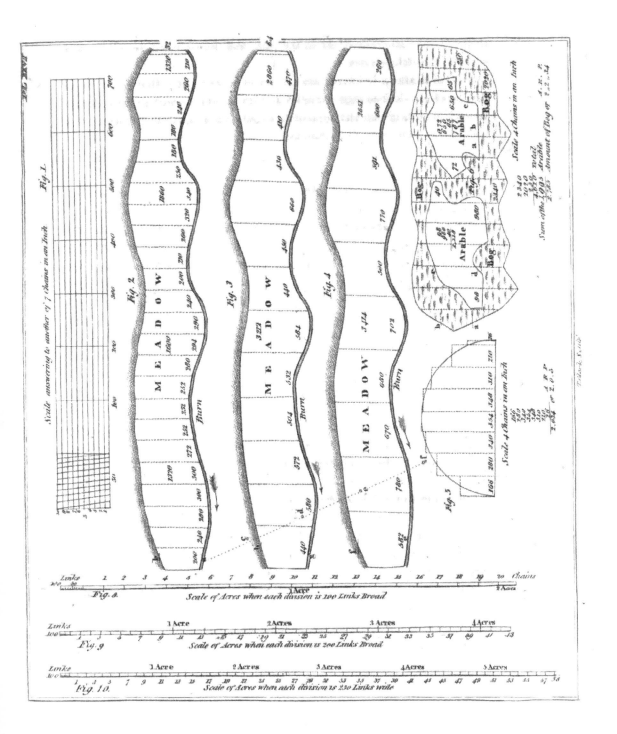

Fig. 1.

Scale answering to another of 5 Chains in an Inch

Fig. 2

M E A D O W

Fig. 3

M E A D O W

Fig. 4

M E A D O W

Scale 4 Chains in an Inch

Arable

Bog

Arable

Bog Earth

Scale 4 Chains in an Inch

Fig. 5

Turn

Turn

Turn

Links 1 2 3 4 5 6 7 8 9 10 11 12 13 14 15 16 17 18 19 20 Chains

Fig. 8. 1 Acre Scale of Acres when each division is 100 Links Broad 2 Acres

Links 1 Acre 2 Acres 3 Acres 4 Acres

Fig. 9 Scale of Acres when each division is 200 Links Broad

Links 1 Acre 2 Acres 3 Acres 4 Acres 5 Acres

Fig. 10. Scale of Acres when each division is 250 Links wide

tion. Square the diameter 720 × 720, which is 51840 × 7854, as described in Page 126, which amounts to 4.07151 for the area of a circle, the half of it is 2.03575 for the content of the semicircle. It would have turned out the same thing, in place of squaring the diameter, to have multiplied the half of it, which is 360, into the whole diameter, thus 720 × 360 is 259000, which again × .7854 = 203575 or 2 acres 0 roods 5 falls. (See the *Plate Fig. 5.*)

Plate XXVI. (*Fig.* 6.)

Represents a bog meadow, with two pieces of dry arable land surrounded by the bog. The only correct and expeditious method of ascertaining the area is by dividing it into distances of 100 links each, as in fig. 2. The parallel lines should be drawn in upon the rough plan, either with red ink or a black lead pencil through the whole figure. It is presumed, from what has already been said, this method will appear very evident. It is done by taking a number of lengths of the different columns, and applying the whole extent to the plotting scale, 1000 then becomes an acre; you insert the number of acres and decimals of an acre in the columns, and add them up into one sum; then go over the two pieces of arable land in the same way, and if there are any corners or small pieces that do not occupy the whole breadth of a column, take the length and breadth of them, and multiply the length by the breadth, and insert the decimals in their proper places on the rough plan: when all is gone over, add each spot of the arable land together, and subtract the sum from the total. (See the *Plate Fig. 6.*)

Suppose you begin at a, and extend the foot of the compasses to b; then remove the compasses to the low end of the 2d column, and make a mark with the point next you; keep one foot of the compasses in that mark, and extend the other to the upper part of the column over both the bog and arable ground; do the same in every column (or square) till you take in the 7th square, and apply the extent between the compasses to the scale of acres, which is 2.340 acres, which insert in the column left off at; begin again in the next column, and take in five more of the divisions, and apply the extent to the scale of acres, which is 2.020 acres, which also insert in the column; lastly, take the length of the next column, which is

250 parts of an acre; add them all up into one sum, which is 4.610 acres. The next thing to be done is to take the length and breadth of the small square on the left in the arable land, which, when multiplied, the product is .098, which insert; then take the length and breadth of the small piece on the right hand, and multiply them, and the product is .040; add those distances to the amount of the other columns which is ·980 and that piece of arable land is 1.118 acres: begin again on the other piece of arable land in the middle of the bog, and take the length and breadth of the left hand small piece, and multiply the length by the breadth, which is .072 parts or decimals of an acre, which insert in that column; begin again at a, and extend the compasses over the arable land; then put one foot in b, and make a mark towards yourself, and extend the compasses from that mark to the far side of the arable land; then put one foot of the compasses in c, and let the other foot extend towards yourself, and make a mark; then extend the other foot over the arable land, and apply the compasses to the scale of acres, which is .650 parts of an acre, which insert on your rough plan; then take the length and breadth of the small piece on the right hand and multiply them together, and the product is .065 decimals of an acre; add all the three distances together and the sum .787 decimals of an acre; then add the amount of this piece of arable land to the other piece of arable land, and the sum is 1.905, which subtract out of the total sum, which is 4.610 acres, and there remains 2.715 acres of bog meadow, = 2 acres 2 roods 34 perches; and the sum of the two pieces of arable land is 1 acre 3 roods 25 perches.

From what has been stated, and the variety of methods pointed out of calculating the contents or areas of land, although some of them may at first view appear a little complicated to a learner, yet I entertain little doubt that, after a minute and strict examination of them, with a little practice and a careful inspection of the figures in this work, he will be enabled, in a short time, to cast up the contents, with expedition and accuracy, of regular, as well as the most irregular fields to be met with in practice. Numerous valuable treatises have been published, but have seldom gone farther than illustrating straight lines, triangles, trapeziums, and figures of five, six, seven, or eight sides, and are in general deficient for giving a beginner a just idea of all the varieties he may expect to meet with in practice. It is well known that many estates are bounded by very crooked lines, curved boundaries, and many serpentine turns and windings are frequently met with in the interior parts of grounds. This has induced me to give rather a detailed account of one of the most useful parts of surveying. The equalizing of irregular boundaries, to facilitate the calculations, and which has not been as yet thoroughly explained, will be found not only expeditious, but correct, even to a nicety, in reducing irregular boundaries to straight lines; which land-surveyors ought to make themselves masters of, particularly in dividing a crooked march or boundary betwixt the proprietors of two adjacent farms, who wish to have a straight boundary in preference to a zigzag one; and this a surveyor may sometimes have occasion to do.

Plate XXVI. (*Fig.* 8.)

Represents a scale of acres, where each division is 100 links or a chain wide. Ten of those divisions make 1 acre, twenty make 2 acres, thirty make 3 acres, and so on.

Plate XXVI. (*Fig.* 9.)

Represents a scale of acres, where each division is 200 links or 2 chains wide. Ten of the small divisions on the scale then become an acre, twenty make 2 acres, thirty make 3 acres, and so on.

Plate XXVI. (*Fig.* 10.)

Represents a scale of acres, where each division is 250 links wide; ten of the small divisions on the scale make 1 acre, twenty make 2 acres, and so on.

For example, take any length you please, suppose an inch and a half, between your compasses, and apply that extent to any of the scales of acres, suppose to the scale of four chains in an inch, which will reach to 600 decimals of an acre: or, if you apply the same extent to the scale of acres of 250 links wide, it will extend to 1500, which is equal to 1 acre and 500 decimals of an acre.

Again, if you apply the same extent to the scale of acres of 200 links wide, it will reach to 1225, or 1 acre and 225 decimals of an acre.

ART. II. EQUALIZING DIFFERENT FIGURES TO REDUCE THEM TO TRIANGLES, &c.

Plate XXVII. (Fig. 1.)

Suppose the four-sided square A B C D is to be reduced to a triangle whose area will be the same.   1st, Produce or extend one of the sides, suppose A D; then lay a parallel ruler or the T square with its companion upon the points B and D, and move it parallel to C; and where the edge of the ruler crosses the produced line, make a mark as at E; then draw the line E B, and it is done.   It would be the same thing if you pricked off upon the produced line the length of one of the sides, suppose A D, by putting one foot of the compasses in D, the other will extend to E; draw the line E B, and it will be the same as the former.

Plate XXVII. (Fig. 2.)

Suppose the four-sided figure *a b c d* is to be reduced to a triangle whose area will be equal to the parallelogram.   1st, Produce the line *a b*, lay the T square upon the points *d* and *b*, and move it parallel to *c*, and make a mark upon the produced line *a b* at *e*; lastly, draw the line *e d*, and it is done; or you may take the length of *a b*, and put one foot of the compasses in *b*, and the other will reach to *e*, on the produced line; then draw the hypothenuse as before.

Plate XXVII. (Fig. 3.)

Suppose the four-sided figure (called a rhombois) is to be reduced to a triangle, whose area will be equal to the figure *f g h i*; extend the line *f g*, and lay the T square upon the points *g* and *i*; move it parallel to *h*, and make a mark where the edge of the T or parallel ruler cuts the produced line *f g*, and make a mark upon the produced line at *k*; then draw the line *k i*, which will be the same area as the rhombois.

Plate XXVII. (Fig. 4.)

Let the figure *m n o p* be reduced to a triangle whose area will be equal to the trapezium. 1st, Extend the line *m p*; then lay the ruler upon the points *p* and *n*, and move the T or a parallel ruler parallel to *o*, and make a mark where the edge cuts the produced line at *q*; then draw the hypothenuse from *q* to *n*, and it is finished.

Plate XXVII. (Fig. 5.)

Let the figure r s t u v, of five sides, be reduced to a triangle whose area will be the same as the figure. 1st, Produce the line v r both ways; that is to say, past r on the left and past v on the right; then lay the T upon r and t, and move it parallel to s, and make a mark upon the produced line on the left at x; then lay the T upon the points v and t; move it parallel to u, and make a mark on the produced line on the right at w; then draw the hypothenuse line x t, and also the line t w; and the triangle will be equal to the five-sided figure r s t u v.

Plate XXVII. (Fig. 6.)

Let the six-sided figure a b c d e f be reduced to a triangle of the same dimensions or area. 1st, Produce or extend the base a f to the left of a and to the right of f, then lay the parallel ruler or T upon the angles a and c, and move it parallel to b, and make a mark upon the produced line on the left of a at h; then lay the ruler upon the mark at h and the point d, and move it forward to the point c, and where the edge of the ruler cuts the produced line make a mark, at i; then lay the parallel ruler or T upon the point f and d, and move it parallel to e; and where the edge of the ruler cuts the extended line on the right of f make a mark, at g; lastly, draw in the hypothenuse from i to d and from d to g, and extend the base from f to g and from a to i, and it is finished.

Plate XXVII. (Fig. 7.)

Is a seven-sided figure, i k l m n o p. First extend the base i p a considerable way on the right past p, and apply the ruler or the T to p and

T

n; move it parallel to o, and where the edge of the ruler cuts the base line at 1 make a mark; then lay the parallel ruler upon the mark 1 and the angle at m and move it parallel to n; and make a mark where the edge of the ruler crosses the extended line at 2; then lay the ruler upon the mark 2 and the angle l, and move it parallel to m, and where the edge cuts the produced line, make a mark at 3; then lay the ruler upon the mark 3 and the angle k, and move it parallel to l; make a mark upon the extended line at 4; then draw the hypothenuse from k to the mark at 4, and the triangle is formed; which reduces the seven-sided figure i k l m n o to a three-sided one whose content is the same, and may be calculated, as all other triangles are done, by multiplying the hypothenuse by half the perpendicular let fall thereon from the opposite angle l.

Plate XXVII. (Fig. 8.)

Is an irregular field of ten sides to be reduced to a four sided figure. First produce the line KA past A; then lay the parallel ruler, or the T square upon the points A and C, and move it parallel to B; where the edge of the T crosses the produced line, make a mark as at 1; then draw a line from the mark 1, through the angle C, which extend past C; then lay the T upon C and E, and move it parallel to D; make a mark at 2, on the extended line 1 C; then lay the T upon the mark 2 and the angle F and move it parallel to E, and where the edge cuts the extended line make a mark, at 3, on the produced line 1 C; then lay the parallel ruler or T upon the mark 3 and the angle G, and move it parallel to the angle F, and where the edge cuts the extended line 1 C make a mark, at 4; then draw the line from the mark 4 through the angle G, which produce past G; this will reduce the four sides CD, DE, EF, and FG, to one side; then apply the T to the angles G and I, and move it parallel to H, and where the edge cuts the line 4 G make a mark, as at 5; then lay the ruler upon the mark 5 and the angle K, and move it parallel to the angle I, and where the edge cuts the produced line 4 G make a mark at 6; then draw the line from 6 to K and the short line from A to 1, which reduces the ten-sided figure to one of four sides, which is calculated by dividing it into 2 triangles, or one trapezium, as is drawn in on the figure by a diagonal and perpendiculars let fall thereon.

Plate XXVII. (Fig. 9.)

Represents a very irregular boundary, which it is proposed to reduce to one mean line by equalizing the different sides. 1st, Extend the line HA below A; then lay the parallel ruler upon the points A and c, and move it parallel to b; where the edge of the ruler cuts the produced line below A make a mark as at 1; then lay the ruler upon the mark at 1 and the angle d, move it parallel to c, and make a mark at 2 on the dotted line AH; then lay the ruler upon the mark 2 and the angle e, move it parallel to d, and make a mark upon the dotted line at 3; then lay the ruler upon the mark 3 and the angle f, move it parallel to e, and make a mark upon the dotted line at 4; then lay the ruler upon the mark 4 and the angle at g, and move it parallel to f, making a mark at 5 on the produced line below A; then lay the ruler upon the point 5 and B, and move it parallel to the angle g, and make a mark upon the dotted line at 6; then draw the line through the mark 6 to B, which equalizes the boundary line of 7 sides to one line; and the triangle may be cast up by one calculation, which will amount to 2 acres 1 rood 29 perches.

Another method may be used for ascertaining the contents of the above Fig. 9. which is, by dividing it into equal divisions of 100 links wide. In that case 10 chains in length is one acre; the length of each column is set down under it in decimals of an acre (see Plate XXVI.); when they are added together the sum amounts to 2.424, which is equal to 2 acres 1 rood 28 perches. The method of dividing irregular fields, like the above, by equal distances, is particularly described in Areas Plate XXVI.; which will be found the most expeditious method of finding the contents of such irregular boundaries as Figure 9.

Plate XXVII. (Fig. 10.)

Is the same irregular figure of 8 sides divided into six triangles, which are all calculated separately, and which, when summed up, amount to 2 acres 1 rood 28 perches, the same as the other, which is calculated by equal divisions of 100 links each.

Plate XXVII. (*Fig.* 11.)

Represents another method of calculating the same figure *viz.* by dividing it into 3 triangles and four trapeziums. The content turns out much the same as the others when the different calculations are added up in onesu m.

There are other methods than those that have already been defined for the calculations of triangles, trapeziums, squares, and irregular figures, to find out the contents ; but none of them deserve notice except the following.

Many surveyors draw lines with red ink all over their rough plans, squares of equal distances, each of which they make $316\frac{2}{10}$ links each side ; then each square becomes an acre, which they number ; and from these calculate all the small pieces, which they either add or deduct according as they are either within or without the squares. If the amount of the whole corresponds nearly to a former calculation, they rest satisfied that their calculation is right. If they do not agree the surveyor examines the different fields by the number of squares in each field till he finds out his error, and then recalculates that field over again where a wrong calculation has been committed.

A good method of casting up the contents and proving the calculations of triangles, trapeziums, squares, or irregular figures, is by a table of logarithms, which is done in the following manner.

Suppose the square, Plate II. Fig. 6, each side of which is 800 links ;

Look for that number in the left hand column in a book of logarithms, and opposite it is..2.90809

Look again for the same number 800...2.90809
                                                                                              ————
                                           The sum is...........5.80618

The index being five denotes that you have six figures in the sum, and if the index had been six, there would have been seven figures in the sum, and so on ; the index always reckoning one figure more than the sum.

Then look for the above logarithm 5.80618, paying no regard to the in-

PLATE XXVII.

dex 5, and opposite .80618 in the left hand column under *Numb.* you will find 6400; to which add 2 cyphers; the index being 5 gives 6.40000=6 acres 1 rood 24 perches.

Again suppose the parallelogram *Plate* II. *Fig.* 7, which is 1167 links long and 305 wide ;

Look what logarithm is opposite 1167, and you will find.............. 3.06707
Look what logarithm is opposite, 305 and you will find.............. 2.48430

$$5.55137$$

Then look what number is opposite the logarithm of .55137, paying no regard to the index 5, which denotes that there are 6 figures in the sum ; the nearest number to the logarithm of 5.55137 is 3559; to which add 2 cyphers, and cut off 5 figures on the right hand, and there remains 3.55900=3 acres 2 roods 9 perches.

Again, suppose the diagonal of a trapezium to be 2200 links, and the half sum of the perpendiculars 840 ;

Look what logarithm is opposite 2200, and you will find.............. 3.34242
Again look what logarithm is opposite 840, and you will find...... 2.92428

$$6.26670$$

Then look what number is opposite .26670, and you will find 1848 ; to which add 3 cyphers. The index being 6 denotes that 7 figures are in the sum ; and when 5 figures are cut of on the right there remain 18 acres, 48000 decimals=18 acres 1 rood 37 perches nearly.

It sometimes occurs that the logarithm of a number is not exactly found in the tables. In that case look for the next less logarithm, and subtract it from the given logarithm; then look for the next greater logarithm, and subtract the next less one from it; then divide it by the difference of the greater and less logarithm found in the table. Thus, suppose the diagonal of a trapezium to be 8748, and the half sum of the perpendicular 4644 ;

Look for the logarithm opposite 8748 links, and opposite it is...... 3.94191
Then look for ditto   ditto   4644   ditto   ditto.......... 3.66689

Given logarithm.................. 7.60880

Then look what number *is* opposite the logarithm of .60880, which is 4062, being 4 of the figures sought ; the index being 7, shews that 8 figures are in the sum.

The logarithm being not exactly found in the table, you must subtract the next less logarithm from the given logarithm ; thus,

> The given logarithm is⸺⸺⸺ 60880
> The next less is⸺⸺⸺⸺⸺ 60874
>
> The difference is 6 for the dividend   6
> To which add 4 cyphers⸺⸺⸺⸺ 6.0000

Then the next larger logarithm is⸺ 60885
Subtract the next less ditto⸺⸺ 60874

Divide by the remainder   11)6.0000(5454 annex this sum
to 4062 and it will be 406.25454   55
=406 acres, 1 rood, 1 perch nearly.

                            50
                            44

                            60
                            55

                            50
                            44

                            6

The following tables for turning perches into acres, roods, and perches poles, or falls, by inspection, are frequently made use of for finding out where a mistake may have been made in the first calculation. It is done by making a scale of perches answering to the plotting scale by which the plan has been protracted and laid down, which will come very near the truth. For example, a perch-pole or fall is 25 links : take 2500 links from your plotting scale, and divide that length into 10 equal divisions; each of those divisions will be 10 perches; then divide either the right or left hand division into 10 equal parts, and each of those divisions will be one perch in length or breadth. With a pair of compasses take off the length of the base of a triangle, and apply it to the above scale of perches, which will shew how many perches it is in length: take half the length of the perpendicular and do the same. Suppose the length of the base is 50 perches and the half of the perpendicular is 9 perches or falls, look for 50 in the left hand column, and for 9 at the top; then with your eye trace the line of 50 till you are immediately under 9 at the top, and in that column you will find 2 acres, 3 roods, and 10 perches.

Again, suppose you have a trapezium the diagonal of which is 220 perches in length, and the half sum of the perpendicular is 80 perches;

	A.	R.	P.
First look out for 200 in the left hand column and opposite it, under 80, is	100	0	0
Then look out for 20 in the left hand column and under 80 you will find	10	0	0
The sum is the amount	110	0	0

Again, suppose you have a triangle the base of which is 19 perches and a half, and the half of the perpendicular is 8 perches;

	A.	R.	P.
Look out for 19 perches in the left hand column and under 8 is	0	3	32
Then for the half perch look for 1 at the top and take the half of 8, which is 4, in the left hand column, and you will find	0	0	4
	0	3	36

All others are done in the same manner, and need no farther illustration.

The following tables and scale will be found useful to gentlemen that have plans of their property, if they wish to know the quantity of ground in any divisions they have made or intend to make on their grounds.

From 1 to 10 Perches, Poles, or Falls wide.

Perches, Poles, or Falls Long	1 Do. Wide			2 Do. Wide			3 Do. Wide			4 Do. Wide			5 Do. Wide			6 Do. Wide			7 Do. Wide			8 Do. Wide			9 Do. Wide			10 Do. Wide		
	A	R	P	A	R	P	A	R	P	A	R	P	A	R	P	A	R	P	A	R	P	A	R	P	A	R	P	A	R	P
1	0	0	1	0	0	2	0	0	3	0	0	4	0	0	5	0	0	6	0	0	7	0	0	8	0	0	9	0	0	10
2	0	0	2	0	0	4	0	0	6	0	0	8	0	0	10	0	0	12	0	0	14	0	0	16	0	0	18	0	0	20
3	0	0	3	0	0	6	0	0	9	0	0	12	0	0	15	0	0	18	0	0	21	0	0	24	0	0	27	0	0	30
4	0	0	4	0	0	8	0	0	12	0	0	16	0	0	20	0	0	24	0	0	28	0	0	32	0	0	36	0	1	0
5	0	0	5	0	0	10	0	0	15	0	0	20	0	0	25	0	0	30	0	0	35	0	1	0	0	1	5	0	1	10
6	0	0	6	0	0	12	0	0	18	0	0	24	0	0	30	0	0	36	0	1	2	0	1	8	0	1	14	0	1	20
7	0	0	7	0	0	14	0	0	21	0	0	28	0	0	35	0	1	2	0	1	9	0	1	16	0	1	23	0	1	30
8	0	0	8	0	0	16	0	0	24	0	0	32	0	1	0	0	1	8	0	1	16	0	1	24	0	1	32	0	2	0
9	0	0	9	0	0	18	0	0	27	0	0	36	0	1	5	0	1	14	0	1	23	0	1	32	0	2	1	0	2	10
10	0	0	10	0	0	20	0	0	30	0	1	0	0	1	10	0	1	20	0	1	30	0	2	0	0	2	10	0	2	20
11	0	0	11	0	0	22	0	0	33	0	1	4	0	1	15	0	1	26	0	1	37	0	2	8	0	2	19	0	2	30
12	0	0	12	0	0	24	0	0	36	0	1	8	0	1	20	0	1	32	0	2	4	0	2	16	0	2	28	0	3	0
13	0	0	13	0	0	26	0	0	39	0	1	12	0	1	25	0	1	38	0	2	11	0	2	24	0	2	37	0	3	10
14	0	0	14	0	0	28	0	1	2	0	1	16	0	1	30	0	2	4	0	2	18	0	2	32	0	3	6	0	3	20
15	0	0	15	0	0	30	0	1	5	0	1	20	0	1	35	0	2	10	0	2	25	0	3	0	0	3	15	0	3	30
16	0	0	16	0	0	32	0	1	8	0	1	24	0	2	0	0	2	16	0	2	32	0	3	8	0	3	24	1	0	0
17	0	0	17	0	0	34	0	1	11	0	1	28	0	2	5	0	2	22	0	2	39	0	3	16	0	3	33	1	0	10
18	0	0	18	0	0	36	0	1	14	0	1	32	0	2	10	0	2	28	0	3	6	0	3	24	1	0	2	1	0	20
19	0	0	19	0	0	38	0	1	17	0	1	36	0	2	15	0	2	34	0	3	13	0	3	32	1	0	11	1	0	30
20	0	0	20	0	1	0	0	1	20	0	2	0	0	2	20	0	3	0	0	3	20	1	0	0	1	0	20	1	1	0
30	0	0	30	0	1	20	0	2	10	0	3	0	0	3	30	1	0	20	1	1	10	1	2	0	1	2	30	1	3	20
40	0	1	0	0	2	0	0	3	0	1	0	0	1	1	0	1	2	0	1	3	0	2	0	0	2	1	0	2	2	0
50	0	1	10	0	2	20	0	3	30	1	1	0	1	2	10	1	3	20	2	0	30	2	2	0	2	3	10	3	0	20
60	0	1	20	0	3	0	1	0	20	1	2	0	1	3	20	2	1	0	2	2	20	3	0	0	3	1	20	3	3	0
70	0	1	30	0	3	20	1	1	10	1	3	0	2	0	30	2	2	20	3	0	10	3	2	0	3	3	30	4	1	20
80	0	2	0	1	0	0	1	2	0	2	0	0	2	2	0	3	0	0	3	2	0	4	0	0	4	2	0	5	0	0
90	0	2	10	1	0	20	1	2	30	2	1	0	2	3	10	3	1	20	3	3	30	4	2	0	5	0	10	5	2	20
100	0	2	20	1	1	0	1	3	20	2	2	0	3	0	20	3	3	0	4	1	20	5	0	0	5	2	20	6	1	0
200	1	1	0	2	2	0	3	3	0	5	0	0	6	1	0	7	2	0	8	3	0	10	0	0	11	1	0	12	2	0
300	1	3	20	3	3	0	5	2	20	7	2	0	9	1	20	11	1	0	13	0	20	15	0	0	16	3	20	18	3	0
400	2	2	0	5	0	0	7	2	0	10	0	0	12	2	0	15	0	0	17	2	0	20	0	0	22	2	0	25	0	0
500	3	0	20	6	1	0	9	1	20	11	2	0	15	2	20	18	3	0	21	3	20	25	0	0	28	0	20	31	1	0
600	3	3	0	7	2	0	11	1	0	15	0	0	18	3	0	22	2	0	26	1	0	30	0	0	33	3	0	37	2	0

From 11 to 20 Perches, Poles, or Falls wide.

Perches Long.	11 Do. Wide.			12 Do. Wide.			13 Do. Wide.			14 Do. Wide.			15 Do. Wide.			16 Do. Wide.			17 Do. Wide.			18 Do. Wide.			19 Do. Wide.			20 Do. Wide.		
	A.	R.	P.	A.	R.	P.	A.	R.	P.	A.	R.	P.	A.	R.	P.	A.	R.	P.	A.	R.	P.	A.	R.	R.	A.	R.	P.	A.	R.	P.
1	0	0	11	0	0	12	0	0	13	0	0	14	0	0	15	0	0	16	0	0	17	0	0	18	0	0	19	0	0	20
2	0	0	22	0	0	24	0	0	26	0	0	28	0	0	30	0	0	32	0	0	34	0	0	36	0	0	38	0	1	0
3	0	0	33	0	0	36	0	0	39	0	1	2	0	1	5	0	1	8	0	1	11	0	1	14	0	1	17	0	1	20
4	0	1	4	0	1	8	0	1	12	0	1	16	0	1	20	0	1	24	0	1	28	0	1	32	0	1	36	0	2	0
5	0	1	15	0	1	20	0	1	25	0	1	30	0	1	35	0	2	0	0	2	5	0	2	10	0	2	15	0	2	20
6	0	1	26	0	1	32	0	1	38	0	2	4	0	2	10	0	2	16	0	2	22	0	2	28	0	2	34	0	3	0
7	0	1	37	0	2	4	0	2	11	0	2	18	0	2	25	0	2	32	0	2	39	0	3	6	0	3	13	0	3	20
8	0	2	8	0	2	16	0	2	24	0	2	32	0	3	0	0	3	8	0	3	16	0	3	24	0	3	32	1	0	0
9	0	2	19	0	2	28	0	2	37	0	3	6	0	3	15	0	3	24	0	3	33	1	0	2	1	0	11	1	0	20
10	0	2	30	0	3	0	0	3	10	0	3	20	0	3	30	1	0	0	1	0	10	1	0	20	1	0	30	1	1	0
11	0	3	1	0	3	12	0	3	23	0	3	34	1	0	5	1	0	16	1	0	27	1	0	38	1	1	9	1	1	20
12	0	3	12	0	3	24	0	3	36	1	0	8	1	0	20	1	0	32	1	1	4	1	1	16	1	1	28	1	2	0
13	0	3	23	0	3	36	1	0	9	1	0	22	1	0	35	1	1	8	1	1	21	1	1	34	1	2	7	1	2	20
14	0	3	34	1	0	8	1	0	22	1	0	36	1	1	10	1	1	24	1	1	38	1	2	12	1	2	26	1	3	0
15	1	0	5	1	0	20	1	0	35	1	1	10	1	1	25	1	2	0	1	2	15	1	2	30	1	3	5	1	3	20
16	1	0	16	1	0	32	1	1	8	1	1	24	1	2	0	1	2	16	1	2	32	1	3	8	1	3	24	2	0	0
17	1	0	27	1	1	4	1	1	21	1	1	38	1	2	15	1	2	32	1	3	9	1	3	26	2	0	3	2	0	20
18	1	0	38	1	1	16	1	1	34	1	2	12	1	2	30	1	3	8	1	3	26	2	0	4	2	0	22	2	1	0
19	1	1	9	1	1	28	1	2	7	1	2	26	1	3	5	1	3	24	2	0	3	2	0	22	2	1	1	2	1	20
20	1	1	20	1	2	0	1	2	20	1	3	0	1	3	20	2	0	0	2	0	20	2	1	0	2	1	20	2	2	0
30	2	0	10	2	1	0	2	1	30	2	2	20	2	3	10	3	0	0	3	0	30	3	1	20	3	2	10	3	3	0
40	2	3	0	3	0	0	3	1	0	3	2	0	3	3	0	4	0	0	4	1	0	4	2	0	4	3	0	5	0	0
50	3	1	30	3	3	0	4	0	10	4	1	20	4	2	30	5	0	0	5	1	10	5	2	20	5	3	30	6	1	0
60	4	0	20	4	2	0	4	3	20	5	1	0	5	2	20	6	0	0	6	1	20	6	3	0	7	0	20	7	2	0
70	4	3	10	5	1	0	5	2	30	6	0	20	6	2	10	7	0	0	7	1	30	7	3	20	8	1	10	8	3	0
80	5	2	0	6	0	0	6	2	0	7	0	0	7	2	0	8	0	0	8	2	0	9	0	0	9	2	0	10	0	0
90	6	0	30	6	3	0	7	1	10	7	3	20	8	1	30	9	0	0	9	2	10	10	0	20	10	2	30	11	1	0
100	6	3	20	7	2	0	8	0	20	8	3	0	9	1	20	10	0	0	10	2	20	11	1	0	11	3	20	12	2	0
200	13	3	0	15	0	0	16	1	0	17	2	0	18	3	0	20	0	0	21	1	0	22	2	0	23	3	0	25	0	0
300	20	2	20	22	2	0	24	1	20	26	1	0	28	0	20	30	0	0	31	3	20	33	3	0	35	2	20	37	2	0
400	27	2	0	30	0	0	32	2	0	35	0	0	37	2	0	40	0	0	42	2	0	45	0	0	47	2	0	50	0	0
500	34	1	20	37	2	0	40	2	20	43	3	0	46	3	20	50	0	0	53	0	20	56	1	0	59	1	20	62	2	0
600	41	1	0	45	0	0	48	3	0	52	2	0	56	1	0	60	0	0	63	3	0	67	2	0	71	1	0	75	0	0

From 21 to 30 Perches, Poles, or Falls wide.

Perches Long.	21 Do. Wide.			22 Do. Wide.			23 Do. Wide.			24 Do. Wide.			25 Do. Wide.			26 Do. Wide.			27 Do. Wide.			28 Do. Wide.			29 Do. Wide.			30 Do. Wide.		
	A	R	P	A	R	P	A	R	P	A	R	P	A	R	P	A	R	P	A	R	P	A	R	P	A	R	P	A	R	P
1	0	0	21	0	0	22	0	0	23	0	0	24	0	0	25	0	0	26	0	0	27	0	0	28	0	0	29	0	0	30
2	0	1	2	0	1	4	0	1	6	0	1	8	0	1	10	0	1	12	0	1	14	0	1	16	0	1	18	0	1	20
3	0	1	23	0	1	26	0	1	29	0	1	32	0	1	35	0	1	38	0	2	1	0	2	4	0	2	7	0	2	10
4	0	2	4	0	2	8	0	2	12	0	2	16	0	2	20	0	2	24	0	2	28	0	2	32	0	2	36	0	3	0
5	0	2	25	0	2	30	0	2	35	0	3	0	0	3	5	0	3	10	0	3	15	0	3	20	0	3	25	0	3	30
6	0	3	6	0	3	12	0	3	18	0	3	24	0	3	30	0	3	36	1	0	2	1	0	8	1	0	14	1	0	20
7	0	3	27	0	3	34	1	0	1	1	0	8	1	0	15	1	0	22	1	0	29	1	0	36	1	1	3	1	1	10
8	1	0	8	1	0	16	1	0	24	1	0	32	1	1	0	1	1	8	1	1	16	1	1	24	1	1	32	1	2	0
9	1	0	29	1	0	38	1	1	7	1	1	16	1	1	25	1	1	34	1	2	3	1	2	12	1	2	21	1	2	30
10	1	1	10	1	1	20	1	1	30	1	2	0	1	2	10	1	2	20	1	2	30	1	3	0	1	3	10	1	3	20
11	1	1	31	1	2	2	1	2	13	1	2	24	1	2	35	1	3	6	1	3	17	1	3	28	1	3	39	2	0	10
12	1	2	12	1	2	24	1	2	36	1	3	8	1	3	20	1	3	32	2	0	4	2	0	16	2	0	28	2	1	0
13	1	2	33	1	3	6	1	3	19	1	3	32	2	0	5	2	0	18	2	0	31	2	1	4	2	1	17	2	1	30
14	1	3	14	1	3	28	2	0	2	2	0	16	2	0	30	2	1	4	2	1	18	2	1	32	2	2	6	2	2	20
15	1	3	35	2	0	10	2	0	25	2	1	0	2	1	15	2	1	30	2	2	5	2	2	20	2	2	35	2	3	10
16	2	0	16	2	0	32	2	1	8	2	1	24	2	2	0	2	2	16	2	2	32	2	3	8	2	3	24	3	0	0
17	2	0	37	2	1	14	2	1	31	2	2	8	2	2	25	2	3	2	2	3	19	2	3	36	3	0	13	3	0	30
18	2	1	18	2	1	36	2	2	14	2	2	32	2	3	10	2	3	28	3	0	6	3	0	24	3	1	2	3	1	20
19	2	1	39	2	2	18	2	2	37	2	3	16	2	3	35	3	0	14	3	0	33	3	1	12	3	1	31	3	2	10
20	2	2	20	2	3	0	2	3	20	3	0	0	3	0	20	3	1	0	3	1	20	3	2	0	3	2	20	3	3	0
30	3	3	30	4	0	20	4	1	10	4	2	0	4	2	30	4	3	20	5	0	10	5	1	0	5	1	30	5	2	20
40	5	1	0	5	2	0	5	3	0	6	0	0	6	1	0	6	2	0	6	3	0	7	0	0	7	1	0	7	2	0
50	6	2	10	6	3	20	7	0	30	7	2	0	7	3	10	8	0	20	8	1	30	8	3	0	9	0	10	9	1	20
60	7	3	20	8	1	0	8	2	20	9	0	0	9	1	20	9	3	0	10	0	20	10	2	0	10	3	20	11	1	0
70	9	0	30	9	2	20	10	0	10	10	2	0	10	3	30	11	1	20	11	3	10	12	1	0	12	2	30	13	0	20
80	10	2	0	11	0	0	11	2	0	12	0	0	12	2	0	13	0	0	13	2	0	14	0	0	14	2	0	15	0	0
90	11	3	10	12	1	20	12	3	30	13	2	0	14	0	10	14	2	20	15	0	30	15	3	0	16	1	10	16	3	20
100	13	0	20	13	3	0	14	1	20	15	0	0	15	2	20	16	1	0	16	3	20	17	2	0	18	0	20	18	3	0
200	26	1	0	27	2	0	28	3	0	30	0	0	31	1	0	32	2	0	33	3	0	35	0	0	36	1	0	37	2	0
300	39	1	20	41	1	0	43	0	20	45	0	0	46	3	20	48	3	0	50	2	20	52	2	0	54	1	20	56	1	0
400	52	2	0	55	0	0	57	2	0	60	0	0	62	2	0	65	0	0	67	2	0	70	0	0	72	2	0	75	0	0
500	65	2	20	68	3	0	71	3	20	75	0	0	78	0	20	81	1	0	84	1	20	87	2	0	90	2	20	93	3	0
600	78	3	0	82	2	0	86	1	0	90	0	0	93	3	0	97	2	0	101	1	0	105	0	0	108	3	0	112	2	0

From 31 to 38 Perches, Poles, or Falls wide.

Each cell below gives **A. R. P.** (Acres, Roods, Perches).

Perches Long.	31 Do. Wide.	32 Do. Wide.	33 Do. Wide.	34 Do. Wide.	35 Do. Wide.	36 Do. Wide.	37 Do. Wide.	38 Do. Wide.
1	0 0 31	0 0 32	0 0 33	0 0 34	0 0 35	0 0 36	0 0 37	0 0 38
2	0 1 22	0 1 24	0 1 26	0 1 28	0 1 30	0 1 32	0 1 34	0 1 36
3	0 2 13	0 2 16	0 2 19	0 2 22	0 2 25	0 2 28	0 2 31	0 2 34
4	0 3 4	0 3 8	0 3 12	0 3 16	0 3 20	0 3 24	0 3 28	0 0 32
5	0 3 35	1 0 0	1 0 5	1 0 10	1 0 15	1 0 20	1 0 25	1 0 30
6	1 0 26	1 0 32	1 0 38	1 1 4	1 1 10	1 1 16	1 1 22	1 1 28
7	1 1 17	1 1 24	1 1 31	1 1 38	1 2 5	1 2 12	1 2 19	1 2 26
8	1 2 8	1 2 16	1 2 24	1 2 32	1 3 0	1 3 8	1 3 16	1 3 24
9	1 2 39	1 3 8	1 3 17	1 3 26	1 3 35	2 0 4	2 0 13	2 0 22
10	1 3 30	2 0 0	2 0 10	2 0 20	2 0 30	2 1 0	2 1 10	2 1 20
11	2 0 21	2 0 32	2 1 3	2 1 14	2 1 25	2 1 36	2 2 7	2 2 18
12	2 1 12	2 1 24	2 1 36	2 2 8	2 2 20	2 2 32	2 3 4	2 3 16
13	2 2 3	2 2 16	2 2 29	2 3 2	2 3 15	2 3 28	3 0 1	3 0 14
14	2 2 34	2 3 8	2 3 32	2 3 36	3 0 10	3 0 24	3 0 38	3 1 12
15	2 3 25	3 0 0	3 0 15	3 0 30	3 1 5	3 1 20	3 1 35	3 2 10
16	3 0 16	3 0 32	3 1 8	3 1 24	3 2 0	3 2 16	3 2 32	3 3 8
17	3 1 7	3 1 24	3 2 1	3 2 18	3 2 35	3 3 12	3 3 29	4 0 6
18	3 1 38	3 2 16	3 2 34	3 3 12	3 3 30	4 0 8	4 0 26	4 1 4
19	3 2 29	3 3 8	3 3 27	4 0 6	4 0 25	4 1 4	4 1 23	4 2 2
20	3 3 20	4 0 0	4 0 20	4 1 0	4 1 20	4 2 0	4 2 20	4 3 0
30	5 3 10	6 0 0	6 0 30	6 1 20	6 2 10	6 3 0	6 3 30	7 0 20
40	7 3 0	8 0 0	8 1 0	8 2 0	8 3 0	9 0 0	9 1 0	9 2 0
50	9 2 30	10 0 0	10 1 10	10 2 20	10 3 30	11 1 0	11 2 10	11 3 20
60	11 2 20	12 0 0	12 1 20	12 3 0	13 0 20	13 2 0	13 3 20	14 1 0
70	13 2 10	14 0 0	14 1 30	14 3 20	15 0 10	15 3 0	16 0 30	16 2 20
80	15 2 0	16 0 0	16 2 0	17 0 0	17 1 0	18 0 0	18 2 0	19 0 0
90	17 1 30	18 0 0	18 2 10	19 0 20	19 1 30	20 1 0	20 3 10	21 1 20
100	19 1 30	20 0 0	20 2 20	21 1 0	21 3 20	22 2 0	23 0 20	23 3 0
200	38 3 0	40 0 0	41 1 0	42 2 0	43 1 0	45 0 0	46 1 0	47 2 0
300	58 0 20	60 0 0	61 3 20	63 3 0	64 3 20	67 2 0	69 1 20	71 1 0
400	77 2 0	80 0 0	82 2 0	85 0 0	87 2 0	90 0 0	92 2 0	95 0 0
500	96 3 20	100 0 0	103 0 20	106 1 0	109 1 20	112 2 0	115 2 20	118 3 0
600	116 1 0	120 0 0	123 3 0	127 2 0	131 1 0	135 0 0	138 3 0	142 2 0

From 39 to 46 Perches, Poles, or Falls wide.

Perches Long.	39 Do. Wide			40 Do. Wide			41 Do. Wide			42 Do. Wide			43 Do. Wide			44 Do. Wide			45 Do. Wide			46 Do. Wide		
	A.	R.	P.	A.	R.	P.	A.	R.	P.	A.	R.	P.	A.	R.	P.	A.	R.	P.	A.	R.	P.	A.	R.	P.
1	0	0	39	0	1	0	0	1	1	0	1	2	0	1	3	0	1	4	0	1	5	0	1	6
2	0	1	38	0	2	0	0	2	2	0	2	4	0	2	6	0	2	8	0	2	10	0	2	12
3	0	2	37	0	3	0	0	3	3	0	3	6	0	3	9	0	3	12	0	3	15	0	3	18
4	0	3	36	1	0	0	1	0	4	1	0	8	1	0	12	1	0	16	1	0	20	1	0	24
5	1	0	35	1	1	0	1	1	5	1	1	10	1	1	15	1	1	20	1	1	25	1	1	30
6	1	1	34	1	2	0	1	2	6	1	2	12	1	2	18	1	2	24	1	2	30	1	2	36
7	1	2	33	1	3	0	1	3	7	1	3	14	1	3	21	1	3	28	1	3	35	2	0	2
8	1	3	32	2	0	0	2	0	8	2	0	16	2	0	24	2	0	32	2	1	0	2	1	8
9	2	0	31	2	1	0	2	1	9	2	1	18	2	1	27	2	1	36	2	2	5	2	2	14
10	2	1	30	2	2	0	2	2	10	2	2	20	2	2	30	2	3	0	2	3	10	2	3	20
11	2	2	29	2	3	0	2	3	11	2	3	22	2	3	33	3	0	4	3	0	15	3	0	26
12	2	3	28	3	0	0	3	0	12	3	0	24	3	0	36	3	1	8	3	1	20	3	1	32
13	3	0	27	3	1	0	3	1	13	3	1	26	3	1	39	3	2	12	3	2	25	3	2	38
14	3	1	26	3	2	0	3	2	14	3	2	28	3	3	2	3	3	16	3	3	30	4	0	4
15	3	2	25	3	3	0	3	3	15	3	3	30	4	0	5	4	0	20	4	0	35	4	1	10
16	3	3	14	4	0	0	4	0	16	4	0	32	4	1	8	4	1	24	4	2	0	4	2	16
17	4	0	13	4	1	0	4	1	17	4	1	34	4	2	11	4	2	28	4	3	5	4	3	22
18	4	1	12	4	2	0	4	2	18	4	2	36	4	3	14	4	3	32	5	0	10	5	0	28
19	4	2	11	4	3	0	4	3	19	4	3	38	5	0	17	5	0	36	5	1	15	5	1	34
20	4	3	20	5	0	0	5	0	20	5	1	0	5	1	20	5	2	0	5	2	20	5	3	0
30	7	1	10	7	2	0	7	2	30	7	3	20	8	0	10	8	1	0	8	1	30	8	2	20
40	9	3	0	10	0	0	10	1	0	10	2	0	10	3	0	11	0	0	11	1	0	11	2	0
50	12	0	30	12	2	20	12	3	10	13	0	20	13	1	30	13	3	0	14	0	10	14	1	20
60	14	2	20	15	0	0	15	1	20	15	3	0	16	0	20	16	2	0	16	3	30	17	1	0
70	17	0	10	17	2	0	17	3	30	18	1	20	18	3	10	19	1	0	19	2	30	20	0	20
80	19	2	0	20	0	0	20	2	0	21	0	0	21	2	0	22	0	0	22	1	10	23	0	0
90	21	3	30	22	2	0	23	0	10	23	2	10	24	0	30	24	3	0	25	2	10	25	3	20
100	24	1	20	25	0	0	25	2	20	26	1	0	26	3	20	27	2	0	28	0	20	28	3	0
200	48	3	0	50	0	0	51	1	0	52	2	0	53	3	0	55	0	0	56	1	0	57	2	0
300	73	0	20	75	0	0	76	3	20	78	3	0	80	1	20	82	2	0	84	1	20	86	1	0
400	97	2	0	100	0	0	102	2	0	105	0	0	107	2	0	110	0	0	112	2	0	115	0	0
500	121	3	20	125	0	0	128	0	20	131	1	0	134	1	20	137	2	0	140	2	20	143	3	0
600	146	1	0	150	0	0	153	3	0	157	2	0	161	1	0	165	0	0	168	3	0	172	2	0

From 47 to 54 Perches, Poles, or Falls wide.

Perches Long.	47 Do. Wide.			48 Do. Wide.			49 Do. Wide.			50 Do. Wide.			51 Do. Wide.			52 Do. Wide.			53 Do. Wide.			54 Do. Wide.		
	A.	R.	P.	A.	R.	P.	A.	R.	P.	A.	R.	P.	A.	R.	P.	A.	R.	P.	A.	R.	P.	A.	R.	P.
1	0	1	7	0	1	8	0	1	9	0	1	10	0	1	11	0	1	12	0	1	13	0	1	14
2	0	2	14	0	2	16	0	2	18	0	2	20	0	2	22	0	2	24	0	2	26	0	2	28
3	0	3	21	0	3	24	0	3	27	0	3	30	0	3	33	0	3	36	0	3	39	1	0	2
4	1	0	28	1	0	32	1	0	36	1	1	0	1	1	4	1	1	8	1	1	12	1	1	16
5	1	1	35	1	2	0	1	2	5	1	2	10	1	2	15	1	2	20	1	2	25	1	2	30
6	1	3	2	1	3	8	1	3	14	1	3	20	1	3	26	1	3	32	1	3	38	2	0	4
7	2	0	9	2	0	16	2	0	23	2	0	30	2	0	37	2	1	4	2	1	11	2	1	18
8	2	1	16	2	1	24	2	1	32	2	2	0	2	2	8	2	2	16	2	2	24	2	2	32
9	2	2	23	2	2	32	2	3	1	2	3	10	2	3	19	2	3	28	2	3	37	3	0	6
10	2	3	30	3	0	0	3	0	10	3	0	20	3	0	30	3	1	0	3	1	10	3	1	20
11	3	0	37	3	1	8	3	1	19	3	1	30	3	2	1	3	2	12	3	2	23	3	2	34
12	3	2	4	3	2	16	3	2	28	3	3	0	3	3	12	3	3	24	3	3	36	4	0	8
13	3	3	11	3	3	24	3	3	37	4	0	10	4	0	23	4	0	36	4	1	9	4	1	22
14	4	0	18	4	0	32	4	1	6	4	1	20	4	1	34	4	2	8	4	2	22	4	2	36
15	4	1	25	4	2	0	4	2	15	4	2	30	4	3	5	4	3	20	4	3	35	5	0	10
16	4	2	32	4	3	8	4	3	24	5	0	0	5	0	16	5	0	32	5	1	8	5	1	24
17	4	3	39	5	0	16	5	0	33	5	1	10	5	1	27	5	2	4	5	2	21	5	2	38
18	5	1	6	5	1	24	5	2	2	5	2	20	5	2	38	5	3	16	5	3	34	6	0	12
19	5	2	13	5	2	32	5	3	11	5	3	30	6	0	9	6	0	28	6	1	7	6	1	26
20	5	3	20	6	0	0	6	0	20	6	1	0	6	1	20	6	2	0	6	2	20	6	3	0
30	8	3	10	9	0	0	9	0	30	9	1	20	9	2	10	9	3	0	9	3	30	10	0	20
40	11	3	0	12	0	0	12	1	0	12	2	0	12	3	0	13	0	0	13	1	0	13	2	0
50	14	2	30	15	0	0	15	1	10	15	2	20	15	3	30	16	1	0	16	2	10	16	3	20
60	17	2	20	18	0	0	18	1	20	18	3	0	19	0	20	19	2	0	19	3	20	20	1	0
70	20	2	10	21	0	0	21	1	30	21	3	20	22	1	10	22	3	0	23	0	30	23	2	20
80	23	2	0	24	0	0	24	2	0	25	0	0	25	2	0	26	0	0	26	2	0	27	0	0
90	26	1	30	27	0	0	27	2	10	28	0	20	28	2	30	29	1	0	29	3	10	30	1	20
100	29	1	20	30	0	0	30	2	20	31	1	0	31	3	20	32	2	0	33	0	20	33	3	0
200	58	3	0	60	0	0	61	1	0	62	2	0	63	3	0	65	0	0	66	1	0	67	2	0
300	88	0	20	90	0	0	91	3	20	93	3	0	95	2	20	97	2	0	99	1	20	101	1	0
400	117	2	0	120	0	0	122	2	0	125	0	0	127	2	0	130	0	0	132	2	0	135	0	0
500	146	3	20	150	0	0	153	0	20	156	1	0	159	1	20	162	2	0	165	2	20	168	3	0
600	176	1	0	180	0	0	183	3	0	187	2	0	191	1	0	195	0	0	198	3	0	202	2	0

x

From 55 to 62 Perches, Poles, or Falls wide.

Perches Long.	55 Do. Wide.			56 Do. Wide.			57 Do. Wide.			58 Do. Wide.			59 Do. Wide.			60 Do. Wide.			61 Do. Wide.			62 Do. Wide.		
	A.	R.	P.	A.	R.	P.	A.	R.	P.	A.	R.	P.	A.	R.	P.	A.	R.	P.	A.	R.	P.	A.	R.	P.
1	0	1	15	0	1	16	0	1	17	0	1	18	0	1	19	0	1	20	0	1	21	0	1	22
2	0	2	30	0	2	32	0	2	34	0	2	36	0	2	38	0	3	0	0	3	2	0	3	4
3	1	0	5	1	0	8	1	0	11	1	0	14	1	0	17	1	0	20	1	0	23	1	0	26
4	1	1	20	1	1	24	1	1	28	1	1	32	1	1	36	1	2	0	1	2	4	1	2	8
5	1	2	35	1	3	0	1	3	5	1	3	10	1	3	15	1	3	20	1	3	25	1	3	30
6	2	0	10	2	0	16	2	0	22	2	0	28	2	0	34	2	1	0	2	1	6	2	1	12
7	2	1	25	2	1	32	2	1	39	2	2	6	2	2	13	2	2	20	2	2	27	2	2	34
8	2	3	0	2	3	8	2	3	16	2	3	24	2	3	32	3	0	0	3	0	8	3	0	16
9	3	0	15	3	0	24	3	0	33	3	1	2	3	1	11	3	1	20	3	1	29	3	1	38
10	3	1	30	3	2	0	3	2	10	3	2	20	3	2	30	3	3	0	3	3	10	3	3	20
11	3	3	5	3	3	16	3	3	27	3	3	38	4	0	9	4	0	20	4	0	31	4	1	2
12	4	0	20	4	0	32	4	1	4	4	1	16	4	1	28	4	2	0	4	2	12	4	2	24
13	4	1	35	4	2	8	4	2	21	4	2	34	4	3	7	4	3	20	4	3	33	5	0	6
14	4	3	10	4	3	24	4	3	38	5	0	12	5	0	26	5	1	0	5	1	14	5	1	28
15	5	0	25	5	1	0	5	1	15	5	1	30	5	2	5	5	2	20	5	2	35	5	3	10
16	5	2	0	5	2	16	5	2	32	5	3	8	5	3	24	6	0	0	6	0	16	6	0	32
17	5	3	15	5	3	32	6	0	9	6	0	26	6	1	3	6	1	20	6	1	37	6	2	14
18	6	0	30	6	1	8	6	1	26	6	2	4	6	2	22	6	3	0	6	3	18	6	3	36
19	6	2	5	6	2	24	6	3	3	6	3	22	7	0	1	7	0	20	7	0	39	7	1	18
20	6	3	20	7	0	0	7	0	20	7	1	0	7	1	20	7	2	0	7	2	20	7	3	0
30	10	1	10	10	2	0	10	2	30	10	3	20	11	0	10	11	1	0	11	1	30	11	2	20
40	13	3	0	14	0	0	14	1	0	14	2	0	14	3	0	15	0	0	15	1	0	15	2	0
50	17	0	30	17	2	0	17	3	10	18	0	20	18	1	30	18	3	0	19	0	10	19	1	20
60	20	2	20	21	0	0	21	1	20	21	3	0	22	0	20	22	2	0	22	3	20	23	1	0
70	24	0	10	24	2	0	24	3	30	25	1	20	25	3	10	26	1	0	26	2	30	27	0	20
80	27	2	0	28	0	0	28	2	0	29	0	0	29	2	0	30	0	0	30	2	20	31	0	0
90	30	3	30	31	2	0	32	0	10	32	2	20	33	0	30	33	3	0	34	1	10	34	3	20
100	34	1	20	35	0	0	35	2	20	36	1	0	36	3	20	37	2	0	38	0	20	38	3	0
200	68	3	0	70	0	0	71	1	0	72	2	0	73	3	0	75	0	0	76	1	0	77	2	0
300	103	0	20	105	0	0	106	3	20	108	3	0	110	2	20	112	2	0	114	1	20	116	1	0
400	137	2	0	140	0	0	142	2	0	145	0	0	147	2	0	150	0	0	152	2	0	155	0	0
500	171	3	20	175	0	0	178	0	20	181	1	0	184	1	20	187	2	0	190	2	20	193	3	0
600	206	1	0	210	0	0	213	3	0	217	2	0	221	1	0	225	0	0	228	3	0	232	2	0

From 63 to 70 Perches, Poles, or Falls wide.

Perches Long.	63 Do. Wide A	R	P	64 Do. Wide A	R	P	65 Do. Wide A	R	P	66 Do. Wide A	R	P	67 Do. Wide A	R	P	68 Do. Wide A	R	P	69 Do. Wide A	R	P	70 Do. Wide A	R	P
1	0	1	23	0	1	24	0	1	25	0	1	26	0	1	27	0	1	28	0	1	29	0	1	30
2	0	3	6	0	3	8	0	3	10	0	3	12	0	3	14	0	3	16	0	3	18	0	3	20
3	1	0	29	1	0	32	1	0	35	1	0	38	1	1	1	1	1	4	1	1	7	1	1	10
4	1	2	12	1	2	16	1	2	20	1	2	24	1	2	28	1	2	32	1	2	36	1	3	0
5	1	3	35	2	0	0	2	0	5	2	0	10	2	0	15	2	0	20	2	0	25	2	0	30
6	2	1	18	2	1	24	2	1	30	2	1	36	2	2	2	2	2	8	2	2	14	2	2	20
7	2	3	1	2	3	8	2	3	15	2	3	22	2	3	29	2	3	36	3	0	3	3	0	10
8	3	0	24	3	0	32	3	1	0	3	1	8	3	1	16	3	1	24	3	1	32	3	2	0
9	3	2	7	3	2	16	3	2	25	3	2	34	3	3	3	3	3	12	3	3	21	3	3	30
10	3	3	30	4	0	0	4	0	10	4	0	20	4	0	30	4	1	0	4	1	10	4	1	20
11	4	1	13	4	1	24	4	1	35	4	2	6	4	2	17	4	2	28	4	2	39	4	3	10
12	4	2	36	4	3	8	4	3	20	4	3	32	5	0	4	5	0	16	5	0	28	5	1	0
13	5	0	19	5	0	32	5	1	5	5	1	18	5	1	31	5	2	4	5	2	17	5	2	30
14	5	2	2	5	2	16	5	2	30	5	3	4	5	3	18	5	3	32	6	0	6	6	0	20
15	5	3	25	6	0	0	6	0	15	6	0	30	6	1	5	6	1	20	6	1	35	6	2	10
16	6	1	8	6	1	24	6	2	0	6	2	16	6	2	32	6	3	8	6	3	24	7	0	0
17	6	2	31	6	3	8	6	3	25	7	0	2	7	0	19	7	0	36	7	1	13	7	1	30
18	7	0	14	7	0	32	7	1	10	7	1	28	7	2	6	7	2	24	7	3	2	7	3	20
19	7	1	37	7	2	16	7	2	35	7	3	14	7	3	33	8	0	12	8	0	31	8	1	10
20	7	3	20	8	0	0	8	0	20	8	1	0	8	1	20	8	2	0	8	2	20	8	3	0
30	11	3	10	12	0	0	12	0	30	12	1	20	12	2	10	12	3	0	12	3	30	13	0	20
40	15	3	0	16	0	0	16	1	0	16	2	0	16	3	0	17	0	0	17	1	0	17	2	0
50	19	2	30	20	0	0	20	1	10	20	2	20	20	3	30	21	1	0	21	2	10	21	3	20
60	23	2	20	24	0	0	24	1	20	24	3	0	25	0	20	25	2	0	25	3	20	26	1	0
70	27	2	10	28	0	0	28	1	30	28	3	20	29	1	10	29	3	0	30	0	30	30	2	20
80	31	2	0	32	0	0	32	2	0	33	0	0	33	2	0	34	0	0	34	2	0	35	0	0
90	35	1	30	36	0	0	36	2	10	37	0	20	37	2	30	38	1	0	38	3	10	39	1	20
100	39	1	20	40	0	0	40	2	20	41	1	0	41	3	20	42	2	0	43	0	20	43	3	0
200	78	3	0	80	0	0	81	1	0	82	2	0	83	3	0	85	0	0	86	1	0	87	2	0
300	118	0	20	120	0	0	121	3	20	123	3	0	125	2	20	127	2	0	130	1	20	131	1	0
400	157	2	0	160	0	0	162	2	0	165	0	0	167	2	0	170	0	0	172	2	0	175	0	0
500	196	3	20	200	0	0	203	0	20	206	1	0	209	1	20	212	2	0	215	2	20	218	3	0
600	236	1	0	240	0	0	243	3	0	247	2	0	151	1	0	255	0	0	258	3	0	262	2	0

From 71 to 78 Perches, Poles, or Falls wide.

Perches Long	71 Do. Wide			72 Do. Wide			73 Do. Wide			74 Do. Wide			75 Do. Wide			76 Do. Wide			77 Do. Wide			78 Do. Wide		
	A.	R.	P.	A.	R.	P.	A.	R.	P.	A.	R.	P.	A.	R.	P.	A.	R.	P.	A.	R.	P.	A.	R.	P.
1	0	1	31	0	1	32	0	1	33	0	1	34	0	1	35	0	1	36	0	1	37	0	1	38
2	0	3	22	0	3	24	0	3	26	0	3	28	0	3	30	0	3	32	0	3	34	0	3	36
3	1	1	13	1	1	16	1	1	19	1	1	22	1	1	25	1	1	28	1	1	31	1	1	34
4	1	3	4	1	3	8	1	3	12	1	3	16	1	3	20	1	3	24	1	3	28	1	3	32
5	2	0	35	2	1	0	2	1	5	2	1	10	2	1	15	2	1	20	2	1	25	2	1	30
6	2	2	26	2	2	32	2	2	38	2	3	4	2	3	10	2	3	16	2	3	22	2	3	28
7	3	0	17	3	0	24	3	0	31	3	0	38	3	1	5	3	1	12	3	1	19	3	1	26
8	3	2	8	3	2	16	3	2	24	3	2	32	3	3	0	3	3	8	3	3	16	3	3	24
9	3	3	39	4	0	8	4	0	17	4	0	26	4	0	35	4	1	4	4	1	13	4	1	22
10	4	1	30	4	2	0	4	2	10	4	2	20	4	2	30	4	3	0	4	3	10	4	3	20
11	4	3	21	4	3	32	5	0	3	5	0	14	5	0	25	5	0	36	5	1	7	5	1	18
12	5	1	12	5	1	24	5	1	36	5	2	8	5	2	20	5	2	32	5	3	4	5	3	16
13	5	3	3	5	3	16	5	3	29	6	0	2	6	0	15	6	0	28	6	1	1	6	1	4
14	6	0	34	6	1	8	6	1	22	6	1	36	6	2	10	6	2	24	6	2	38	6	3	12
15	6	2	25	6	3	0	6	3	15	6	3	30	7	0	5	7	0	20	7	0	35	7	1	10
16	7	0	16	7	0	32	7	1	8	7	1	24	7	2	0	7	2	16	7	2	32	7	3	8
17	7	2	7	7	2	24	7	3	1	7	3	18	7	3	35	8	0	12	8	0	29	8	1	0
18	7	3	38	8	0	16	8	0	34	8	1	12	8	1	30	8	2	8	8	2	26	8	3	4
19	8	1	29	8	2	8	8	2	27	8	3	6	8	3	25	9	0	4	9	0	23	9	1	2
20	8	3	20	9	0	0	9	0	20	9	1	0	9	1	20	9	2	0	9	2	20	9	3	0
30	13	1	10	13	2	0	13	2	30	13	3	20	14	0	10	14	1	0	14	1	30	14	2	20
40	17	3	0	18	0	0	18	1	0	18	2	20	18	3	0	19	0	0	19	1	10	19	2	0
50	22	0	30	22	2	0	22	3	10	23	0	20	23	1	30	23	3	0	24	0	10	24	1	20
60	26	2	20	27	0	0	27	1	20	27	3	0	28	0	20	28	2	0	28	3	20	29	1	0
70	31	0	10	31	2	0	31	3	10	32	1	20	32	3	10	33	1	0	33	2	30	34	0	20
80	35	2	0	36	0	0	36	2	0	37	0	0	37	2	0	38	0	0	38	2	0	39	0	0
90	39	3	30	40	2	0	41	0	10	41	2	20	42	0	30	42	3	0	43	1	10	43	3	20
100	41	1	20	45	0	0	45	2	20	46	1	0	46	3	20	47	2	0	48	0	20	48	3	0
200	83	3	0	90	0	0	91	1	0	92	2	0	93	3	0	95	0	0	96	1	0	97	2	0
300	133	0	20	135	0	0	136	3	20	138	3	0	140	2	20	142	2	0	144	1	20	146	1	0
400	177	2	0	180	0	0	182	2	0	185	0	0	187	2	0	190	0	0	192	2	0	195	0	0
500	221	3	20	225	0	0	228	0	20	231	1	0	234	1	30	237	2	0	240	2	20	243	3	0
600	266	1	0	270	0	0	273	3	0	277	2	0	281	1	0	285	0	0	288	3	0	292	2	0

From 79 to 86 Perches, Poles, or Falls wide.

Perches Long.	79 Do. Wide.			80 Do. Wide.			81 Do. Wide.			82 Do Wide.			83 Do. Wide.			84 Do. Wide.			85 Do. Wide.			86 Do. Wide.		
	A.	R.	P.	A.	R.	P.	A.	R.	P.	A.	R.	P.	A.	R.	P.	A.	R.	P.	A.	R.	P.	A.	R.	P.
1	0	1	39	0	2	0	0	2	1	0	2	2	0	2	3	0	2	4	0	2	5	0	2	6
2	0	3	38	1	0	0	1	0	2	1	0	4	1	0	6	1	0	8	1	0	10	1	0	12
3	1	1	37	1	2	0	1	2	3	1	2	6	1	2	9	1	2	12	1	2	15	1	2	18
4	1	3	36	2	0	0	2	0	4	2	0	8	2	0	12	2	0	16	2	0	20	2	0	24
5	2	1	35	2	2	0	2	2	25	2	2	10	2	2	15	2	2	20	2	2	25	2	2	30
6	2	3	34	3	0	0	3	0	6	3	0	12	3	0	18	3	0	24	3	0	30	3	0	36
7	3	1	33	3	2	0	3	2	7	3	2	14	3	2	21	3	2	28	3	2	35	3	3	2
8	3	3	32	4	0	0	4	0	8	4	0	16	4	0	24	4	0	32	4	1	0	4	1	8
9	4	1	31	4	2	0	4	2	9	4	2	8	4	2	27	4	2	36	4	3	5	4	3	14
10	4	3	30	5	0	0	5	0	10	5	0	20	5	0	30	5	1	0	5	1	10	5	1	20
11	5	1	29	5	2	0	5	2	11	5	2	22	5	2	33	5	3	4	5	3	15	5	3	26
12	5	3	28	6	0	0	6	0	12	6	0	24	6	0	36	6	1	8	6	1	20	6	1	32
13	6	1	27	6	2	0	6	2	13	6	2	26	6	2	39	6	3	12	6	3	25	6	3	38
14	6	3	26	7	0	0	7	0	14	7	0	28	7	1	2	7	1	16	7	1	30	7	2	4
15	7	1	25	7	2	0	7	2	15	7	2	30	7	3	5	7	3	20	7	3	35	8	0	10
16	7	3	24	8	0	0	8	0	16	8	0	32	8	1	8	8	1	24	8	2	0	8	2	16
17	8	1	23	8	2	0	8	2	17	8	2	34	8	3	11	8	3	28	9	0	5	9	0	22
18	8	3	22	9	0	0	9	0	18	9	0	36	9	1	14	9	1	32	9	2	10	9	2	28
19	9	1	21	9	2	0	9	2	19	9	2	38	9	3	17	9	3	36	10	0	15	10	0	34
20	9	3	20	10	0	0	10	0	20	10	1	0	10	1	20	10	2	0	10	2	20	10	3	0
30	14	3	10	15	0	0	15	0	30	15	1	20	15	2	10	15	3	0	15	3	30	16	0	20
40	19	3	0	20	0	0	20	1	0	20	2	0	20	3	0	21	0	0	21	1	0	21	2	0
50	24	2	30	25	0	0	25	1	10	25	2	20	25	3	30	26	1	0	26	2	10	26	3	20
60	29	2	20	30	0	0	30	1	20	30	3	0	31	0	20	31	2	0	31	3	20	32	1	0
70	34	2	10	35	0	0	35	1	30	35	3	20	36	1	10	36	3	0	37	0	30	37	2	20
80	39	2	0	40	0	0	40	2	0	41	0	0	41	2	0	42	0	0	42	2	0	43	0	0
90	44	1	30	45	0	0	45	2	10	46	0	20	46	2	30	47	1	0	47	3	10	48	1	20
100	49	1	20	50	0	0	50	2	20	51	1	0	51	3	20	52	2	0	53	0	20	53	3	0
200	98	3	0	100	0	0	101	1	0	102	2	0	103	3	0	105	0	0	106	1	0	107	2	0
300	148	0	20	150	0	0	151	3	20	153	3	0	155	2	20	157	2	0	159	1	20	161	1	0
400	197	2	0	200	0	0	202	2	0	205	0	0	207	2	0	210	0	0	212	2	0	215	0	0
500	246	3	20	250	0	0	253	0	20	256	1	0	259	1	20	262	2	0	265	2	20	268	3	0
600	296	1	0	300	0	0	303	3	0	307	2	0	311	1	0	315	0	0	318	3	0	322	2	0

Y

From 87 to 94 Perches, Poles, or Falls wide.

Perches Long.	87 Do. Wide.			88 Do. Wide.			89 Do. Wide.			90 Do. Wide.			91 Do. Wide.			92 Do. Wide.			93 Do. Wide.			94 Do. Wide.		
	A.	R.	P.	A.	R.	P.	A.	R.	P.	A.	R.	P.	A.	R.	P.	A.	R.	P.	A.	R.	P.	A.	R.	P.
1	0	2	7	0	2	8	0	2	9	0	2	10	0	2	11	0	2	12	0	2	13	0	2	14
2	1	0	14	1	0	16	1	0	18	1	0	20	1	0	22	1	0	24	1	0	26	1	0	28
3	1	2	21	1	2	24	1	2	27	1	2	30	1	2	33	1	2	36	1	2	39	1	3	2
4	2	0	28	2	0	32	2	0	36	2	1	0	2	1	4	2	1	8	2	1	12	2	1	16
5	2	2	35	2	3	0	2	3	5	2	3	10	2	3	15	2	3	20	2	3	25	2	3	30
6	3	1	2	3	1	8	3	1	14	3	1	20	3	1	26	3	1	32	3	1	18	3	2	4
7	3	3	9	3	3	16	3	3	23	3	3	30	3	3	37	4	0	4	4	0	11	4	0	18
8	4	1	16	4	1	24	4	1	32	4	2	0	4	2	8	4	2	16	4	2	24	4	2	32
9	4	3	23	4	3	32	5	0	1	5	0	10	5	0	19	5	0	28	5	0	37	5	1	6
10	5	1	30	5	2	0	5	2	10	5	2	20	5	2	30	5	3	0	5	3	10	5	3	20
11	5	3	37	6	0	8	6	0	19	6	0	30	6	1	1	6	1	12	6	1	23	6	1	34
12	6	2	4	6	2	16	6	2	28	6	3	0	6	3	12	6	3	24	6	3	36	7	0	8
13	7	0	11	7	0	24	7	0	37	7	1	10	7	1	23	7	1	35	7	2	8	7	2	21
14	7	2	18	7	2	32	7	3	6	7	3	20	7	3	34	8	0	8	8	0	22	8	0	36
15	8	0	25	8	1	0	8	1	15	8	1	30	8	2	5	8	2	20	8	2	35	8	3	10
16	8	2	32	8	3	8	8	3	24	9	0	0	9	0	16	9	0	32	9	1	8	9	1	24
17	9	0	39	9	1	16	9	1	33	9	2	10	9	2	27	9	3	4	9	3	21	9	3	38
18	9	3	6	9	3	24	10	0	2	10	0	20	10	0	38	10	0	38	10	1	16	10	1	34
19	10	1	13	10	1	32	10	2	11	10	2	30	10	3	9	10	3	28	11	0	7	11	0	26
20	10	3	20	11	0	0	11	0	20	11	1	0	11	1	20	11	2	0	11	2	20	11	3	0
30	16	1	10	16	2	0	16	2	30	16	3	20	17	0	10	17	1	0	17	1	30	17	2	20
40	21	3	0	22	0	0	22	1	0	22	2	0	22	3	0	23	0	0	23	1	0	23	2	0
50	27	0	30	27	2	0	27	3	10	28	0	20	28	1	30	28	3	0	29	0	10	29	1	20
60	32	2	20	33	0	0	33	1	20	33	3	0	34	0	20	34	2	0	34	3	20	35	1	0
70	38	0	10	38	2	0	38	3	30	39	1	20	39	3	10	40	1	0	40	2	30	41	0	20
80	43	2	0	44	0	0	44	2	0	45	0	0	45	2	0	46	0	0	46	2	0	47	0	0
90	48	3	30	49	2	0	50	0	10	50	2	20	51	0	30	51	3	0	52	1	10	52	3	20
100	54	1	20	55	0	0	55	2	20	56	1	0	56	3	20	57	2	0	58	0	20	58	3	0
200	108	3	0	110	0	0	111	1	0	112	2	0	113	3	0	115	0	0	116	1	0	117	2	0
300	163	0	20	165	0	0	166	3	20	168	3	0	170	2	20	172	2	0	174	1	20	176	1	0
400	217	2	0	220	0	0	222	2	0	225	0	0	227	2	0	230	0	0	232	2	0	235	0	0
500	271	3	20	275	0	0	278	0	20	281	1	0	284	1	20	287	2	0	290	2	20	293	3	0
600	326	1	0	330	0	0	333	3	0	337	2	0	341	1	0	345	0	0	348	3	0	352	2	0

From 95 to 102 Perches, Poles, or Falls wide.

Perches Long	95 Do. Wide.			96 Do. Wide.			97 Do. Wide.			98 Do. Wide.			99 Do. Wide.			100 Do. Wide.			101 Do. Wide.			102 Do. Wide.		
	A.	R.	P.	A.	R.	R.	A.	R.	P.	A.	R.	P.	A.	R.	P.	A.	R.	P.	A.	R.	P.	A.	R.	P.
1	0	2	15	0	2	16	0	2	17	0	2	18	0	2	19	0	2	20	0	2	21	0	2	22
2	1	0	30	1	0	32	1	0	34	1	0	36	1	0	38	1	1	0	1	1	2	1	1	4
3	1	3	5	1	3	8	1	3	11	1	3	14	1	3	17	1	3	20	1	3	23	1	3	26
4	2	1	20	2	1	24	2	1	28	2	1	32	2	1	36	2	2	0	2	2	4	2	2	8
5	2	3	35	3	0	0	3	0	5	3	0	10	3	0	15	3	0	20	3	0	25	3	0	30
6	3	2	10	3	2	16	3	2	22	3	2	28	3	2	34	3	3	0	3	3	6	3	3	12
7	4	0	25	4	0	32	4	0	39	4	1	6	4	1	13	4	1	20	4	1	27	4	1	34
8	4	3	0	4	3	8	4	3	16	4	3	24	4	3	32	5	0	0	5	0	8	5	0	16
9	5	1	15	5	1	24	5	1	33	5	2	2	5	2	11	5	2	20	5	2	29	5	2	38
10	5	3	30	6	0	0	6	0	10	6	0	20	6	0	30	6	1	0	6	1	10	6	1	20
11	6	2	5	6	2	16	6	2	27	6	2	38	6	3	9	6	3	20	6	3	31	7	0	2
12	7	0	20	7	0	32	7	1	4	7	1	16	7	1	28	7	2	0	7	2	12	7	2	24
13	7	2	35	7	3	8	7	3	21	7	3	34	8	0	7	8	0	20	8	0	33	8	1	6
14	8	1	10	8	1	24	8	1	38	8	2	12	8	2	26	8	3	0	8	3	14	8	3	28
15	8	3	25	9	0	0	9	0	15	9	0	30	9	1	5	9	1	20	9	1	35	9	2	10
16	9	2	0	9	2	16	9	2	32	9	3	8	9	3	24	10	0	0	10	0	16	10	0	32
17	10	0	15	10	0	32	10	1	9	10	1	26	10	2	3	10	2	20	10	2	33	10	3	14
18	10	2	30	10	3	8	10	3	26	11	0	4	11	0	22	11	1	0	11	1	18	11	1	36
19	11	1	5	11	1	24	11	2	3	11	2	22	11	3	1	11	3	20	11	3	39	12	0	18
20	11	3	20	12	0	0	12	0	20	12	1	0	12	1	20	12	2	0	12	2	20	12	3	0
30	17	3	10	18	0	0	18	0	30	18	1	20	18	2	10	18	3	0	18	3	30	19	0	20
40	23	3	0	24	0	0	24	1	0	24	2	0	24	3	0	25	0	0	25	1	0	25	2	0
50	29	2	30	30	0	0	30	1	10	30	2	20	30	3	30	31	1	0	31	2	10	31	3	20
60	35	2	20	36	0	0	36	1	20	36	3	0	37	0	20	37	2	0	37	3	20	38	1	0
70	41	2	10	42	0	0	42	1	30	42	3	20	43	1	10	43	3	0	44	0	30	44	2	20
80	47	2	0	48	0	0	48	2	0	49	0	0	49	2	0	50	0	0	50	2	0	51	0	0
90	53	1	30	54	0	0	54	2	10	55	0	20	55	2	30	56	1	0	56	3	10	57	1	20
100	59	1	20	60	0	0	60	2	20	61	1	0	61	3	20	62	2	0	63	0	20	63	3	0
200	118	3	0	120	0	0	121	1	0	122	2	0	123	3	0	125	0	0	126	1	0	127	2	0
300	178	0	20	180	0	0	181	3	20	183	3	0	185	2	20	187	2	0	189	1	20	191	1	0
400	237	2	0	240	0	0	242	2	0	245	0	0	247	2	0	250	0	0	252	2	0	255	0	0
500	296	3	20	300	0	0	303	0	20	306	1	0	309	1	20	312	2	0	315	2	20	318	3	0
600	356	1	0	360	0	0	363	3	0	367	2	0	371	1	0	375	0	0	378	3	0	382	2	0

ART. III. CONTAINING USEFUL TABLES FOR THE REDUCTION OF MEASURES.

ENGLISH LONG MEASURE.

Inches.							
7.92	one Link.						
12	1.51	one Foot.					
36	4.54	3	one Yard.				
198	25	16	5.5	one Pole or Perch.			
792	100	66	22	4	one Chain.		
7920	1000	660	220	40	10	one Furlong.	
63360	8000	5280	1760	320	80	8	one Mile.

ENGLISH SQUARE MEASURE.

Sq. Inches.	Sq. Links					
62.7264	one Link.					
144	2.29	one Foot.				
1296	20.66	9	one Yard.			
39204	625	272.25	30.25	one Perch.		
1568160	25000	10890	1210	40	one Rood.	
6272640	100000	43560	4840	160	4	one Acre.

SCOTS LONG MEASURE.

Inches.						
8.88	one Link.					
12	1.35	one Foot.				
37	4.16	3.08	one Ell.			
222	25	18.5	6	one Rood.		
880	100	74	24	4	one Chain.	
71040	8000	5920	1920	320	80	one Mile.

SCOTS SQUARE MEASURE.

Sq. Inches.	Sq. Links.					
78.8544	one Link.					
144	1.82	one Foot.				
1369	17.36	9.50	one Ell.			
49284	625	342.25	36	one Fall.		
1971360	25000	13690	1440	40	one Rood.	
7885440	100000	54760	5760	160	4	one Acre.

IRISH LONG MEASURE.

Inches.						
9.53	one Link.					
12	1.19	one Foot.				
36	3.57	3	one Yard.			
252	25	21	7	one Perch.		
1008	100	84	28	4	one Chain.	
80640	8000	6720	2240	320	80	one Mile.

IRISH SQUARE MEASURE.

Inches.	Sq. Links.					
106.2144	one Link.					
144	1.42	one Foot.				
1296	12.78	9	one Yard.			
66384	625	441	49	one Perch.		
2655360	25000	17640	1960	40	one Rood.	
10621440	100000	70560	7840	160	4	one Acre.

TABLE, for ascertaining, by inspection, the number of Roods and Perches contained in the two first Decimals of an Acre.

Dec.	Roods and Perches.			Dec.	Roods and Perches.			Dec.	Roods and Perches.		
	R.	P.	Pts.		R.	P.	Pts.		R	P.	Pts.
01	0	01	.6	34	1	14	.4	67	2	27	.2
02	0	03	.2	35	1	16	.0	68	2	28	.8
03	0	04	.8	36	1	17	.6	69	2	30	.4
04	0	06	.4	37	1	19	.2	70	2	32	.0
05	0	08	.0	38	1	20	.8	71	2	33	.6
06	0	09	.6	39	1	22	.4	72	2	35	.2
07	0	11	.2	40.	1	24	.0	73	2	36	.8
08	0	13	.8	41	1	25	.6	74	2	38	.4
09	0	14	.4	42	1	27	.2	75	3	0	.0
10	0	16	.0	43	1	28	.8	76	3	1	.6
11	0	17	.6	44	1	30	.4	77	3	3	.2
12	0	19	.2	45	1	32.	0	78	3	4	.8
13	0	20	.8	46	1	33	.6	79	3	6	.4
14	0	22	.4	47	1	35	.2	80	3	8	.0
15	0	24	.0	48	1	36	.8	81	3	9	.6
16	0	25	.6	49	1	38	.4	82	3	11	.2
17	0	27	.2	50	2	0	.0	83	3	13	.8
18	0	28	.8	51	2	1	.6	84	3	14	.4
19	0	30	.4	52	2	3	.2	85	3	16	.0
20	0	32	.0	53	2	4	.8	86	3	17	.6
21	0	33	.6	54	2	6	.4	87	3	19	.2
22	0	35	.2	55	2	8	.0	88	3	20	.8
23	0	36	.8	56	2	9	.6	89	3	22	.4
24	0	38	.4	57	2	11	.2	90	3	24	.0
25	1	0	.0	58	2	13	.8	91	3	25	.6
26	1	1	.6	59	2	14	.4	92	3	27	.2
27	1	3	.2	60	2	16	.0	93	3	28	.8
28	1	4	.8	61	2	17	.6	94	3	30	.4
29	1	6	.4	62	2	19	.2	95	3	32	.0
30	1	8	.0	63	2	20	.8	96	3	33	.6
31	1	9	.6	64	2	22	.4	97	3	35	.2
32	1	11	.2	65	2	24	.0	98	3	36	.8
33	1	12	.8	66	2	25	.4	99	3	38	.4

Decimals of an Acre.

The last figure is only the decimal of a Perch or Fall.

TABLE,
Shewing the proportion of English Measure to Scots and Irish.

Eng. Acres.	Scots Measure.			Eng. Perch.	Scots Falls.				Eng. Acres.	Irish Measure.			Eng. Perch.	Irish Perches.			
	A.	R.	F.		A.	R.	F.	Pts		A.	R.	F.		A.	R.	P.	Pts
1	0	3	7	1	0	0	0	$\frac{8}{10}$	1	0	2	19	1	0	0	0.6	
2	1	2	14	2	0	0	1.6		2	1	0	37	2	0	0	1.2	
3	2	1	21	3	0	0	2.4		3	1	3	16	3	0	0	1.8	
4	3	0	29	4	0	0	3.2		4	2	1	34	4	0	0	2.4	
5	3	3	36	5	0	0	4		5	3	0	13	5	0	0	3	
6	4	3	3	6	0	0	4.8		6	3	2	32	6	0	0	3.7	
7	5	2	10	7	0	0	5.6		7	4	1	11	7	0	0	4.3	
8	6	1	18	8	0	0	6.4		8	4	3	30	8	0	0	4.9	
9	7	0	25	9	0	0	7.2		9	5	2	19	9	0	0	5.5	
10	7	3	33	10	0	0	8		10	6	0	28	10	0	0	6.1	
11	8	3	0	11	0	0	8.8		11	6	3	7	11	0	0	6.7	
12	9	2	7	12	0	0	9.5		12	7	1	24	12	0	0	7.4	
13	10	1	15	13	0	0	10.3		13	8	0	5	13	0	0	8	
14	11	0	22	14	0	0	11.1		14	8	2	22	14	0	0	8.6	
15	11	3	29	15	0	0	11.9		15	9	1	1	15	0	0	9.2	
16	12	2	36	16	0	0	12.7		16	9	3	20	16	0	0	9.8	
17	13	2	4	17	0	0	13.5		17	10	1	39	17	0	0	10.4	
18	14	1	11	18	0	0	14.3		18	11	0	18	18	0	0	11.1	
19	15	0	18	19	0	0	15.1		19	11	2	37	19	0	0	11.7	
20	15	3	25	20	0	0	15.9		20	12	1	16	20	0	0	12.3	
21	16	2	33	21	0	0	16.7		21	12	3	35	21	0	0	12.9	
22	17	2	0	22	0	0	17.5		22	13	2	14	22	0	0	13.5	
23	18	1	7	23	0	0	18.3		23	14	0	33	23	0	0	14.1	
24	19	0	14	24	0	0	19.1		24	14	3	12	24	0	0	14.8	
25	19	3	22	25	0	0	19.9		25	15	1	31	25	0	0	15.4	
26	20	2	29	26	0	0	20.7		26	16	0	10	26	0	0	16	
27	21	1	36	27	0	0	21.5		27	16	2	29	27	0	0	16.6	
28	22	1	4	28	0	0	23.1		28	17	1	8	28	0	0	17.2	
29	23	0	11	29	0	0	23.9		29	17	3	27	29	0	0	17.8	
30	23	3	18	30	0	0	24.7		30	18	2	3	30	0	0	18.5	
40	31	3	11	31	0	0	25.5		40	24	2	32	31	0	0	19.1	
50	39	3	3	32	0	0	26.3		50	30	3	20	32	0	0	19.7	
60	47	2	37	33	0	0	27.1		60	37	0	8	33	0	0	20.3	
70	55	2	29	34	0	0	27.9		70	43	0	36	34	0	0	20.9	
80	63	2	22	35	0	0	28.7		80	49	1	24	35	0	0	21.6	
90	71	2	15	36	0	0	29.5		90	55	2	9	36	0	0	22.2	
100	79	2	2	37	0	0	30.2		100	61	3	0	37	0	0	22.8	
				38	0	8	31.1						38	0	0	23.4	
Roods				39	0	0	31.9		Roods				39	0	0	24	
1	0	0	32						1	0	0	25					
2	0	1	23						2	0	1	10					
3	0	2	15						3	0	1	35					

The following Table is for shewing the number of square links to be added to each acre, when land in England, Scotland, and Ireland, is measured by a chain longer than the standard measure, to recover what is lost by the chains stretching, which they commonly do after being used for some time. A land-measurer cannot be too careful with his chain: after having adjusted it, before he sets out upon a survey, he ought to fix upon some spot on the ground, and stretch it out, and drive in two pins or stakes, and, every morning before he goes out, to try if it has encreased any thing in length, and to make it shorter by taking out a ring or two. The table will be found useful in making an allowance. For example, if the English chain has stretched six inches, and if you have surveyed a field of fifty acres, you have an allowance to make of 1521 square links for each acre; which, multiplied by 50, the number of acres, shows that the measure is short by 3 roods and 2 poles nearly, which ought to be added to the 50 acres.

ENGLISH.			SCOTS.			IRISH.		
Length of Chain.		Square Links add to each Acre.	Length of Chain.		Square Links add to each Acre.	Length of Chain.		Square Links add to each Acre.
Ft.	In.	Sq. Links.	Ft.	In.	Sq. Links.	Ft.	In.	Sq. Links.
66	1	00252	74	1	226	84	1	200
66	2	506	74	2	452	84	2	400
66	3	759	74	3	678	84	3	600
66	4	1013	74	4	904	84	4	800
66	5	1360	74	5	1130	84	5	1000
66	6	1521	74	6	1356	84	6	1200
66	7	1774	74	7	1582	84	7	1400
66	8	2027	74	8	1708	84	8	1600
66	9	2280	74	9	1934	84	9	1800
66	10	2533	74	10	2160	84	10	2000
66	11	2788	74	11	2486	84	11	2200
67		3040	75		2712	85		2400

Suppose the Scots chain to have stretched 8 inches, and you have measured a field of 60 acres, you have an allowance to make of 1708 square links, which, multiplied by 60, shows that you must add 1 acre and 4 falls to the 60 acres. On the other hand, if the chain should be found too short 8 inches in 60 acres, 1 acre and 4 falls must be subtracted.

TABLE,

Shewing the breadth and length required in Perches, Feet, and Inches, to make an Acre.

Breadth in Perches.	Length to make an Acre. Per.	Ft.	In.		Length in Perches.	Breadth to make an Acre. Per.	Ft.	In.
1	160	0	0		25	6	6	2
2	88	0	0		26	6	2	6
3	53	4	0		27	5	15	4
4	40	0	0		28	5	11	9
5	32	0	0		29	5	8	6
6	26	11	0		30	5	5	6
7	22	14	3		31	5	2	4
8	20	0	0		32	5	0	0
9	17	12	10		33	4	14	0
10	16	0	0		34	4	11	7
11	14	9	0		35	4	9	5
12	13	5	6		36	4	7	4
13	12	5	1		37	4	5	4

Length in Perches.	Breadth to make an Acre. Per.	Ft.	In.		Length in Perches.	Breadth to make an Acre. Per.	Ft.	In.
					38	4	3	2
					39	4	1	8
					40	4	0	0
14	11	7	1		41	3	14	2
15	10	11	0		42	3	13	4
16	10	0	0		43	3	11	10
17	9	6	6		44	3	10	6
18	8	14	1		45	3	9	2
19	8	6	10		46	3	7	10
20	8	0	0		47	3	6	8
21	7	10	6		48	5	5	6
22	7	4	0½		49	3	4	6
23	6	15	8		50	3	3	3
24	6	11	0		51	3	2	1

TABLE,

Shewing the length of an Acre, in Chains, Links, and parts of a Link.

Chains.	Chains.	Links.	Pts.		Chains.	Chains.	Links.	Pts.	
1	10	00	.000	1 acre.	11	0	90	.909	1 acre
2	5	00	.000	do.	12	0	83	.333	do.
3	3	33	.333	do.	13	0	76	.923	do.
4	2	50	.000	do.	14	0	71	.429	do.
5	2	00	.000	do.	15	0	66	.666	do.
6	1	66	.666	do.	16	0	62	.500	do.
7	1	42	.285	do.	17	0	58	.824	do.
8	1	25	.000	do.	18	0	55	.555	do.
9	1	11	.111	do.	19	0	53	.631	do.
10	1	00	.000	do.	20	0	50	.000	do.

TABLE, shewing how many feet and decimals of a foot, also how many perches and decimals of a perch, are contained in English chains and links, from one link to 100 chains.

TABLE, shewing how many feet and decimals of a foot, also how many falls and decimals of a fall, are contained in Scots chains and links, from one link to 100 chains.

Links.	Ft. Pts.	P. Dec.	Ch.	Feet.	P.	Links.	Ft. Pts.	Fls. Pts.	Ch.	Feet.	Falls.
1	.66	.4	1	66	4	1	74	.4	1	74	4
2	1.32	.8	2	132	8	2	1.48	.8	2	148	8
3	2.98	.12	3	198	12	3	2.22	.12	3	222	12
4	2.64	.16	4	264	16	4	2.96	.16	4	296	16
5	3.30	.20	5	330	20	5	3.70	.20	5	370	20
6	3.96	.24	6	396	24	6	4.44	.24	6	444	24
7	4.62	.28	7	462	28	7	5.18	.28	7	518	28
8	5.28	.32	8	528	32	8	5.92	.32	8	592	32
9	5.94	.36	9	594	36	9	6.66	.36	9	666	36
10	6.60	.40	10	660	40	10	7.40	.40	10	740	40
20	13.20	.80	20	1320	80	20	14.80	.80	20	1480	80
30	19.80	1.20	30	1980	120	30	22.20	1.20	30	2220	120
40	26.40	1.60	40	2640	160	40	29.60	1.60	40	2960	160
50	33. 0	2	50	3300	200	50	37.00	2	50	3700	200
60	39.40	2.40	60	3940	240	60	44.40	2.40	60	4440	240
70	46.80	2.80	70	4620	280	70	51.80	2.80	70	5180	280
80	52.20	3.20	80	5280	320	80	59.20	3.20	80	5920	320
90	59.40	3.60	90	5940	360	90	66.60	3.60	90	6660	360
100	66. 0	4	100	6600	400	100	74.00	4	100	7400	400

By the above Table it is required to know how many perches are in 8 chains and 88 links English.

1st, look into the Table under chains for 8; in the column under perches is 32

2d, look for 80 under links, and in the column under perches is...... 3.20

3d, look under links for 8........... 32

Answer, 36 perches and 12 dec......36.12

Again, how many feet are there in 8 chains 80 links?

Look for 8 chains in the column under chains, and in the column under feet is..............528.32

Again look under links for 80, and opposite it is............... 52.20

Then look for 8 links, and opposite it is 5.28

Answer.....585.80

By the above Table it is required to know how many feet are in 9 Scots chains and 90 links.

Look into the Table under chains for 90, and in the column under feet is 6660

Again look under links for 90, and in the column under feet is 66.60

Answer.....6726.60

Again it is required to know how many falls are in 9 Scots chains and 90 links.

Look as above under chains for 90, and under falls opposite it is............... 360.00

Again, look under links for 90, and under falls is............... 3.60

Total perches.......363.60

A 2

The following Tables will be found useful to a practical surveyor in turning feet into links, which he has frequently to do, as dimensions are often taken, either with a chain divided into feet or a tape. The quickest method to obtain the contents in acres roods and perches is, to bring the feet into links.

For example, if you wish to know how many English links there are in 4590 feet,

                                                                    Links. Dec.

Look into the Table for 4000 feet, and opposite it is......6060.606
Again look   do.   for   500 do.   and opposite it is...... 757.575
Again look   do.   for   90 do.   and opposite it is...... 136.363
                                                            ─────────
Add up the sum, which amounts to English links 6954.544

Or, if you want to know how many Scots links are in the same number of feet,

                                                                    Links. Dec.

Look into the next page (*Page* 172) for 4000 feet, and oppo-
    site it is..5405.40
Again look   do.   for 500 do. and opposite it is........ 676.67
Again look   do.   for 90 do. and opposite it is........ 121.62
                                                            ─────────
Add up the sum, which amounts to Scots links......6202.69

Irish links are found out in the same way as above.

N. B. The decimals of a link or fractional parts are inserted, but a land-surveyor seldom thinks of adding them up. If the decimal is under 50, he takes no notice of it; but if it is above 50, he adds one link to the last figure.

TABLE,

Shewing how many English Links are in Feet, from one Foot to 12,000.

Feet.	Links.	Dec.	Feet.	Links.	Dec.	Feet.	Links.	Dec.
1	1	510	41	62	121	81	122	727
2	3	030	42	63	636	82	124	242
3	4	545	43	65	151	83	125	757
4	6	060	44	66	666	84	127	292
5	7	575	45	68	181	85	128	575
6	9	090	46	69	696	86	130	303
7	10	606	47	71	211	87	131	818
8	12	121	48	72	726	18	133	333
9	13	636	49	74	241	89	134	848
10	15	150	50	75	756	90	136	363
11	16	666	51	77	271	91	137	878
12	18	181	52	78	786	92	139	393
13	19	696	53	80	301	93	140	908
14	21	211	54	81	816	94	142	423
15	22	726	55	83	331	95	143	938
16	24	262	56	84	846	96	145	454
17	25	757	57	86	361	97	146	969
18	27	272	58	87	876	98	148	484
19	28	575	59	89	393	99	150	——
20	30	303	60	90	908	100	151.	515
21	31	818	61	92	425	200	303	030
22	33	333	62	93	940	300	454	545
23	34	848	63	95	455	400	606	060
24	36	363	64	96	070	500	757	575
25	37	878	65	98		600	909	090
26	39	393	66	100		700	1060	606
27	40	908	67	101		800	1212	121
28	42	423	68	103	030	900	1363	636
29	43	938	69	104	545	1000	1515	151
30	45	454	70	106	060	2000	3030	303
31	46	969	71	107	576	3000	4545	454
32	48	484	72	109	091	4000	6060	606
33	50	——	73	110	606	5000	7575	757
34	51	515	74	112	121	6000	9090	909
35	53	030	75	113	637	7000	10606	060
36	54	545	76	115	152	8000	12121	212
37	56	060	77	116	667	9000	13636	363
38	57	575	78	118	181	10000	15151	513
39	59	090	79	119	696	11000	16666	666
40	60	606	80	121	212	12000	18180	161

TABLE,

For turning Feet into Scots Links, from one Foot to 30,000.

Feet.	Links.	Dec.	Feet.	Links.	Dec.	Feet.	Links.	Dec.
1	1	35	41	55	40	81	109	45
2	2	70	42	56	76	82	110	80
3	4	05	43	58	12	83	112	15
4	5	40	44	59	47	84	113	50
5	6	75	45	60	80	85	114	85
6	8	10	46	62	16	86	116	22
7	9	46	47	63	51	87	117	57
8	10	80	48	64	86	88	118	92
9	12	16	49	66	21	89	120	27
10	13	51	50	67	56	90	121	62
11	14	67	51	68	91	91	122	97
12	16	21	52	70	26	92	124	32
13	17	57	53	71	61	93	125	67
14	18	92	54	72	96	94	127	02
15	20	27	55	74	31	95	128	37
16	21	62	56	75	66	96	129	72
17	22	97	57	77	01	97	131	07
18	24	32	58	78	36	98	132	42
19	25	67	59	79	71	99	133	77
20	27	02	60	81	06	100	135	13
21	28	38	61	82	41	200	270	26
22	29	74	62		76	300	405	39
23		09	63	85	11	400	540	54
24	32	44	64	86	46	500	675	67
25	33	79	65		81	600	810	80
26	35	13	66		16	700	945	93
27	36	49	67		58	800	1081	06
28	37	84	68	91	89	900	1216	21
29	39	19	69	93	24	1000	1351	34
30	40	54	70	94	59			
						2000	2702	68
31	41	89	71	95	94	3000	4054	05
32	43	24	72	97	29	4000	5405	40
33	44	59	73	98	64	5000	6756	75
34	45	94	74	100	—	6000	8108	08
35	47	29	75	101	35	7000	9459	42
36	48	64	76	102	69	8000	10810	77
37	50	—	77	104	04	9000	12162	21
38	51	35	78	105	39	10000	13513	51
39	52	70	79	106	74	20000	27027	02
40	54	05	80	108	10	30000	40540	53

TABLE,

For turning English Links into Feet, from one Link to 12,000

Links.	Feet.	In. Dec.	Links.	Feet.	In. Dec.	Links.	Feet.	In. Dec.
1	0	7.92	41	27	0.72	81	53	5.52
2	1	3.84	42	27	8.64	82	54	1.44
3	1	11.76	43	28	4.56	83	54	9.36
4	2	7.68	44	29	0.48	84	55	5.28
5	3	3.60	45	29	8.40	85	56	1.20
6	3	11.52	46	30	4.32	86	56	4.12
7	4	7.44	47	31	0.24	87	57	5.04
8	5	3.36	48	31	8.16	88	58	0.96
9	5	11.28	49	32	4.08	89	58	8.88
10	6	7.20	50	33	0.00	90	59	4.80
11	7	3.12	51	33	7.92	91	60	0.72
12	7	11.04	52	34	3.84	92	60	8.64
13	8	.96	53	34	11.76	93	61	4.56
14	9	2.88	54	35	7.68	94	62	0.48
15	9	10.80	55	36	3.60	95	62	8.40
16	10	6.72	56	36	11.52	96	63	4.32
17	11	2.64	57	37	7.44	97	64	0.24
18	11	10.56	58	38	3.36	98	64	8.16
19	12	6.48	59	38	11.28	99	65	4.08
20	13	2.40	60	39	7.20	100	66	0
21	13	10.32	61	40	3.12	200	132	0
22	14	6.24	62	40	11.04	300	198	0
23	15	2.16	63	41	6.96	400	264	0
24	15	10.08	64	42	2.88	500	330	0
25	16	6.00	65	42	10.80	600	396	0
26	17	1.92	66	43	6.72	700	462	0
27	17	9.84	67	44	2.64	800	528	0
28	18	5.76	68	44	10.56	900	594	0
29	19	1.68	69	45	6.48	1000	660	0
30	19	9.60	70	46	2.40	2000	1320	0
31	20	5.52	71	46	10.32	3000	1980	0
32	21	1.44	72	47	6.24	4000	2640	0
33	21	9.36	73	48	2.16	5000	3300	0
34	22	5.28	74	48	10.08	6000	3960	0
35	23	1.20	75	49	6.00	7000	4620	0
36	23	9.12	76	50	1.92	8000	5280	0
37	24	5.04	77	50	9.84	9000	5940	0
38	25	0.96	78	51	5.76	10000	6600	0
39	25	8.88	79	52	1.68	11000	7260	0
40	26	4.80	80	52	9.60	12000	7920	0

TABLE,
For turning Scots Links into Feet, from one Link to 12,000.

Links.	Feet.	In. Dec.	Feet.	Links.	In. Dec.	Links.	Feet.	In. Dec.
1	0	8.88	41	30	4.08	81	59	11.22
2	1	5.76	42	31	0.96	82	60	8.16
3	2	2.64	43	31	9.84	83	61	5.04
4	2	11.52	44	32	6.72	84	62	1.92
5	3	8.40	45	33	3.60	85	62	10.80
6	4	5.28	46	34	0.48	86	63	7.68
7	5	2.16	47	34	9.36	87	64	4.56
8	5	11.04	48	35	6.24	88	65	1.44
9	6	7.92	49	36	3.12	89	65	10.32
10	7	4.80	50	37	0.00	90	66	7.22
11	8	1.68	51	37	8.88	91	67	4.00
12	8	10.56	52	38	5.76	92	68	0.96
13	9	7.44	53	39	2.64	93	68	9.84
14	10	4.32	54	39	11.52	94	69	6.72
15	11	1.20	55	40	8.40	95	70	3.60
16	11	10.08	56	41	5.28	96	71	0.48
17	12	6.96	57	42	2.16	97	71	9.36
18	13	3.84	58	42	11.04	98	72	6.24
19	14	0.72	59	43	7.92	99	73	3.12
20	14	9.60	60	44	4.80	100	4	0
21	15	6.48	61	45	1.68	200	148	0
22	16	3.36	62	45	10.56	300	222	0
23	17	0.24	63	46	7.44	400	262	0
24	17	9.12	64	47	4.32	500	370	0
25	18	6.00	65	48	1.20	600	444	0
26	19	2.88	66	48	10.08	700	518	0
27	19	11.76	67	49	6.96	800	592	0
28	20	8.64	68	50	3.84	900	666	0
29	21	5.52	69	51	0.72	1000	740	0
30	22	2.40	70	51	9.56	2000	1480	0
31	22	11.28	71	52	6.48	3000	2220	0
32	23	8.16	72	53	3.36	4000	2960	0
33	24	5.04	73	54	0.24	5000	3700	0
34	25	1.92	74	54	9.12	6000	4440	0
35	25	10.80	75	55	6.00	7000	5180	0
36	26	7.68	76	56	2.88	8000	5920	0
37	27	4.56	77	56	11.76	9000	6660	0
38	28	1.44	78	57	8.64	10000	7400	0
39	28	10.32	79	58	5.52	11000	8140	0
40	29	7.20	80	59	2.40	12000	8880	0

TABLE,
For turning Irish Links into Feet, from one Link to 12,000.

Links.	Feet.	In. Dec.	Links.	Feet.	In. Dec.	Links.	Feet.	In. Dec.
1	0	10.08	41	34	5.28	81	68	0.48
2	1	8.16	42	35	3.36	82	68	10.56
3	2	6.24	43	36	1.44	83	69	8.64
4	3	4.32	44	36	11.52	84	70	6.72
5	4	2.40	45	37	9.60	85	71	4.80
6	5	0.48	46	38	7.68	86	72	2.88
7	5	10.56	47	39	5.76	87	73	0.96
8	6	8.64	48	40	3.84	88	73	11.04
9	7	6.72	49	41	1.92	89	74	9.12
10	8	4.80	50	42	0.00	90	75	7.20
11	9	2.88	51	42	10.08	91	76	5.28
12	10	0.96	52	43	8.16	92	77	3.36
13	10	11.04	53	44	6.24	93	78	1.44
14	11	9.12	54	45	4.32	94	78	11.52
15	12	7.20	55	46	2.40	95	79	9.60
16	13	5.28	56	47	0.48	96	80	7.68
17	14	3.36	57	47	10.56	97	81	5.76
18	15	1.44	58	48	8.64	98	82	3.84
19	15	11.52	59	49	6.72	99	83	1.92
20	16	9.60	60	50	4.80	100	84	0
21	17	7.68	61	51	2.88	200	168	0
22	18	5.76	62	52	0.96	300	252	0
23	19	3.84	63	52	11.04	400	336	0
24	20	1.92	64	53	9.12	500	420	0
25	21	0.00	65	54	7.20	600	504	0
26	21	10.08	66	55	5.28	700	588	0
27	22	8.16	67	56	3.36	800	672	0
28	23	6.24	68	57	1.44	900	756	0
29	24	4.32	69	57	11.52	1000	840	0
30	25	2.40	70	58	9.60			
						2000	1680	0
31	26	0.48	71	59	7.68	3000	2520	0
32	26	10.56	72	60	5.76	4000	3360	0
33	27	8.64	73	61	3.84	5000	4200	0
34	28	6.72	74	62	1.92	6000	5040	0
35	29	4.80	75	63	0.00	7000	5880	0
36	30	2.88	76	63	10.08	8000	6720	0
37	31	0.96	77	64	8.16	9000	7560	0
38	31	11.04	78	65	6.24	10000	8400	0
39	32	9.12	79	66	4.32	11000	9240	0
40	33	7.20	80	67	2.40	12000	10800	0

The foregoing Tables for reducing links into feet will be found useful to gentlemen and land-surveyors, in ascertaining the length in feet, where dimensions are measured with a chain, or if the distances are measured upon a plan by the scale and compasses. They will also be found useful for finding out the number of feet in length of a stone wall, or the cutting a drain, which in general is calculated in feet.

In many parts of England the customary acre differs very materially from the statute measure of an acre, which is 160 perches, each perch being 16 feet and a half. In some counties 15 feet is reckoned a perch. in other counties 18 feet, 21 feet, and in Cheshire 24 feet.

In some counties they reckon 120 perches 1 acre to the tenantry, which is but 3 roods statute measure; so that the tenant loses one acre in four. Suppose his farm consisted of 100 customary acres, he has only 75 statute acres, which diminishes his farm 25 acres.

Suppose a tenant takes a farm of 100 customary acres, at 15 feet per perch, he loses nearly one acre in five, or 17 acres nearly in 100 acres statute measure.

If a farmer takes a farm of 100 acres, reckoning 18 feet per perch customary measure, he then gains nearly 16 acres of statute measure in 100 acres.

If a farmer takes a farm of 100 acres, reckoning 21 feet per perch, he then gains nearly two acres in five, or nearly 38 acres one rood in 100.

If a farmer takes a farm in Cheshire, reckoning 24 feet per perch, he gains nearly 52 acres and a half in 100 acres of Cheshire measure.

In order to give the learner an idea of the manner of reducing customary measure into statute measure, I shall lay down the following general rule.

As the square of one sort of measure is to the square of the other, so is the area of the one to the area of the other.

For example, supposing 100 acres customary measure, at 18 feet per perch, how much of statute measure?

```
                        18                272.25)32400.000000(119.00686 Statute measure.
                        18                27225               A.  R.  F.
    16.5                --                -----             = 119  0  1
    16.5               144                51750
    ----               18                 27225
     825               ---                -----
     990               324                245250
     165               100                245025
    ----                                  -----
272.25 : 100 : : 32400                    225000
                                          217800
                                          -----
                                          72000
                                          54450
                                          -----
                                          175500
                                          163350
                                          -----
                                          12150
```

Again, suppose a farm of 100 acres customary measure at 15 feet per perch, allowing 160 perches to an acre, how much ground is there of statute measure?

```
    16.5                              272.25)22500000000(82.64461 Statute measure.
    16.5               15             217800              A.  R.  F.
    ----               15             ------            = 82  2  33
     825               --             72000
     990               75             54450
     165               15             ------
    ----                              175500
272.25 : 100 : : 225                  163350
                                      ------
                                      121500
                                      108900
                                      ------
                                      126000
                                      108900
                                      ------
                                      171000
                                      166350
                                      ------
                                      46500
```

c c

TABLES

For turning Roods and Perches into Money.

Roods.	At 1s. per Acre.				At 2s. per Acre.				At 3s. per Acre.				At 4s. per Acre.				At 5s. per Acre.			
	L.	S.	D.	F. P.	L.	S.	D.	F. P.	L.	S.	D.	F. P.	L.	S.	D.	F. P.	L.	S.	D.	F. P.
1	0	0	3	0.0	0	0	0	0.$\frac{5}{10}$	0	0	9	0.0	0	1	0	0.0	0	1	3	0.0
2	0	0	6	0.0	0	0	0	1.0	0	1	6	0.0	0	2	0	0.0	0	2	0	0.0
3	0	0	9	0.0	0	0	0	1.6	0	2	3	0.0	0	3	0	0.0	0	3	9	0.0
Perches.																				
1	0	0	0	0.$\frac{1}{r}$	0	0	0	0.6	0	0	0	0.9	0	0	0	1.2	0	0	0	1.5
2	0	0	0	0.6	0	0	0	1.2	0	0	0	1.8	0	0	0	2.4	0	0	0	3.0
3	0	0	0	0.9	0	0	0	1.8	0	0	0	2.7	0	0	0	3.6	0	0	1	0.5
4	0	0	0	1.2	0	0	0	2.4	0	0	0	3.6	0	0	1	0.8	0	0	1	2.0
5	0	0	0	1.5	0	0	0	3.0	0	0	1	0.5	0	0	1	2.0	0	0	1	3.5
6	0	0	0	1.8	0	0	0	3.6	0	0	1	1.4	0	0	1	3.2	0	0	2	1.0
7	0	0	0	2.1	0	0	1	0.2	0	0	1	2.3	0	0	2	0.4	0	0	2	2.5
8	0	0	0	2.4	0	0	1	0.8	0	0	1	3.2	0	0	2	1.6	0	0	3	0.0
9	0	0	0	2.7	0	0	1	1.4	0	0	2	0.1	0	0	2	2.8	0	0	3	1.5
10	0	0	0	3.0	0	0	1	2.0	0	0	2	1.0	0	0	3	0.0	0	0	3	3.0
11	0	0	0	3.3	0	0	1	2.6	0	0	2	1.9	0	0	3	1.2	0	0	4	0.5
12	0	0	0	3.6	0	0	1	3.2	0	0	2	2.8	0	0	3	2.4	0	0	4	2.0
13	0	0	0	3.9	0	0	1	3.8	0	0	2	3.7	0	0	3	3.6	0	0	4	3.5
14	0	0	1	0.2	0	0	2	0.4	0	0	3	0.6	0	0	4	0.8	0	0	5	1.0
15	0	0	1	0.5	0	0	2	1.0	0	0	3	1.5	0	0	4	2.0	0	0	5	2.5
16	0	0	1	0.8	0	0	2	1.6	0	0	3	2.4	0	0	4	3.2	0	0	6	0.0
17	0	0	1	1.1	0	0	2	2.2	0	0	3	3.3	0	0	5	0.4	0	0	6	1.5
18	0	0	1	1.4	0	0	2	2.8	0	0	4	0.2	0	0	5	1.6	0	0	6	3.0
19	0	0	1	1.7	0	0	2	3.4	0	0	4	1.1	0	0	5	2.8	0	0	7	0.5
20	0	0	1	2.0	0	0	3	0.0	0	0	4	2.0	0	0	6	0.0	0	0	7	2.0
21	0	0	1	2.3	0	0	3	0.6	0	0	4	2.9	0	0	6	1.2	0	0	7	3.5
22	0	0	1	2.6	0	0	3	1.2	0	0	4	3.8	0	0	6	2.4	0	0	8	1.0
23	0	0	1	2.9	0	0	3	1.8	0	0	5	0.7	0	0	6	3.6	0	0	8	2.5
24	0	0	1	3.2	0	0	3	2.4	0	0	5	1.6	0	0	7	0.8	0	0	9	0.0
25	0	0	1	3.5	0	0	3	3.0	0	0	5	2.5	0	0	7	2.0	0	0	9	1.5
26	0	0	1	3.8	0	0	3	3.6	0	0	5	3.4	0	0	7	3.2	0	0	9	3.0
27	0	0	2	0.1	0	0	4	0.2	0	0	6	0.3	0	0	8	0.4	0	0	10	0.5
28	0	0	2	0.4	0	0	4	0.8	0	0	6	1.2	0	0	8	1.6	0	0	10	2.0
29	0	0	2	0.7	0	0	4	1.4	0	0	6	2.1	0	0	8	2.8	0	0	10	3.5
30	0	0	2	1.0	0	0	4	2.0	0	0	6	3.0	0	0	9	0.0	0	0	11	1.0
31	0	0	2	1.3	0	0	4	2.6	0	0	6	3.9	0	0	9	1.2	0	0	11	2.5
32	0	0	2	1.6	0	0	4	3.2	0	0	7	0.8	0	0	9	2.4	0	1	0	0.0
33	0	0	2	1.9	0	0	4	3.8	0	0	7	1.7	0	0	9	3.6	0	1	0	1.5
34	0	0	2	2.2	0	0	5	0.4	0	0	7	2.6	0	0	10	0.8	0	1	0	3.0
35	0	0	2	2.5	0	0	5	1.0	0	0	7	3.5	0	0	10	2.0	0	1	1	0.5
36	0	0	2	2.8	0	0	5	1.6	0	0	8	0.4	0	0	10	3.2	0	1	1	2.0
37	0	0	2	3.1	0	0	5	2.2	0	0	8	1.3	0	0	11	0.4	0	1	1	3.5
38	0	0	2	3.4	0	0	5	2.8	0	0	8	2.2	0	0	11	1.6	0	1	2	1.0
39	0	0	2	3.7	0	0	5	3.4	0	0	8	3.1	0	0	11	2.8	0	1	2	2.5

Roods	At 6s. per Acre.				At 7s. per Acre.				At 8s. per Acre.				At 9s. per Acre.				At 10s. per Acre.			
	L.	s.	D.	F. P.	L.	s.	D.	F. P.	L.	s.	D.	F. P.	L.	s.	D.	F. P.	L.	s.	D.	F. P.
1	0	1	6	0.0	0	1	9	.0.0	0	2	0	0.0	0	2	3	0.0	0	2	6	0.0
2	0	3	0	0.0	0	3	6	0.0	0	4	0	0·0	0	4	6	0.0	0	5	0	0.0
3	0	4	6	0.0	0	5	3	0.0	0	6	0	0.0	0	6	9	0.0	0	7	6	0.0
Perches 1	0	0	0	1.8	0	0	0	2.1	0	0	0	2.4	0	0	0	2.7	0	0	0	3.0
2	0	0	0	3.6	0	0	1	0.2	0	0	1	0.8	0	0	1	1.4	0	0	1	2.0
3	0	0	1	1.4	0	0	1	2.3	0	0	1	3.2	0	0	2	0.1	0	0	2	1.0
4	0	0	1	3.2	0	0	2	0.4	0	0	1	1.6	0	0	2	2.8	0	0	3	0.0
5	0	0	2	1.0	0	0	2	2.5	0	0	3	0.0	0	0	3	1.5	0	0	3	3.0
6	0	0	2	2.8	0	0	3	0.6	0	0	3	2.4	0	0	4	0.2	0	0	4	2.0
7	0	0	3	0.6	0	0	3	2.7	0	0	4	0.8	0	0	4	2.9	0	0	5	1.0
8	0	0	3	2.4	0	0	4	0.8	0	0	4	3.2	0	0	5	1.6	0	0	6	0.0
9	0	0	4	0.2	0	0	4	2.9	0	0	5	1.6	0	0	6	0.3	0	0	6	3.0
10	0	0	4	2.0	0	0	5	1.0	0	0	6	0.0	0	0	6	3.0	0	0	7	2.0
11	0	0	4	3.8	0	0	5	3.1	0	0	6	2.4	0	0	7	1.7	0	0	8	1.0
12	0	0	5	1.6	0	0	6	1.2	0	0	7	0.8	0	0	8	0.4	0	0	9	0.0
13	0	0	5	3.4	0	0	6	3.3	0	0	7	3.2	0	0	8	3.1	0	0	9	3.0
14	0	0	5	1.2	0	0	7	1.4	0	0	8	1·6	0	0	9	1.8	0	0	10	2.0
15	0	0	6	3.0	0	0	7	3.5	0	0	9	0.0	0	0	10	0.5	0	0	11	1.0
16	0	0	7	0.8	0	0	8	1.6	0	0	9	2.4	0	0	10	3.2	0	1	0	0.0
17	0	0	7	2.6	0	0	8	3.7	0	0	10	0.8	0	0	11	1.9	0	1	0	3.0
18	0	0	8	0.4	0	0	9	1.8	0	0	10	3.2	0	1	0	0.6	0	1	1	2.0
19	0	0	8	2.2	0	0	9	3.9	0	0	11	1.6	0	1	0	3.3	0	1	2	1.0
20	0	0	9	0.0	0	0	10	2.0	0	1	0	0.0	0	1	1	2.0	0	1	3	0.0
21	0	0	9	1.8	0	0	11	0.1	0	1	0	2.4	0	1	2	0.7	0	1	3	3.0
22	0	0	9	3.6	0	0	11	2.2	0	1	1	0.8	0	1	2	3.4	0	1	4	2.0
23	0	0	10	1.4	0	1	0	0.3	0	1	1	3.2	0	1	3	2.1	0	1	5	1.0
24	0	0	10	3.2	0	1	0	2.4	0	1	2	1.6	0	1	4	0.8	0	1	6	0.0
25	0	0	11	1.0	0	1	1	0.5	0	1	3	0.0	0	1	4	3.5	0	1	6	3.0
26	0	0	11	2.8	0	1	1	2.6	0	1	3	2.4	0	1	5	2.2	0	1	7	2.0
27	0	1	0	0.6	0	1	2	0.7	0	1	4	0.8	0	1	6	0.9	0	1	8	1.0
28	0	1	0	2.4	0	1	2	2.8	0	1	4	3.2	0	1	6	3.6	0	1	9	0.0
29	0	1	1	0.2	0	1	3	0.9	0	1	5	1.6	0	1	7	2.3	0	1	9	3.0
30	0	1	1	2.0	0	1	3	3.0	0	1	6	0.0	0	1	8	1.0	0	1	10	2.0
31	0	1	1	3.8	0	1	4	1.1	0	1	6	2.4	0	1	8	3.7	0	1	11	1.0
32	0	1	2	1.6	0	1	4	3.2	0	1	7	0.8	0	1	9	2.4	0	2	0	0.0
33	0	1	2	3.4	0	1	5	1.3	0	1	7	3.2	0	1	10	1.1	0	2	0	3.0
34	0	1	3	1.2	0	1	5	3.4	0	1	8	1.6	0	1	10	3.8	0	2	1	2.0
35	0	1	3	3.0	0	1	6	1.5	0	1	9	0.0	0	1	11	2.5	0	2	2	1.0
36	0	1	4	0.8	0	1	6	3.6	0	1	9	2.4	0	2	0	1.2	0	2	3	0.0
37	0	1	4	2.6	0	1	7	1.7	0	1	10	0.8	0	2	0	3.9	0	2	3	3.0
38	0	1	5	0.4	0	1	7	3.8	0	1	10	3.2	0	2	1	2.6	0	2	4	2.0
39	0	1	5	2.2	0	1	8	1.9	0	1	11	1.6	0	2	2	1.3	0	2	5	1.0

Roods.	At 11s. per Acre.				At 12s. per Acre.				At 13s. per Acre.				At 14s. per Acre.				At 15s. per Acre.			
	L.	S.	D.	F.P.	L.	S.	D.	F.P.	L.	S.	D.	F.P.	L.	S.	D.	F.P.	L.	S.	D.	F.P.
1	0	2	9	0.0	0	3	0	0.0	0	3	3	0.0	0	3	6	0.0	0	3	9	0.0
2	0	5	6	0.0	0	6	0	0.0	0	6	6	0.0	0	7	0	0.0	0	7	6	0.0
3	0	8	3	0.0	0	9	0	0.0	0	9	9	0.0	0	10	6	0.0	0	11	3	0.0
Perches																				
1	0	0	0	3.3	0	0	0	3.6	0	0	0	3.9	0	0	1	0.2	0	0	1	0.5
2	0	0	1	2.6	0	0	1	3.2	0	0	1	3.8	0	0	2	0.4	0	0	2	1.0
3	0	0	2	1.9	0	0	2	2.8	0	0	2	3.7	0	0	3	0.6	0	0	3	1.5
4	0	0	3	1.2	0	0	3	2.4	0	0	3	3.6	0	0	4	0.8	0	0	4	2.0
5	0	0	4	0.5	0	0	4	2.0	0	0	4	3.5	0	0	5	1.0	0	0	5	2.5
6	0	0	4	3.8	0	0	5	1.6	0	0	5	3.4	0	0	6	1.2	0	0	6	3.0
7	0	0	5	3.1	0	0	6	1.2	0	0	6	3.3	0	0	7	1.4	0	0	7	3.5
8	0	0	6	2.4	0	0	7	0.8	0	0	7	3.2	0	0	8	1.6	0	0	9	0.0
9	0	0	7	1.7	0	0	8	0.4	0	0	8	3.1	0	0	9	1.8	0	0	10	0.5
10	0	0	8	1.0	0	0	9	0.0	0	0	9	3.0	0	0	10	2.0	0	0	11	1.0
11	0	0	9	0.3	0	0	9	3.6	0	0	10	2.9	0	0	11	2.2	0	1	0	1.5
12	0	0	9	3.6	0	0	10	3.2	0	0	11	2.8	0	1	0	2.4	0	1	1	2.0
13	0	0	10	2.9	0	0	11	2.8	0	1	0	2.7	0	1	1	2.6	0	1	2	2.5
14	0	0	11	2.2	0	1	0	2.4	0	1	1	2.6	0	1	2	2.8	0	1	3	3.0
15	0	1	0	1.5	0	1	1	2.0	0	1	2	2.5	0	1	3	3.0	0	1	4	3.5
16	0	1	1	0.8	0	1	2	1.6	0	1	3	2.4	0	1	4	3.2	0	1	6	0.0
17	0	1	2	0.1	0	1	3	1.2	0	1	4	2.3	0	1	5	3.4	0	1	7	0.5
18	0	1	2	3.4	0	1	4	0.8	0	1	5	2.2	0	1	6	3.6	0	1	8	1.0
19	0	1	3	2.7	0	1	5	0.4	0	1	6	2.1	0	1	7	3.8	0	1	9	1.5
20	0	1	4	2.0	0	1	6	0.0	0	1	7	2.0	0	1	9	0.0	0	1	10	2.0
21	0	1	5	1.3	0	1	6	3.6	0	1	8	1.9	0	1	10	0.2	0	1	11	2.5
22	0	1	6	0.6	0	1	7	3.2	0	1	9	1.8	0	1	11	0.4	0	2	0	3.0
23	0	1	6	3.9	0	1	8	2.8	0	1	10	1.7	0	2	0	0.6	0	2	1	3.5
24	0	1	7	3.2	0	1	9	2.4	0	1	11	1.6	0	2	1	0.8	0	2	3	0.0
25	0	1	8	2.5	0	1	10	2.0	0	2	0	1.5	0	2	2	1.0	0	2	4	0.5
26	0	1	9	1.8	0	1	11	1.6	0	2	1	1.4	0	2	3	1.2	0	2	5	1.0
27	0	1	10	1.1	0	2	0	1.2	0	2	2	1.3	0	2	4	1.4	0	2	6	1.5
28	0	1	11	0.4	0	2	1	0.8	0	2	3	1.2	0	2	5	1.6	0	2	7	2.0
29	0	1	11	3.7	0	2	2	0.4	0	2	4	1.1	0	2	6	1.8	0	2	8	2.5
30	0	2	0	3.0	0	2	3	0.0	0	2	5	1.0	0	2	7	2.0	0	2	9	3.0
31	0	2	1	2.3	0	2	3	3.6	0	2	6	0.9	0	2	8	2.2	0	2	10	3.5
32	0	2	2	1.6	0	2	4	3.2	0	2	7	0.8	0	2	9	2.4	0	3	0	0.0
33	0	2	3	0.9	0	2	5	2.8	0	2	8	0.7	0	2	10	2.6	0	3	1	0.5
34	0	2	4	0.2	0	2	6	2.4	0	2	9	0.6	0	2	11	2.8	0	3	2	1.0
35	0	2	4	3.5	0	2	7	2.0	0	2	10	0.5	0	3	0	3.0	0	3	3	1.5
36	0	2	5	2.8	0	2	8	1.6	0	2	11	0.4	0	3	1	3.2	0	3	4	2.0
37	0	2	6	2.1	0	2	9	1.2	0	3	0	0.3	0	3	2	3.4	0	3	5	2.5
38	0	2	7	1.4	0	2	10	0.8	0	3	1	0.2	0	3	3	3.6	0	3	6	3.0
39	0	2	8	0.7	0	2	11	0.4	0	3	2	0.1	0	3	4	3.8	0	3	7	3.5

Roods.	At 16s. per Acre.				At 17s. per Acre.				At 18s. per Acre.				At 19s. per Acre.				At 20s. per Acre.			
	L.	S.	D.	F. P.	L.	S.	D.	F. P.	L.	S.	D.	F. P.	L.	S.	D.	F. P.	L.	S.	D.	F. P.
1	0	4	0	0.0	0	4	3	0.0	0	4	6	0.0	0	4	9	0.0	0	5	0	0.0
2	0	8	0	0.0	0	8	6	0.0	0	9	0	0·0	0	9	6	0.0	0	10	0	0.0
3	0	12	0	0.0	0	12	9	0.0	0	13	6	0.0	0	14	3	0.0	0	15	0	0.0
Perches. 1	0	0	1	0.8	0	0	1	1.1	0	0	1	1.4	0	0	1	1.7	0	0	2	2.1
2	0	0	2	1.6	0	0	2	2·2	0	0	2	2.8	0	0	1	3.4	0	0	3	0.0
3	0	0	3	2.4	0	0	3	3.3	0	0	4	0.2	0	0	4	1.1	0	0	4	2.0
4	0	0	4	3.2	0	0	5	0.4	0	0	5	1.6	0	0	5	2.8	0	0	6	0.0
5	0	0	6	0.0	0	0	6	1.5	0	0	6	3.0	0	0	7	0.5	0	0	7	2.0
6	0	0	7	0.8	0	0	7	2.6	0	0	8	0.4	0	0	8	2.2	0	0	9	0.0
7	0	0	8	1.6	0	0	8	3.7	0	0	9	1.8	0	0	9	3.9	0	0	10	2.0
8	0	0	9	2.4	0	0	10	0.8	0	0	10	3.2	0	0	11	1.6	0	1	0	0.0
9	0	0	10	3.2	0	0	11	1.9	0	1	0	0.6	0	1	0	3.3	0	1	1	2.0
10	0	1	0	0.0	0	1	0	3.0	0	1	1	2.0	0	1	2	1.0	0	1	3	0.0
11	0	1	1	0.8	0	1	2	0.1	0	1	2	3.4	0	1	3	2.7	0	1	4	2.0
12	0	1	2	1.6	0	1	3	1.2	0	1	4	0.8	0	1	5	0.4	0	1	6	0.0
13	0	1	3	2.4	0	1	4	2.3	0	1	5	2.2	0	1	6	2.1	0	1	7	2.0
14	0	1	4	3.2	0	1	5	3.4	0	1	6	3·6	0	1	7	3.8	0	1	9	0.0
15	0	1	6	0.0	0	1	7	0.5	0	1	8	1.0	0	1	9	1.5	0	1	10	2.0
16	0	1	7	0.8	0	1	8	1.6	0	1	9	2.4	0	1	10	3.2	0	2	0	0.0
17	0	1	8	1.6	0	1	9	2.7	0	1	10	3.8	0	2	0	0.9	0	2	1	2.0
18	0	1	9	2.4	0	1	10	3.6	0	2	0	1.2	0	2	1	2.6	0	2	3	0.0
19	0	1	10	3.2	0	2	0	0.9	0	2	1	2.6	0	2	3	0.3	0	2	4	2.0
20	0	2	0	0.0	0	2	1	2.0	0	2	3	0.0	0	2	4	2.0	0	2	6	0.0
21	0	2	1	0.8	0	2	2	3.1	0	2	4	1.4	0	2	5	3.7	0	2	7	2.0
22	0	2	2	1.6	0	2	4	0.2	0	2	5	2.8	0	2	7	1.4	0	2	9	0.0
23	0	2	3	2.4	0	2	5	1.3	0	2	7	0.2	0	2	8	3.1	0	2	10	2.0
24	0	2	4	3.2	0	2	6	2.4	0	2	8	1.6	0	2	10	0.8	0	3	0	0.0
25	0	2	6	0.0	0	2	7	3.5	0	2	9	3.0	0	2	11	2.5	0	3	1	2.0
26	0	2	7	0.8	0	2	9	0.6	0	2	11	0.4	0	3	1	0.2	0	3	3	0.0
27	0	2	8	1.6	0	2	10	1.7	0	3	0	1.8	0	3	2	1.9	0	3	4	2.0
28	0	2	9	2.4	0	2	11	2.8	0	3	1	3.2	0	3	3	3.6	0	3	6	0.0
29	0	2	10	3.2	0	3	0	3.9	0	3	3	0.6	0	3	5	1.3	0	3	7	2.0
30	0	3	0	0.0	0	3	2	1.0	0	3	4	2.0	0	3	6	3.0	0	3	9	0.0
31	0	3	1	0.8	0	3	3	2.1	0	3	5	3.4	0	3	8	0.7	0	3	10	2.0
32	0	3	2	1.6	0	3	4	3.2	0	3	7	0.8	0	3	9	2.4	0	4	0	0.0
33	0	3	3	2.4	0	3	6	0.3	0	3	8	2.2	0	3	11	0.1	0	4	1	2.0
34	0	3	4	3.2	0	3	7	1.4	0	3	9	3.6	0	4	0	1.8	0	4	3	0.0
35	0	3	6	0.0	0	3	8	2.5	0	3	11	1.0	0	4	1	3.5	0	4	4	2.0
36	0	3	7	0.8	0	3	9	3.6	0	4	0	2.4	0	4	3	1.2	0	4	6	0.0
37	0	3	8	1.6	0	3	11	0.7	0	4	1	38	0	4	4	2.9	0	4	7	2.0
38	0	3	9	2.4	0	4	0	1.8	0	4	3	1.2	0	4	6	0.6	0	4	9	0.0
39	0	3	10	3.2	0	4	1	2.9	0	4	4	2.6	0	4	7	2.3	0	4	10	2.0

D d

Roods.	At L.2 per Acre.				At L.3 per Acre.				At L.4 per Acre.				At L.5 per Acre.				At L.6 per Acre.			
	L.	S.	D.	F.P.	L.	S.	D.	F.P.	L.	S.	D.	F.P.	L.	S.	D.	F.P.	L.	S.	D.	F.P.
1	0	10	0	0.0	0	15	0	0.0	1	0	0	0.0	1	5	0	0.0	1	10	0	0.0
2	1	0	0	0.0	1	10	0	0.0	2	0	0	0.0	2	10	0	0.0	3	0	0	0.0
3	1	10	0	0.0	2	5	0	0.0	3	0	0	0.0	3	15	0	0.0	4	10	0	0.0
Perches.																				
1	0	0	3	0.0	0	0	4	2.0	0	0	6	0.0	0	0	7	2.0	0	0	9	0.0
2	0	0	6	0.0	0	0	9	0.0	0	1	0	0.0	0	1	3	0.0	0	1	6	0.0
3	0	0	9	0.0	0	1	1	1.2	0	1	6	0.0	0	1	10	2.0	0	2	3	0.0
4	0	1	0	0.0	0	1	6	0.0	0	2	0	0.0	0	2	6	0.0	0	3	0	0.0
5	0	1	3	0.0	0	1	10	2.0	0	2	6	0.0	0	3	1	2.0	0	3	9	0.0
6	0	1	6	0.0	0	2	3	0.0	0	3	0	0.0	0	3	9	0.0	0	4	6	0.0
7	0	1	9	0.0	0	2	7	2.0	0	3	6	0.0	0	4	4	2.0	0	5	3	0.0
8	0	2	0	0.0	0	3	0	0.0	0	4	0	0.0	0	5	0	0.0	0	6	0	0.0
9	0	2	3	0.0	0	3	4	2.0	0	4	6	0.0	0	5	7	2.0	0	6	9	0.0
10	0	2	6	0.0	0	3	9	0.0	0	5	0	0.0	0	6	3	0.0	0	7	6	0.0
11	0	2	9	0.0	0	4	1	2.0	0	5	6	0.0	0	6	10	2.0	0	8	3	0.0
12	0	3	0	0.0	0	4	6	0.0	0	6	0	0.0	0	7	6	0.0	0	9	0	0.0
13	0	3	3	0.0	0	4	10	2.0	0	6	6	0.0	0	8	1	2.0	0	9	9	0.0
14	0	3	6	0.0	0	5	3	0.0	0	7	0	0.0	0	8	9	0.0	0	10	6	0.0
15	0	3	9	0.0	0	5	7	2.0	0	7	6	0.0	0	9	4	2.0	0	11	3	0.0
16	0	4	0	0.0	0	6	0	0.0	0	8	0	0.0	0	10	0	0.0	0	12	0	0.0
17	0	4	3	0.0	0	6	4	2.0	0	8	6	0.0	0	10	7	2.0	0	12	9	0.0
18	0	4	6	0.0	0	6	9	0.0	0	9	0	0.0	0	11	3	0.0	0	13	6	0.0
19	0	4	9	0.0	0	7	1	2.0	0	9	6	0.0	0	11	10	2.0	0	14	3	0.0
20	0	5	0	0.0	0	7	6	0.0	0	10	0	0.0	0	12	6	0.0	0	15	0	0.0
21	0	5	3	0.0	0	7	10	2.0	0	10	6	0.0	0	13	1	2.0	0	15	9	0-0
22	0	5	6	0.0	0	8	3	3.0	0	11	0	0.0	0	13	9	0.0	0	16	6	0.0
23	0	5	9	0.0	0	8	7	2.0	0	11	6	0.0	0	14	4	2.0	0	17	3	0.0
24	0	6	0	0.0	0	9	0	0.0	0	12	0	0.0	0	15	0	0.0	0	18	0	0.0
25	0	6	3	0.0	0	9	4	2.0	0	12	6	0.0	0	15	7	2.0	0	18	9	0.0
26	0	6	6	0.0	0	9	9	0.0	0	13	0	0.0	0	16	3	0.0	0	19	6	0.0
27	0	6	9	0.0	0	10	1	2.0	0	13	6	0.0	0	16	10	2.0	1	0	3	0.0
28	0	7	0	0.0	0	10	6	0.0	0	14	0	0.0	0	17	6	0.0	1	1	0	0.0
29	0	7	3	0.0	0	10	10	2.0	0	14	6	0.0	0	18	1	2.0	1	1	9	0.0
30	0	7	6	0.0	0	11	3	0.0	0	15	0	0.0	0	18	9	0.0	1	2	6	0.0
31	0	7	9	0.0	0	11	7	2.0	0	15	6	0.0	0	19	4	2.0	1	3	3	0.0
32	0	8	0	0.0	0	12	0	0.0	0	16	0	0.0	1	0	0	0.0	1	4	0	0.0
33	0	8	3	0.0	0	12	4	2.0	0	16	6	0.0	1	0	7	2.0	1	4	9	0.0
34	0	8	6	0.0	0	12	9	0.0	0	17	0	0.0	1	1	3	0.0	1	5	6	0.0
35	0	8	9	0.0	0	13	1	2.0	0	17	6	0.0	1	1	10	2.0	1	6	3	0.0
36	0	9	0	0.0	0	13	6	0.0	0	18	0	0.0	1	2	6	0.0	1	7	0	0.0
37	0	9	3	0.0	0	13	10	2.0	0	18	6	0.0	1	3	1	2.0	1	7	9	0.0
38	0	9	6	0.0	0	14	3	0.0	0	19	0	0.0	1	3	9	0.0	1	8	6	0.0
39	0	9	9	0.0	0	14	7	2.0	0	19	6	0.0	1	4	4	2.0	1	9	3	0.0

The foregoing Tables for reducing roods, perches, poles, or falls, into money, will be found useful to a surveyor or a land valuator for ascertaining the value of an estate.

Example 1st. Suppose it is required to turn 3 roods and 36 perches or falls into cash, valued at 18s. per acre.

Look for 18s. at the top column, and for 3 roods in

the left hand column, and under 18, and opposite 3 roods, is L. 0 13 6

Again, look for 36 perches or falls in the left hand column,

and under 18s. in the top column, is   -   -   -   0 4 0$\frac{1}{2}$

Value - L. 0 17 6$\frac{1}{2}$

Example 2d. Suppose 2 roods and 39 perches or poles, valued at 11s. per acre, is required to be turned into money.

Look at the top column for 11s. and in the left hand column

for 2 roods, and opposite it, under 11s. is   -   -   -   L. 0 5 6

Again, look for 39 perches in the left column, and opposite

it, under 11, is   -   -   -   -   -   -   -   0 2 8$\frac{7}{13}$

Value - L. 0 8 2$\frac{7}{13}$

Example 3d. Suppose 15 acres 3 roods and 14 perches, valued at 12s. per acre, is to be turned into cash.

First multiply 15 acres by 12s. the quotient is 180s. equal to L. 9 0 0

Then look at the top column for 12s. and opposite 3 roods, is   0 9 0

Then opposite 14 perches, and under 12s. is   -   -   0 1 0$\frac{1}{2}$

Value - L. 9 10 0$\frac{1}{2}$

Example 4th. Suppose 20 acres 1 rood and 35 perches or falls, valued at L.3 10s. per acre.

First, L.3 10s. is = 70s. which multiplied by 20 acres, is

1400s. =   -   -   -   -   -   -   -   -   -   L.70 0 0

Then look into the table for L.3, and opposite 1 rood, is   0 15 0

Again, look into the table for L.3, and opposite 35 perches, is   0 13 1$\frac{1}{2}$

Then look into the table for 10s. and opposite 1 rood, is   0 2 6

Again, look into the table for 10s. and opposite 35 perches, is   0 2 2$\frac{1}{4}$

Value - L.71 12 9$\frac{1}{4}$

Another method for turning acres, roods, perches, poles or falls, into money, I frequently accomplish by the table for reducing acres, roods, &c. into square links, Page 187. and multiply by the amount per acre the ground is valued at, suppose 70s. per acre.

Thus 20 acres, when turned into square links, is   -   -   20.00000

1 rood,   -   -   -   do.   -   is   -   -   25000

35 perches, poles, or falls,   do.   -   is   -   -   21875

20,46875

The calculation thus 20.46875

70s. the amount per acre.

Shillings 1432.81250

12

Pence 9.75000

4

Farthings 3.0000

1432 Shillings, is   -   -   -   L.71 12   0

,81250 Decimals of Shillings, is   -   0   0   9

.75000 Decimals of Pence, is   -   0   0   0¾

L.71 12   9¾ the same as by the

Tables.

MEASURING TIMBER.

As in the measuring either standing or cut timber, a land-surveyor is often employed to ascertain the solid contents in feet, the following Table will be found very expeditious for that purpose. The Table needs little explanation. As every person knows that the length and girth must be taken before the contents can be known, I shall here only mention what way the girth is taken.

Suppose a tree from the bottom to the top tapers equally all the way; take the girth or circumference in the middle, and divide it by 4, which gives what is called, in customary measure, the quarter girth, or *side of the square*; that is to say, when the bark is cut off the tree, and squared, it has four equal sides; and the girth being taken in the middle of the tree gives a mean thickness: but as many trees are unequal, in that case it will be necessary to take the girth or circumference of the tree in three, four, five, or six places, and add all the different girths into one sum, suppose five girths; dividing the sum by five, gives a mean, and by dividing the mean girth by four, gives the side of the square commonly called the quarter girth. Whatever number of times the girth has been taken, the sum of the girths must be divided by that number, and be particular in taking the girths nearly at equal distances.

TABLE for measuring Timber.

Quarter Girth.	Area.	Quarter Girth.	Area.	Quarter Girth.	Area.
Inches.	F. Dec.	Inches.	F. Dec.	Inches.	F. Dec.
6	.250	16½	1.890	26½	4.876
6¼	.294	17	2.006	27	5.062
7	.340	17½	2.126	27½	5.252
7½	.390	18	2.250	28	5.444
8	.444	18½	2.376	28½	5.640
8½	.501	19	2.506	29	5.840
9	.562	19½	2.640	29½	6.040
9½	.626	20	2.717	30	6.250
10	.694	20½	2.917	30½	6.459
10½	.766	21	3.062	31	6.739
11	840	21½	3.209	31½	6.902
11½	.918	22	3.362	32	6.111
12	1.000	22½	3.516	32½	7.335
12½	1.085	23	3.673	33	7.569
13	1.174	23½	3.835	33½	7.792
13½	1.265	24	4.000	34	8.028
14	1.361	24½	4.168	34½	8.260
14½	1.460	25	4.340	35	8.507
15	1.562	25½	4.516	35½	8.707
15½	1.668	26	4.692	36	8.930
16	1.777				

N. B. The number of the area opposite the quarter girth, in the right hand column in the table, must be multiplied by the length of the plank or tree in feet, and the product will be the content in feet and parts of a foot.

Suppose a plank to be 22 feet long, and the mean quarter girth 14 inches, look into the table for 14 inches, and opposite, in the right hand column, and under area, is 1.361; which, multiplied by 22, is equal to 29 feet, 942 decimals; and if you multiply the decimals by 12, is 29 feet, 11 inches, $\frac{504}{1000}$.

Again, suppose a tree to be 30 feet long, 60 inches girth at the thick end, 40 inches girth in the middle, and 20 inches girth at the small end, add up all the girths into one sum, which is 120; which sum, divided by three, the quotient is 40 inches for a mean girth; then divide 40 by four, which is 10 for the quarter girth; lastly, look into the table for the number opposite 10 inches, and you will find .694; which number, multiplied by 30, the length of the tree, the quotient is 20 feet, 820 parts, or 20 feet, 9 inches, $\frac{84}{100}$.

5

ART. IV. OF THE DIVIDING OF LAND.

The dividing of land may be considered as a principal part of a land-measurer's business, as he is frequently employed in dividing such amongst sundry tenants and proprietors, according to the proportion of their claims. In many instances, the division relates only to the quantity that each claimant is entitled to ; and in others, the quality as well as quantity must be taken into account.   The first operation that a land-surveyor has to perform, is to ascertain accurately, by some of the methods before mentioned, the content or area of the whole land ; and a correct draught of it is to be made out upon a large scale.

The following Table will be found very useful for such divisions, as acres, roods, falls or perches, for reducing them into square links.

TABLE, pointing out the number of Square Links contained in Acres, Roods, and Perches.

Acres.	Sq. Links.	Perch.	Sq. Links.
1	100000	1	0625
2	200000	2	1250
3	300000	3	1875
4	400000	4	2500
5	500000	5	3125
6	600000	6	3750
7	700000	7	4375
8	800000	8	5000
9	900000	9	5625
10	1000000	10	6250
11	1100000	11	6875
12	1200000	12	7500
13	1300000	13	8125
14	1400000	14	8750
15	1500000	15	9375
16	1600000	16	10000
17	1700000	17	10625
18	1800000	18	11250
19	1900000	19	11875
20	2000000	20	12500
30	3000000	21	13125
40	4000000	22	13750
50	5000000	23	14375
60	6000000	24	15000
70	7000000	25	15625
80	8000000	26	16250
90	9000000	27	16875
100	10000000	28	17500
200	20000000	29	18125
300	30000000	30	18750
400	40000000	31	19375
500	50000000	32	20000
600	60000000	33	20625
700	70000000	34	21250
800	80000000	35	21875
Roods		36	22500
1	25000	37	23125
2	50000	38	23750
3	75000	39	24375
4	100000	40	25000

Plate XXVII. (*Fig.* 12.)

Suppose the square A B C D consists of ten acres; two and a half acres were sold; how far will it reach up the enclosure, parallel with the side A B? Look into the table, p. 187. for shewing how many square links are in 2 acres, 2 roods, which by the Table is 250000; which divide by 1000, the length of the side A B, and the quotient is 250 links, which must be measured from A to e on the side A D. The same distance must be measured on the line B C to e, and the dotted line ee is the line of division, which is 2½ acres, parallel with the side A B, and leaves 7 acres 2 roods in the field e e D C.

Plate XXVII. (*Fig.* 13.)

The four-sided figure E F G H consists of 12 acres 1 rood 11 perches, and it is required to measure off five acres parallel with the side H E, which is 1270 links long. Look into the table how many square links are in 5 acres, which by the Table is 500000; which divide by 1270, the length of the side H E, the quotient is 394⅞ links; measure off that distance from H to i on the side H G, and the same distance on the side E F to i; the dotted line ii is the division, and is parallel with H E; the land next H E being 5 acres, and the land next G F is 7 acres 1 rood 11 perches.

Plate XXVII. (*Fig.* 14.)

The triangle I K L contains 4 acres 2 roods, which has to be divided between two men, one to have 1 acre 2 roods 35 perches, and the other to have 2 acres 3 roods 5 perches. The length of the line K I is 1000, and the division to be made from L, to fall upon the base L K, 2 acres 3 roods 5 perches, by the table is 278125 square links; which divide by 500, half the length of the base K I; the quotient is 556 links, which must be laid off perpendicular from the line K L upon I K to h; then draw the dotted line L h, which makes the division. Or it may be done thus: If 4 acres 2 roods, which by the Table is 450000 square links, what will 278125 give upon the line K I? Answer, 618 links; which lay off from K on the line towards I, which will reach to h; draw in the dotted line from

L to h, which makes the division next K 2 acres 3 roods 5 perches, and the division next I 1 acre 2 roods 35 perches.

Plate XXVII. (*Fig.* 15.)

The triangle L M N consists of 5 acres 20 perches, which has to be divided betwixt three proprietors from the angle at M; the person next N to get 2 acres, and the person next L to get 1 acre 19 perches, the length of the line M N is 930 links by the Table; 2 acres is 200000 square links; which divided by 465, half the length of M N, the quotient is 432, which must be laid off perpendicular from the line M N till it intersect the line N L at i; then draw in the dotted line from M to i, which finishes the 2 acre share; then measure the length of M L, which is 1060. One acre and 19 perches or falls by the table is 111875 square links; which divide by 530, half of the length of the line M L; the quotient is 211, which must be laid off perpendicular with the line M L, and will intersect the line L N at K; draw in the dotted line from k to M, which divides it into 3 triangles, *viz.* M N i 2 acres, M i k 2 acres 1 perch, and the triangle M k L is 1 acre 19 perches, laid down upon a scale of ten chains in an inch.

Plate XXVII. (*Fig.* 16.)

The triangle O P Q consists of 12 acres, and has to be divided into halves parallel with the line O P. First from 12 acres deduct 6, there remain 6 acres; which turned into square links by the Table (see *Page* 187.) amounts to 600000; the length of the line O Q is 1330, the square of which is 176900, the half is 884450, the square root of which is 920; which must be measured off from O to m on the O Q line. The dotted line m m laid off parallel with O P divides the triangle in halves.

Plate XXVIII. (*Fig.* 1.)

The triangular field L M N, which has to be divided betwixt three men, consists of 12 acres; one man to have 3 acres, a second to have 4 acres, and the third to have 5 acres, and the division of all three to commence from O. First, draw an obscure line from O to the angle M; the length of the base L N is 2400 links; then say, if 12 acres give 2400 links, what will 3 acres give? divide 300000 (the square links in 3 acres) by 2400, the quotient is 600 : which lay off from L to P, and leave a mark ; then say, if 12 acres give 2400, what will 4 acres give? This is found by the table to be 400000 ; which sum divided by 2400 gives 800 ; which lay off upon the base line from P to Q, and leave a mark. Again say, if 12 acres give 2400, what will 5 acres give? This by the table is 500000 square links ; which divided by 2400 gives 1000 ; which distance lay off from Q, and if it coincides with the angle at N you are certain no mistake is made : you then lay a parallel ruler upon the obscure line O M, and move it parallel to the mark left at P ; and where it intersects the line L M, make a mark at S ; draw the line O S, which finishes Lot 1st. You then lay the parallel ruler again upon the obscure line O M, and move it parallel to the mark at Q, and make a mark upon the line M N where the edge of the ruler crosses it at R. Lastly, draw the line O R, which divides the triangle according to the proportion required. A variety of other examples might be given to divide triangles into any number of shares; but as a land-measurer seldom meets with land lying in such regular forms, it will be necessary to give a few examples, which may be of service to him when he is called upon to divide irregular pieces of land. 1st, The general method used by land-measurers is, after having measured the ground proposed to be divided with great accuracy, and having plotted it upon a large scale, to draw a line (by guess) upon the protracted rough draught, and calculate how much is contained between the promiscuous line and the boundary ; if too little, what is required must be added, suppose it wanted 1 acre 2 roods, which, turned into square links by the table, is 150000. This number, divided by the length of the guessed line, which suppose is 900 links, the quotient is 166 links, and is to be laid off parallel with the guessed line, which should be drawn in upon the rough plan, and the quantity of acres and decimals inserted. 2d. Draw another line by guess for the 2d division, and cast up the contents. If it is too large it must be made less ; suppose it is 3 roods 5 perches, turn it into square links by the table, which is .78125, and divide it by the length of the last guessed line, which measures upon the plan 750 ; the quotient is 104 links ; which distance must be laid off upon the plan parallel with the guessed line. This will divide the field into three shares, which must now be staked off upon the ground. This may be very expeditiously done in the following manner: Take the rough plan to the field, and with scale and compasses measure from any corner on the plan you know to the first division on the plan, suppose it is 5 chains; measure the same distance on the ground, and drive in a stake for the first division; then measure and see how far it is with the scale and compasses upon the plan to the next division, from any point you know, both on the plan and the ground, suppose 150 links; measure off that distance on the ground from the corner, and drive in a stake for the next division; then go to the other side of the field, and find out some place you know, both upon the plan and on the ground, and measure upon the plan how many links it is to the first division line, which suppose 850; measure off that distance upon the ground, and drive in a stake, and, if you think it necessary, you may drive in three or four additional stakes in a line from the one stake to the other; then measure on your plan a distance of 20 links that the 2d division line is from an angle you know; measure 20 links from that angle on the ground, and drive in a stake; and if you think proper you may drive in three or four more stakes in a line from one stake to another, which finishes the division; and the number of acres in each division should be inserted on the plan.

Plate XXVIII. (Fig. 2.)

A B C D is a long square field laid down from a scale of 20 chains in an inch, and contains 25 acres. The proprietor sold 9 acres 2 roods, and wished it staked off parallel with the line A D. The distance from A to D is 10 chains: look into the table p. 187. how many square links there are in 9 acres 2 roods, which is 9.50000; when divided by 1000 links, the length of A D, the quotient is 950; which distance lay off with the scale and compasses upon the plan, which will reach from A D to e e. He likewise sold 5 acres 2 roods 25 perches parallel with the line B C, which is 10 chains or 1000 links in length, which by the table is 565625 square links; which number divided by 1000, the length of B C, gives 565; which lay off with the scale parallel with the line C B, which will extend to f f; let the same distances be measured off upon the ground as are laid off with the scale and compasses on the plan, and the divisions are finished.

Plate XXVIII. (*Fig. 3.*)

Suppose the square field E F G H, containing 55 acres 3 roods 8 perches, was to be divided into 10 acres, 8 acres, 12 acres, and 7 acres, and the remainder next G F to be another lot of 18 acres 3 roods 8 perches. First, look into the table, and see how many square links there are in ten acres, which will be found to contain 1000000; divide it by the shortest side E H 1800, and the quotient is 550; which distance take off from the scale of 20 chains in an inch, and lay it off upon the plan parallel with the line E H, which will extend to h h; then look into the table for the square links in 8 acres, which is 800000, and divide it by 1800, the length of h h, and the quotient is 444; which distance being laid off from h h, will reach to i i; then look into the table for the square links in 12 acres, which is 1200000; this divided by 1800, the length of i i, the quotient will be 666; which lay off, and it will extend from i i to k k. Lastly, look into the table for the square links that there are in 7 acres: this is found to be 700000; that number divided by the length of k k, 1800, the quotient is 388, which lay off from the scale from k k, and it will extend to m m, and the remaining lot will be 18 acres 3 roods 8 perches.

Plate XXVIII. (*Fig. 4.*)

Represents the outline of a farm consisting of 236 acres 3 roods 12 perches, which the proprietor wished to divide into two farms of equal dimensions. After an exact survey and plan made out upon a large scale, it was divided into triangles and trapeziums. The area of each was inserted upon the large plan, merely to give an idea where a promiscuous line could be drawn, not far from where the division would run. Accordingly a line was drawn from C C, represented in the plan with wide dots, to distinguish it from the other dotted lines drawn for the purpose of dividing it into triangles and trapeziums for ascertaining the area. The trapezium A is 82 acres 5 perches, the triangle B is 17 acres 2 roods 16 perches, and the triangle D is 6 acres 1 rood 19 perches; when added to gether, the sum is 106 acres, which is short of half the farm by 12 acres 1 rood 26 perches. The next thing to be done is to measure the length of the guessed line C C upon the plan, which is 3300; then look into the table how many square links are in 12 acres 1 rood 26 perches, which is 12.35200; when this is divided by 3300 (the length of the guessed line C C) the quotient is 374; which lay off parallel with the line C C, which will divide the farm into two equal parts, by drawing in the division line E E.

In dividing of land, the measurer in general keeps an account of the number of links wanting to make up the division, as he has to drive stakes in the ground, and to measure off the number of chains and links, from some angle that he knows upon the field, to the line of division.

Plate XXVIII. (Fig. 5.)

Suppose 15 acres were to be staked off from the irregular field A B C D, which consists of 40 acres: from the point A first measure the boundary carefully round from A by B towards C, till you think you have been nearly half way round to C; take an angle, and measure from C to A; then plot all you have measured, and lay it down upon a large scale, and cast up the contents, which you find is considerably more than you want; you then draw a line by guess from A to B upon the plan, and, after calculating it, you find it is only 11 acres 2 roods 32 perches, which is short of 15 acres by 3 acres 2 roods 8 perches. Look into the table for the number of square links contained in 3 acres 2 roods 8 perches, viz. 355000; then measure the length of the line A B, which is 1950, and divide 355000 by that number, the quotient is $182\frac{1}{2}$ for the breadth of a parallelogram; which distance must be doubled on account of its being a triangle; then lay off from the scale 365, being twice $182\frac{1}{2}$, from B to the boundary at D; then draw the line D A upon the plan, and measure off the distance 365 on the ground, and drive in stakes from D to A, and it is finished, leaving 25 acres on one side, and 15 on the other of the division line.

Plate XX. (Fig. 3.)

Is to be divided into four equal parts from a spring at A, and each division to have the benefit of the water. First measure the whole field correctly, and also the situation of the spring; plot the field with great care from a large scale, and calculate it by some of the methods (before mentioned in Areas), which is found to consist of 90 acres, the fourth of which is 22 acres 2 roods for each share. Draw a line from A to B, and another line by guess, which is dotted, to D; then calculate the trapezium A B C D; which is short of 22 acres 2 roods, by 2 acres 2 roods 3 perches; when turned into square links by the table it is 251875; divide it by 910, half the length of the dotted line A D, the quotient is 276; which distance lay off by the scale to k; then draw the line from A to k, which is one enclosure of 22 acres 2 roods; then draw a line by guess, which is dotted, from A to F, and calculate upon the plan the trapezium A k E F, which is found too large by 476320 square links; which sum divide by 1245, half the length of the dotted line A F, the quotient is 555, which distance lay off from the scale upon the line E F, perpendicular from the line A F, which will finish the division A k E i; then draw a line by guess, which is dotted, from A to C, and calculate the trapezium i F G A upon the plan, which is short of 22 acres 2 roods by 22180 square links; which sum divide by 830, half the length of the line A G, the quotient is 267; which lay off with the scale perpendicular to m; then draw the line A m, which finishes the division. However, it will be convenient to calculate the division A m H i b. If it answers to 22 acres 2 roods, you are certain of its accuracy; if it does not agree, the calculations must be made over again.

Plate XXVIII. (Fig. 6.)

Suppose the piece of land represented by A B C D E containing 60 acres is to be divided betwixt K and L, the division to be made from C, K having a right for the value of L.70 a-year, and L having a right to L.90 a-year. First add L.70 and L.90 together, the sum of which is L.160; turn the acres into square links by the table, which is 6000000;

	Sq. Links.		Sq. Links	A.	R.	P.
Then say, if L.160 give 6000000, what will L.70 give?	*Answer*	2625000=	26	1	0,	K's share
if L.160 give 6000000, what will L.90 give?	....	3375000=	33	3	0,	L's share

Then from the point c draw the dotted line by guess to g, which calculate. Now, suppose you find it is short of K's share by 625000 square links, divide this by 1000, half the length of c g, and the quotient is 625, which distance lay off upon the line A E from g, which will reach to F; then draw in the line F C, which divides the field according to the required valuation, giving quantity proportionable to quality.

Plate XXVIII. (*Fig. 7.*)

Represents a large field consisting of 79 acres 1 rood, which has to be divided into 3 divisions, giving quantity for quality; and the divisions are to go from A and B, and to fall upon the line E D. The first is valued at 30s. per acre, the 2d at 40s. per acre, and the 3d at 50s. per acre; the land was accurately measured, and a plan made out upon a large scale.

The different shares were made out thus: by adding 30s. 40s. and 50s. into one sum, they amount to 120; and 79 acres 1 rood, when turned into square links by the table, is 7925000.

	Sq. Links.	Sq. Links.	A. R. P.
Then, if 120s. gives 30s. what will 7925000 give?	*Answer*	1981250 = 19 3 10,	First Share.
120s. gives 40s. what will 7925000 give?	....	2641666 = 26 1 27,	Second Share.
120s. gives 50s. what will 7925000 give?	....	3302083 = 33 0 3,	Third Share.

To make out the division upon the plan, draw a line by guess from A to g. After calculating, it is found too much by 215000 square links; this sum divided by 1300, half the length of the line A g, the quotient is 165; lay off that distance upon the line E D towards E from g, and it will extend to h; draw in the division line A h, which finishes the 1st Lot. A line is drawn from B to i by guess: after calculating A g i B it exceeded the proportionate share by 457000 square links; which divided by 1250, half the length of the line B i, the quotient is 360, which distance when laid off from i extends to k; a line drawn from k to B finishes the 2d and 3d divisions. If it is thought proper, lot 3d may be calculated as a check; if it amounts to 33 acres 9 roods, it is right.

Plate XXVIII. (*Fig.* 8.)

Is a common where there are four claimants A, B, C, and D; each of whom have a right to feed cattle upon it. A had a right to feed 6, B 4, C 3, and D but 1. And it was mutually agreed amongst them, that each claimant should have his proportion of the common according to the number of cattle he kept. The grazing of each was valued worth five pounds per year. The common was carefully measured, and a plan of the same made out upon a large scale, the contents of which amounted to 40 acres = 4000000 square links. Now,

	L. Sq. Links.	L. Sq. Links.	A. R. P.	
A has 6 at L.5 each is L.30, then as	70 : 4000000	: : 30 : 17.14285 =	17 0 23,	A's share.
B has 4 at Do....... is L.20, ...	70 : 4000000	: : 20 : 11.42857 =	11 1 28½,	B's share.
C has 3 at Do....... is L.15, ...	70 : 4000000	: : 15 : 8.57144 =	8 2 11½,	C's share.
D has 1 at Do....... is L. 5, ...	70 : 4000000	: : 5 : 2.85714 =	2 3 17,	D's share.

Total amount per year L.70   Amount, 40.00000 = 40 0 0

By adding up the different shares, the sum is 40 acres; which proves the calculation is right.

To lay off each share upon the plan, and also upon the ground, first draw a line by guess upon the plan, suppose from C do D, parallel with the fence A B; cast up the contents, which is 202400 square links too little, which divide by 2300, the length of C D, the quotient is 88; which lay off with the scale parallel with the dotted line C D, and it will extend to e e; then draw in the division line e e, B's Lot; draw the line f f, and cast up the contents betwixt that line and the division line of A's share e e, which is too large by 3.35000, which divide by 2060, the length of f f, the quotient is 162, which lay off from f f to g g, and draw in B's division, which finishes B's lot. We now come to C's lot: draw a line by guess k k, and cast up the contents, which is too little by 90000 square links, which divide by the length of k k 1630, the quotient is 55 links, which lay off from k k to i i; draw in the division line i i, which finishes C's lot; then measure D's lot. If it answer to 2 acres 3 roods 17 perches, it is right.

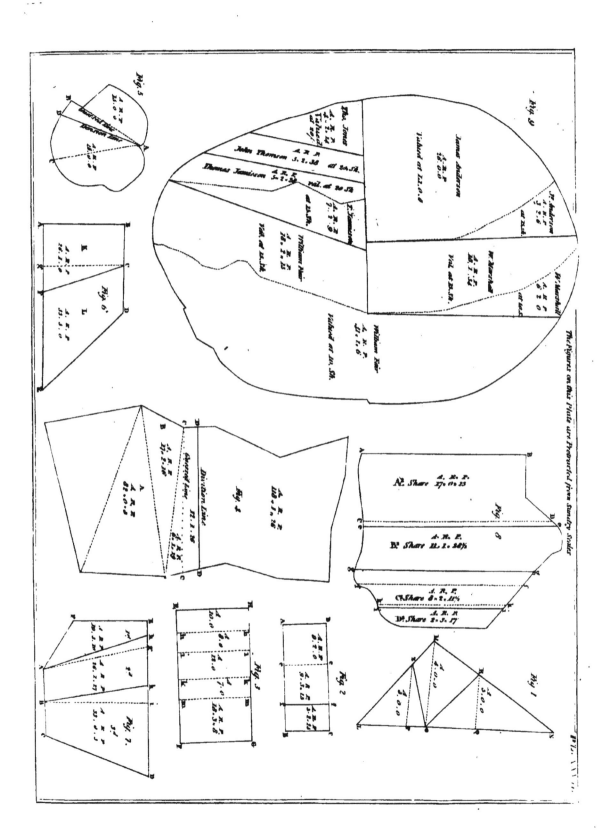

It has been observed before in staking off the different lots upon the ground, that the surveyor ought to be attentive in having all the distances, &c. that refer to his plan ; and by measuring distances from marks that he knows both upon the plan and in the field, he will find very little trouble in laying off the divisions or lots.

Plate XXVIII. (*Fig.* 9.)

Also represents a common, consisting of 137 acres 3 roods 30 perches, which was measured, as also all the different lots of valuation, and a plan made out thereof, and plotted from a large scale. The commissioners, not aware of the great trouble which would occur to the surveyor, divided the common into three different values, and chiefly in curved lines, as may be seen in the small sketch, which, although containing only three different qualities, includes no less than ten different lots to calculate, which makes a survey of this description very difficult to make out and delineate. This common is to be divided between six proprietors, whose claims are as follows :

	L.	s.	d.
James Anderson, Esq. for his estate valued at L.500 yearly	28	13	0¼
William Marshall, Esq. for do. L.300 do.	17	1	11¼
William Fair, Esq. for do. L.600 do.	34	11	9¼
Mr Thomas Jamieson, for do. L.200 do.	11	6	9
Mr John Thompson, for do. L.100 do.	5	14	9
Mr Thomas Jones, for do. L. 80 do.	4	11	9
Total value of the six estates, do. L.1780 Total	102	0	0

The method used to ascertain the valuation per acre is ; as 1780, the total amount of the value of all the estates, is to 102, the total amount of the annual value, so is the valuation of each estate to its annual worth.

For example, to find out James Anderson, Esq.'s value, as 1780 : 102 : : 500 : L.28 13 0½, and so on with all the others, and the sum of each when added gives the total amount.

ɪ f

Contents of the Closure.

	A. R. P.		L s d	L s d
James Anderson, Esq.	26 0 0	Valued at 20 per acre	26 0 0	⎫ 28 13 0½
Do.	3 2 6 do.	15 do.	2 13 0½	⎭
William Marshall	18 1 34 do.	15 do.	13 16 11½	⎫ 17 1 11½
Do.	6 2 0 do.	10 do.	3 5 0	⎭
William Fair, Esq.	41 1 6 do.	10 do.	20 12 10½	⎫ 34 11 9
Do.	18 2 15 do.	15 do.	13 18 10½	⎭
Mr Thomas Jamieson	7 2 9 do.	15 do.	5 13 3	⎫ 11 6 9
Do.	5 2 28 do.	20 do.	5 13 6	⎭
Mr John Thomson	5 2 38 do.	20 do.	5 14 9	5 14 9
Mr Thomas Jones	4 2 14 do.	20 do.	4 11 9	4 11 9

Amount of acres......137 3 30   Amount of Valuations......102 0 0

For an idea of the various calculations requisite to make out the above contents, I shall refer the pupil to the methods of calculating areas, so particularly described in that Section.

Plate XVIII. (Fig. 5.)

We shall now suppose the common-field or run-rigs described before, Plate XVIII. Fig. 3. Page 109. which are situated in the heart of the lord of the manor's estate, and he is anxious to give quantity for quality: Accordingly, an agreement was concluded betwixt the lord of the manor and the different proprietors, that he would enclose each person's property at his own expense in a regular form. The business was referred to arbitrators, and a value put upon Robert Brown's lot, which is 266700 square links, at L.3, 10s. per acre; David Rennie's, 372200 square links, at L.3, 5s. per acre; Thomas Smellie's, 306200 square links, at L.3 per acre; Mrs George, 347800 square links, at L.3 per acre; George Peacock, 597200 square links, at L.3, 5s. per acre; Robert Thomas, 306800 square links, at L.4 per acre; Joseph Dice, 186800 square links, at L.4 per acre; and John Wilson's 460000 square links, at L.3, 5s. per acre; and the ground, that is to be given in exchange is valued at L.2 per acre, which is to be laid off along the side of a straight road, and each division to be eight chains wide.

Below is the length of the respective lot that each proprietor will receive along side of the road.

	Sq. links in the common field.	Sq. links that each proprietor will receive.	Divided by.	Length of each lot.
Robert Brown's lot	266700	466775	800	584
David Rennie's do	372000	604825	do.	758
Thomas Smellie's do	306200	459300	do.	574
Mrs George's do	347800	521200	do.	651
Thomas Peacock's do	597200	1045100	do.	1254
Robert Thomas's do	206800	413600	do.	517
Joseph's Dice's do	186800	373600	do.	467
John Wilson's do	400000	700000	do.	875
	2683500	4584400		
	or	or		

Total of the runrigs 26 3 14   45 1 30 Total land got in exchange.

The quantity of ground which each proprietor is to receive at the side of the road, also the amount of ground which they give in lieu of it to the lord of the manor, is stated below. The method used for finding out the proportions that each proprietor receives is simply thus: If one acre gives L.2, what will any number of acres and decimals of an acre give at what they are valued at per acre? Turn each proprietor's acres, roods, and perches, into square links by the Table in *Page* 187.

The Calculation as under.

	A. R. P.	Sq. links.	L. s.		A. Dec.	L. A. Dec.		A. R. P.
Robert Brown,	2 2 96	=266700 × 8	0	=	9.33450	+ 2 4.66725	=	4 2 25
David Rennie,	3 2 35	=372000 × 3	5	=	12.09650	+ 2 6.04825	=	6 0 7
Thomas Smellie,	3 0 9	=306200 × 3	0	=	9.18600	+ 2 4.59900	=	5 2 1
Mrs George,	3 1 36	=347800 × 3	0	=	10.43400	+ 2 5.21200	=	5 0 34
Thomas Peacock,	5 3 86	=597200 × 3	10	=	20.19600	+ 2 10.45100	=	10 1 32
Robert Thomas,	2 0 21	=413600 × 4	0	=	8.27200	+ 2 4.13600	=	4 0 21
Joseph Dice,	1 3 10	=186800 × 4	0	=	7.37200	+ 2 3.73600	=	3 3 37
John Wilson,	4 0 0	=400000 × 3	10	=	14.00000	+ 2 7.00000	=	7 0 0

What has now been related of dividing land, includes the principles on which all other divisions are made; and with a little practice, a land surveyor will overcome all the obstacles the commissioners often give them, by dividing the different qualities in curved and irregular lots, in place of making every division run as straight as the nature of the ground will admit of.

SECTION FOURTH,

OF LEVELLING.

———————

LEVELLING is the art of finding a line parallel to the horizon at one or more stations, in order to determine how much one place is higher or lower than another, for regulating descents, cutting canals, conveying water, &c. Five or more places are said to be on a level when equally distant from the earth's centre, or a line equally distant from that centre in all its points is a line of true level. The apparent line of level, is the line of sight given by the repeated operations of levels, and rises always higher above the true line of level the greater the distance. However, by the help of tables constructed for the purpose, we can find the difference between the apparent and true line of level; it is by this assistance also we can level to almost any distance by a single operation. I shall not attempt to go over the properties of the circle upon which those tables are constructed, but shall merely give the following position, viz. That the difference between the true and apparent level is equal to the square of the distance between the two places or stations divided by the earth's diameter, and consequently is always proportional to the square of the distance; and by proportioning the excesses of height as the squares of the distances we obtain the useful table, inserted in page 205.

The common methods of levelling are sufficiently correct for masons and paviers work, &c.; but in extensive operations, such as canal levelling, for the purpose of conveying water for a number of miles, too much attention with regard to accuracy cannot be paid to such operations; and in such cases it is necessary to take the difference between the true and apparent level into the account.

The most complete level is the *Spirit Level*, invented by the celebrated artist Ramsden, see *Plate* VIII. *Fig.* 9. I shall not take up the surveyor's time with a long and tedious description of this instrument, being well aware that a few minutes inspection of the instrument itself will give a better idea of its construction and use than the most lengthened detail. Its principal parts is a telescope A A, in the tube of which cross wires are fixed and adjusted by means of four small screws. The horizontal wire cuts the object at the time of an observation; under the telescope is fixed a brass tube, inclosing one of glass containing spirits; this tube is hermetically sealed, and the spirits occupy the whole of its internal cavity all to a bubble of air, which settles exactly in the middle of the glass when the instrument is level. The telescope and level are supported by two forked uprights called Ys, owing to their resemblance to that letter; under the Ys are milled headed screws, working against collars, for the purpose of raising or depressing the telescope and level. The level is fastened to the telescope by means of capstan screws, which adjust it exactly parallel with the axis of the telescope; two bars at right angles to the Ys support a compass, for the purpose of taking magnetic bearings. The instrument turns round on a socket fastened to the legs. There are two parallel plates, fastened together by means of a ball and socket; these plates contain four screws, B B, which screw the upper plate thereof, and act against the under, for the purpose of levelling the whole instrument; which is done by raising and lowering the screws till you find the bubble in the glass tube exactly in the middle; which done, turn the instrument at right angles to its former situation. If it is not level, the screws must be raised or depressed till it is so, until it appears to be level in any situation the instrument is placed in. There is a clamp screw for the purpose of keeping the instrument tight in the centre, when required, and a tangent screw for moving the instrument easily round with a slow motion. The whole is fixed to three legs, either round or triangular; if the latter, the three legs form into one round pole, and are kept together by means of rings.

The whole is generally packed in a box, for the purpose of being conveyed safely from place to place when not at work in the field.

Various kinds of levels have of late years been invented; but the one I have just given a sketch of, I am inclined to think the best; yet by experience I have found it, as well as most others, more or less liable to error. Alexander Keith, Esq. of Ravelston in Scotland, some years ago invented a level (see *Plate* VIII. *Fig.* 10.), which, when once adjusted, seldom goes wrong. It is composed of a piece of mahogany about six inches long and one inch and a quarter square. At each end is cut a square hole about an inch deep, and the same in width. There is a tube which communicates mercury from the one incision to the other. It has two sights, one for each hole, made very light, and of an equal weight. When placed in the hole upon the mercury, one sight rises as the other sinks, the mercury running always to the level from one hole to the other by means of the tube in the under side; and what ever way you look through the sights, the object cut by the horizontal hair in the sight is always level. After advancing so much in favour of this instrument, it may be asked the reason of its never coming into general use? In reply, I can give no other reason, than that, like many other good inventions, it has been despised on account of its simplicity. I always make use of one to adjust my other long levels before any observation is taken by them. Those levels are not to be purchased, being the invention of a private gentleman, and hitherto not much known.

I shall now describe the best and easiest method of adjusting the spirit level.

Go to some field or meadow that is nearly level; there set up the instrument, and measure out eight or ten chains, leaving a mark, by driving into the earth a small wedge or stake; return to the instrument, and measure out the same distance the opposite way from the centre of the instrument, and drive in a stake to set the level staff on; there leave one of your assistant's with the staff, which should have a vane upon it to slide up and down; send another assistant to the other stake with his staff and vane, and let him place it upon the wedge or stake; then set the instrument level by the four screws B B on the parallel plates, and look through the telescope, and make signs for the assistant you first take an observation

to, to move his vane up or down the staff till you see the horizontal wire
and the black line drawn across the vane to coincide exactly; then make
a sign for him to mark upon his staff with a piece of chalk where the under part of the vane is upon the staff; then turn the telescope round, and
observe if the telescope is level; if not, set it level as before to the other
assistant, and sign to him to put up the staff upon the stake; then cause
him to move the vane up or down till you perceive the horizontal wire and
the mark on the vane to coincide, and cause him to mark the under part
of the vane with chalk upon the staff; for although the instrument should
not be adjusted, the vanes upon the staffs are exactly level. You then remove the instrument to the assistant, and place it up within six or eight
yards of him, and set it level as before, and order him to put up the staff,
and cause him to move the vane up or down till you see the horizontal
hair in the telescope and the mark on the vane to coincide. Whatever
space there is between the first and second marks on the staff, the one assistant must go to the other, and cause him to put his vane either up or down
upon his staff, the same difference there is upon his, with the addition of
$\frac{1}{8}$ of an inch higher for the earth's curvature; then sign to your assistant
to put up his staff upon the stake, and observe that the instrument conti-
nues level; then take an observation to him, and if the horizontal hair in
the telescope and the mark on the vane agrees, the level is right; but if
it should be otherwise, you must move the joint and capstan headed screw
C C, that holds the level to the telescope, either up or down, till you see
through the telescope the horizontal hair or wire to coincide exactly; and
the instrument will be adjusted. The station or level staffs above mentioned
should be 10 or 12 feet in length and about an inch and a quarter square.
It will be convenient to have two shorter ones, about five feet long, to be
used occasionally. The vanes which slide up and down upon the staffs
are sometimes of thin iron, brass, or copper, about four inches in diameter.
The segment of the circle is taken from the under side, and the vane
painted white with oil colour (see *Plate* XXIX. *Fig.* 8.); a black line is
drawn, about the eighth of an inch broad, through the centre of the vane,
which has a spring on the back part of it, to clamp it gently to the staff,
but so contrived, that, with gentle pressure, it can be made to slide along

the staff. The staffs should be exactly divided into feet and inches, and the inches divided into eighths. The feet should be marked with large figures, and numbered upwards; the same ought to be done with the five feet staff, which is only used when the descent exceeds the length of your long staff; in this case the weight or vane is put to the top of the staff, and the five feet staff upon the stake, which should be held as perpendicular as possible, sliding the long staff up close by the short one, and adding whatever height the bottom of the long staff cuts upon the short one, suppose 2 feet 10 inches; which shows that the fall is 12 feet 10 inches, if the long staff is 10 feet long. This your foremost assistant marks; but there is to be deducted the height of the instrument, which suppose is 4 feet; which deducted from 12 feet 10 inches, there remain 8 feet 10 inches of declivity.

Plate VIII.   (*Fig.* 11.)

Represents a pocket level, which is very useful for small operations, such as cutting drains or taking levels, for ascertaining the cutting; also for determining the cubical yards required to be taken out for the foundation of houses, &c. &c. It is commonly made about eight inches in length, of mahogany, with a groove taken out from the upper side to admit a glass tube to go in, which is filled with spirits of wine all to a bubble of air, which shews when it is level, which is done by means of a screw. This instrument is so simple in itself as to require no explanation.

The following Table will be found useful in taking an observation when the instrument cannot be placed at equal distances. In that case, an allowance must be made for the curvature of the earth.

Suppose you have a station that is 80 chains, or one mile in length look into the table for 80 chains, and opposite it, in the right hand column is 8 inches; which shews that the line of sight is 8 inches higher than the true level. Again, suppose you have another station that is 30 chains in length; opposite 30 chains is 1 inch 12 decimals; which shows that the difference betwixt the apparent and true level is 1 inch and 12 decimals,

1

TABLE of the Curvature of the Earth, calculated to the Apparent Level in Inches and Decimals of an Inch, from three Chains to eight Miles.

Chains.	In. Dec.	Chains.	In. Dec.	Chains.	In. Dec.	M. Ch.		Ft. In. Dec.	
3	0.01	16	0.32	29	1.05	0	50	0	3.12
4	0.02	17	0.36	30	1.12	0	55	0	3.78
5	0.03	18	0.37	31	1.19	0	60	0	4.50
6	0.04	19	0.45	32	1.27	0	65	0	5.31
7	0.06	20	0.50	33	1.35	0	70	0	6.12
8	0.08	21	0.55	34	1.44	0	75	0	7.03
9	0.10	22	0.60	35	1.53	0	80	0	8.00
10	0.12	23	0.67	36	1.62	2	0	2	7.8
11	0.15	24	0.72	37	1.71	3	0	5	11.6
12	0.18	25	0.78	38	1.80	4	0	10	7.3
13	0.21	26	0.84	39	1.91	5	0	16	6.9
14	0.24	27	0.91	40	2.00	6	0	23	10.6
15	0.28	28	0.98	45	2.28	7	0	32	5 6
						8	0	42	5.16

Levelling, of all parts of a land-measurer's work, is the easiest attained; yet it requires the greatest nicety, not only in his own observations, but that of his assistants. The most certain method to attain the greatest degree of accuracy, is to carry out a quantity of small stakes or wedges, to be stuck in the ground, about seven or eight inches long and about two inches broad at the top, and tapered off at the bottom that they may the more easily enter the ground. Upon these are placed the station staffs. The assistants should be very attentive to hold the staffs as nearly perpendicular as they can.

A surveyor is frequently employed to convey water from a spring to any particular place, either in open cuts or in pipes. To explain this, we shall suppose the water from a spring is wished to be conveyed to a house at about a mile distance, and a trial is to be made if it is possible to do so. First provide paper, pen, and ink, to each of your assistants, and order the hindmost assistant to set up his staff at the spring; then go in the direction towards the house, and plant up the instrument, and set it level by the screws in the brass plates till the bubble in the glass settle exactly in the middle; order the staffman left at the spring to move the vane up or down upon the staff, till you see it and the horizontal hair in the telescope, and the mark on the vane, to

6 g

coincide; sign to him to mark the feet and inches cut by the bottom part of the vane upon the staff, and to insert them in his field-book; then turn the telescope round to the other assistant whose pole or staff he holds up as perpendicular as possible, make signs to him to slide the vane up or down upon the staff, till you see the hair in the telescope and the mark on the vane to coincide; and cause him to mark the feet and inches cut upon the staff at the under side of the vane, which he also enters in his field-book: you then order the hindmost assistant to go and place his staff exactly where that of the foremost assistant stood: you desire the foremost assistant to go forward, and erect his staff; then plant the instrument as near half way as you can guess between them, and set it level as before; then, by signs, cause the hindmost assistant to raise or depress the vane till you see it and the hair to coincide; he then marks in his field-book, as before, the feet and inches cut on the staff; then turn the telescope about to the foremost assistant, and sign also to him to raise or depress the vane till you perceive through the telescope the hair and the mark drawn across the vane to coincide; then sign to him to mark the feet and inches in his field book cut by the lower edge of the vane upon the staff. Go on exactly in the same manner all the way to the house. This done, the running level is finished.

In comparing each assistant's notes, they turn out as follows:

Hindmost Assistant.				Foremost Assistant.				Difference of Each Station.		
	Ft.	In.	8ths.		Ft.	In.	8ths.	Ft.	In.	8ths.
1. Station	3	4	1	1. Station	4	10	5	1	6	4
2. do.	2	6	0	2. do.	4	4	2	1	10	2
3. do.	4	7	3	3. do.	5	7	6	1	0	3
4. do.	4	1	1	4. do.	6	10	4	2	9	3
5. do.	3	10	0	5. do.	6	1	1	2	3	1
6. do.	4	6	0	6. do.	4	7	7	0	1	7
7. do.	3	11	7	7. do.	4	11	1	0	11	2
8. do.	4	10	6	8. do.	5	8	6	0	10	0
	31	9	2		43	2	0	11	4	6

This shews the difference from the spring head to the house, by the stations, to be only 11 feet, 4 inches, 6 eighths; that is to say, the fall is 11 feet, 4 inches, 6 eighths, from the spring to the house, which is sufficient declivity for the water to run to the house, being only about a mile distant from the spring head; and it is well known that water will run along a pipe at no greater fall than five inches in a mile. In that case the water may run with two great a current, which requires that some of the pipes should be laid nearly level, which in some measure would impede the progress; or in some places the pipes may be laid in a curved direction, which will have a similar effect. There is sometimes a necessity for laying the pipes a little up hill before they reach to the appointed place, to avoid the water running with too great a velocity.

In levelling, it will be proper to observe, that, if the ground will admit of it, if the instrument is planted at equal distances between the back and fore assistant, although the level should be out of its adjustment, the observations will be right, and there will be no occasion for making any allowance for the curvature of the earth; but if you have to take levels where the ground is very uneven, and you have an opportunity of observing a rising ground a little more depressed than where you stand, and a valley betwixt you and that ground, which would take a long time in levelling over, the instrument ought to be very correctly adjusted, and an allowance made for the curvature of the earth. Suppose the ground which is across the valley to be half a mile, then (by the table, p. 205.) 2 inches must be allowed for the curvature, and for which 2 inches the vane must be raised upon the staff above its former situation.

Plate XXIX. (*Fig.* 1.)

Levelling for a rail-way, which requires to be made as level as the ground will admit, the first thing that ought to be done is to take a running level in the same way as described in *Page* 206. in levelling from a spring head to a house, to ascertain the practicability of conveying water to it.

After having ascertained the number of feet in the fall, measure the distance in feet from the place you began to level at to the place you left off at, which suppose 7600 feet, and the fall 10 feet; then divide 7600 by 10, and the quotient is 760; which shews that the level can be brought by cutting and filling up to one in 760, which will make a remarkable easy rail-way. Set up the instrument level at any convenient distance, suppose 800 feet from where the rail-way is to begin; sign to the staffman to move the vane up or down till you see the mark on the vane and the horizontal hair in the telescope to coincide; he then marks with chalk the bottom part of the vane on the staff; the chainmen measure the distance, 800 feet; which distance being doubled, is 1600; then say, if 7600 gives 10 feet, what will 1600 give? which, when calculated, is 2 feet 1 inch 2 eighths, which the vane must be raised upon the staff above the mark. The chainmen then measure 800 feet farther, and the staffman drives in a stake, and erects the staff upon it; if it is too high, he must drive it a little lower with a hand mallet, which he ought to have for that purpose. The observer looks again through the telescope till he sees the horizontal hair and the mark on the vane to coincide. The instrument is then moved and placed at any convenient distance in the line of direction forward, and placed exactly level as before; the staffman puts up his staff upon the stake, and is caused to move the vane higher or lower till the observer sees the mark upon the vane and the hair in the telescope to coincide; he is then to mark with chalk as before. The chainmen then measure from the stake to the instrument, which is 790 feet, which distance doubled is 1580; then 7600 : 10 : : 1580 : 2 feet, 1 inch; this shews that the vane must be raised upon the staff that height; the chainmen then measure 790 forward, and the staffman drives in a stake and places his staff upon it; if the stake is too high it must be driven lower, and raised if too low. After repeated trials the observer at last perceives the cross hairs in the telescope and the mark made by the vane to coincide; which finishes the 2d level. The instrument is then set up, and being levelled, the staffman moves the vane up or down, according to the signs given him, till the hair in the telescope and the mark in the vane coincide. The chainmen then measure the distance to the instrument, which is 720; which doubled, is 1440; which multiplied by 10 and divided by 7600, shews that the vane must be raised 1 foot 10 inches 9 eighths, higher than the last mark. The chainmen then measure forward

720, and the staffman drives in a stake and sets his staff upon it, which finishes the 3d level. Go on in the same manner, whatever may be the number of levels to take. It is no matter at what distance the instrument is placed from the staffman, if you measure the same distance forward that you measured to the instrument. Suppose the instrument was placed 200 feet from the staff, then measure 200 feet forward in the line of direction of the rail-way; when the two distances are added the distance from one stake to another is but 400 feet; that number multiplied by 10 feet, which is the whole of the fall of the rail-way, is 4000, which is less than the whole distance 7600, and shews that the 4000 must be reduced to inches by multiplying it by 12, which amounts to 48000; this when divided by the length of the rail-way gives 6 inches, 2400 parts, × 8 to bring it to the eighth of an inch is 19200 ÷ 7600 is 2 eighths and some odd fractions of the eighth of an inch; which shews that the vane is to be raised upon the staff 6 inches, 2 eighths, above the mark on the staff. Here it will be proper to observe, whatever height the vane is raised upon the staff, the ground is so much lower from one stake to the other. The levelling for turnpike roads is done exactly in the same manner, when the road is required to be brought to an equal ascent.

Plate XXIX. (Fig. 2.)

Is a continuation of the same railway as Fig. 1. but upon more uneven ground, where there is some cutting and banking required to bring it to an equal descent. First take a running level as correctly as possible, and find out what fall there is from C to D, which is 10 feet, and the distance 7510 feet, which is equal to 1 in 751; that is to say, for every 751 feet the rail-way falls 1 foot. In this method care must always be taken to measure the height of the instrument from the ground, and mark it in a field-book. This will point out the lowest ground in making out the section, and the staff will point out the highest ground, by taking the difference from one station to another, which should also be marked in the field-book. After having taken all the different levels and all the distances from one station to another, you have a section of the ground to make out, shewing all the heights, hollows, &c.; which ought to be done very correctly. To do this, first draw a line C B to represent a level; the height of the vane is 1 foot 6 inches, above the ground at No. 1.; the distance from thence to the instrument is 830 feet, and the height of the telescope above the ground is 5 feet; which shews that the fall from No. 1. to the instrument is 3 feet, 6 inches; which protract and lay off from a scale. The distance from the instrument to No. 2. is 580 feet, and the rise is 3 feet; protract this also from the same scale, and it will give the representation of a hollow between 1. and 2. The distance from No. 2. to where the instrument is placed is 260, the fall 4; the distance from the instrument to No. 3. is 870, and the rise is 3; the distance from No. 3. to the instrument is 380, and the fall 5; the distance from the instrument to No. 4. is 220, and the rise 3: protract this also, which will give the hollow between No. 3. and 4. The distance from No. 4. to the instrument is 320, and the fall 5; the distance from the instrument to No. 5. is 500, and the rise 3 feet 9 inches, which gives the representation of the hollow from 4. to 5.; the distance from No. 5. to the instrument is 500, and the fall is 4 feet, 6 inches; and the distance from the instrument to No. 6. is 530, and the rise is 3 feet, 3 inches: protract this, which represents the hollow between 5. and 6. The distance from No. 6. to the instrument is 500, and the fall is 4; the distance from the instrument to No. 7. is 538 feet, and the rise is 3, which represents the hollow between 6. and 7. The distance from No. 7. to the instrument is 450, and the fall 5; the distance from thence to No. 8. is 400, and the rise is 4 feet, 6 inches: protract this, which will represent the hollow between 7. and 8. Again, the distance from the instrument to No. 9. is 610 feet, and the rise 2 feet to D: protract this, and you have a representation of the whole section from C to D. Draw a line from the lowest ground at D to the highest ground at C, which shews what cutting and banking will be required to make the rail-way from C to D of an equal descent.

N. B. One station staff and one staffman answers the same purpose as making use of two, and it is equally the same in taking the levels for a canal.

Plate XXIX.   (*Fig.* 3.)

Shews the method of levelling for a canal.   Adjust the level as has already been described, and place the instrument as near the summit as you can guess; send the staffman the contrary way from where you begin, and let him drive in one of his wedges or stakes and set his staff upon it; sign to him to move the vane higher or lower, till you perceive the horizontal hair in the telescope and the mark across the vane to coincide; the staffman then marks the staff at the bottom part of the vane, and the chain-men measure the distance from the stake to the instrument, which is 720 feet; when the staffman comes up, look how much higher the vane upon the staff is above the height of the instrument, which suppose 4 feet; this shews that there is a cut of 4 feet on the summit.   The chainmen then measure about the same distance forward, and the staffman puts up his staff; if he is too low, the observer signs to him to move upon higher ground, till he sees him nearly upon the same level with the first stake.   The observer then makes motions for him to drive in one of his stakes into the ground, and to set his staff upon it.   If it is too high, the observer signs to him to drive the stake farther into the ground and to put his staff upon it, till such time as the horizontal hair and the mark on the vane coincides. The staffman ought to be very attentive, at every time he places the staff upon the stake, that the vane is exactly at the mark, as the vane is apt sometimes to shift a little in carrying from one station to another.   The instrument is now removed past the staffman (the first level being finished), and placed at any convenient distance; and being levelled, the staffman rubs out all the marks, and puts the staff upon the stake; he then moves the vane up or down till such time as the hair in the telescope and the mark on the vane coincide, and marks the staff as before with chalk.   The chainmen then measure the distance, which is 720 feet, and also the same distance forward from the instrument; the staffman puts up his staff to try if it is near the level; he is then ordered to drive in a stake, which he sets the staff upon; and after repeated trials, moves the stake up and down till such time as the observer sees the hair and the mark on the vane to coincide; which finishes the 2d level.   All others are done in the same way, by placing the instrument at any convenient distance from the man left at the staff. Sometimes you may find it convenient to place it at 5, 6, 7, or 800 feet; but observe particularly, at whatever distance the instrument is placed from one stake, the next stake should be placed nearly at the same distance from the instrument. You may go on in this way for many miles upon a dead level, till you come to some fall in the ground, which must be descended by locks of any number of feet that the ground will admit of, suppose 8 feet each lock. Before proceeding farther, as stakes were drove in at every place the levels were taken, if a plan and section is required, the ground must be again carefully measured with a theodolite and chain, the first measure that was taken being only done in a rough way, merely for erecting the instrument at nearly equal distances. The surveyor will have to return to where the 2d stake was placed, and plant up the theodolite, and take a bearing to the first stake that was drove into the ground, past the cut of 4 feet upon the summit; also a bearing to the 3d stake, and cause the chainmen to measure those distances carefully; and if there are any towns, villages, or farm-houses seen, take bearings to them as in *Plate* XXI. *Fig.* 3. and 4. *Page* 112; so that these distances may be ascertained by intersection from the line of the canal on either side of it. Also, in crossing a road or brook or any little rivulet, insert on a sketch, not only the distance where they are crossed, but also bearings both to the right hand and the left; mark every enclosure you enter into, and leave a mark by digging a hole with a spade at or near every fence. If the canal is to be made, every enclosure will have to be measured, and the quantity of ground ascertained on each side of the canal, and also the quantity of ground occupied by the canal.

I now come to show the best method of taking locks, suppose of 8 feet each: order the staffman to place his staff upon the stake at the end of the level, and plant the instrument level at any convenient distance, suppose 430 feet, from the staff, and order the staffman to slide the vane up or down till you see the hair in the telescope and the mark across the vane to coincide, and cause him to mark with chalk where the under side of the vane is upon the staff; when he comes down to the instrument look how

1

far the mark is upon the staff, and you will find it 1 foot 3 inches; then slide the vane up the staff to 9 feet 3 inches, and order the staffman to go down 6 or 700 feet, and there to put up his staff to see if he be nearly right. If he is too low, call him nearer you, and place his staff, and look again; you then order him to put in one of his stakes, and keep driving the stake till such time as the vane and hair in the telescope coincide; then remove the instrument 3 or 400 feet below the stake and set it level; order the staffman to pull down the vane till such time as you see the hair in the telescope to coincide; he should then mark where the vane is upon the staff, which is 1 foot 6 inches; then raise the vane to 9 feet 6 inches, which is 8 feet above the mark, and cause him to go 4 or 500 feet down on the line of direction, and put up his staff; if you see the vane, order him to drive in a stake. After several trials you will see the hair in the telescope to coincide, which finishes the 2d lock. Every lock required to be taken is done in the same way.

I shall only observe two things more in canal surveying, viz. the method of measuring cuts and banking across glens, gulleys, ravines, or valleys, as they are termed in different parts of the country.

Plate XXIX. (Fig. 3.)

Represents the section of a canal A A, where the instrument was placed; at each station B B is the staff where it was placed; C C, Fig. 8, is the representation of the staff and slider, commonly called the weight or vane, which the staffman holds up as perpendicular as he can when an observation is taken; E is a cutting of 8 feet at the deepest part, and is 850 feet in length; F is another of 11 feet deep, and 920 feet in length; G is another cut of 4 feet deep, and 1440 feet in length; H is a glen or ravine that is almost perpendicular on one side of the brook or burn which was not levelled, being impracticable, but the depth taken from a level stake on the opposite side, and the distance across was fixed by intersection, and calculated by logarithms, to prove if the intersection was right; which by both methods was found to be 920 feet wide. The cutting on each side might have been avoided by going across the brook farther down the bank; but as earth is wanted to fill up the ravine or glen, it is best to make a cut, if the ground will admit of it, before crossing any hollow that cannot be avoided, on purpose to get earth to fill it up.

The cutting, banking, building, and calculation of the probable expence required in cutting a canal, is, however, more the profession of an engineer than a land-surveyor; but as a land-measurer is generally employed under the former, his knowledge of a little of this department, joined to his own, is certainly a great acquisition. I shall now point out the method I have hitherto practised myself.

Suppose the section of the canal, Plate XXIX. *Fig. 3. the cutting of which is to be calculated, the canal being proposed to be 12 feet wide at bottom, 26 feet wide at top, and 4 feet deep.*

First, add 12, the width at bottom, to 26 feet, the width at top, the sum is 38; the half is 19 for a mean, which multiplied by 4, the depth, is 76; which sum multiplied by 7430 feet, the whole length of the canal, the product is 564680 feet; which sum, divided by 27, the number of feet in a cubic yard, is 20914 yards nearly, at 8d. per yard . - - - - - - - - - L. 697 2 8

The cut of four feet deep at the summit is 1440 feet long, 26 feet wide at bottom, and 40 feet wide at top.

Add 26 and 40, which is 66, the half of which is 33 for a mean width; which multiplied by 2, being a mean depth, is 66; which again multiplied by 1440, the whole length of the cut, is 95040; which, divided by 27, the cubic feet in a yard, is 2250 yards, at 8d. per yard, is - -   117 6 8

The cut F at the steep side of the glen is 26 feet wide at bottom, 62 feet wide at top, and 11 feet deep, and 920 feet long.

Add 26 and 62, the sum is 88, the half of which is 44, being a mean width; which multiplied by 5 feet 6 inches, half the depth, being a mean, is 242 feet; which again multiplied by 920, the length of the cut, is 222640; which, divided by 27, the cubic feet in a yard, is 8246 yards, at 8d. - - - - - - - 274 17 4

Carried forward   L. 1089 6 8

Brought forward   L.1089   6   8

The cut E at the opposite side of the glen is 26 feet wide
    at bottom, 52 feet wide at top, 8 feet deep, and 850
    feet long.

Add 26 to 52, the sum is 78, the half is 39 for a mean width;
    which, multiplied by 4, half the depth, is 156; which,
    multiplied by 850, the length, is 132600; which, divided

by 27, is 4911 yards, at 8d. - - - -	163	14	0
To two locks, at L.800 each - - - -	1600	0	0
To an aqueduct across the glen - - - -	150	0	0
To towing path, &c. &c. - - - - -	180	0	0
To ten *per cent*, allowed for unforeseen accidents -	318	6	0

Total expence of cutting a canal 1 mile 3 furlongs and
    45½ yards in length   -   -   -   -   -   L.3501   6   8

Plate XXIX. (*Fig.* 4.)

Represents part of a lake, which the proprietor wished drained either
by an open cast or a mine. The levels being taken, the summit was found
to be 34 feet high above the bed of the lake, and the cut is 1220 feet long,
the ground a stiff clay. In calculating the expense, it was found as
follows : 6 feet wide at bottom + 30 feet wide at top, is 36 feet; the
half is 18 × by 1200 = 21600, which × 17, half the depth, is 367200
cubic feet, which ÷ 27 cubic feet in a yard, is 13600 cubic yards,
at 1s.   -   -   -   -   -   -   -   -   L.680   0   0
Two men took in hand to cut a mine 4 feet deep and 3 feet
    wide at 9s. per running foot, and to put up the sluice, &c.
    at their own expence, for   -   -   -   -   -   540   0   0

    This last method was adopted, not only for being less expensive, but
because it saved the land from being broke into a deep and steep ravine.

Plate XXIX. (*Fig.* 5.)

Represents the section of a road, which has pulls of 1 in 15, 1 in 34, and 1
in 9, in going from the bottom to the top; the height is 30 feet, and the length
480 feet ; 480, divided by 30, is 16; which shows that the road can be
brought to an equal pull of 1 in 16 by cutting 2 feet deep at a, and bank-

ing 3 feet at b. In going down the hill on the other side, the road descends at 1 in 16, 1 in 60, and 1 in 10, the length is 480; which sum divide by 30, the height of the hill, and the quotient is 16; which shews that the hill can be brought on that side to an equal descent of 1 in 16, by cutting 6½ feet at c to the dotted line drawn upon the section.

Plate XXIX. (Fig. 6.)

Is the section of a hollow, which has a descent of 1 in 25, another of 1 in 16, and another of 1 in 13; and it is proposed to make the road of an equal declivity. The length is 610 feet, and the fall is 36 feet. Divide 610 by 36, the quotient is 17 nearly; which shews that the descent can be brought to a fall of 1 in 17 by cutting 4½ feet from the surface at a to the dotted line marked on the section. In ascending the hill from the hollow there is a rise of 1 in 25, another of 1 in 12, another of 1 in 10, and another of 1 in 28; the height is 31 feet, and the whole length is 620 feet; which divided by 31 the quotient is 20; which shews that the ascent can be brought to an equal rise of 1 in 20 by banking 2 feet at b to the dotted line, and cutting 7 feet deep from the surface at c.

Plate XXIX. (Fig. 7.)

Represents an excellent little instrument, which was invented by Messrs. Miller and Adie, mathematical instrument makers in Edinburgh, which enables the inspector and contractor of roads to ascertain the ascents and descents of a road with greater facility and precision than has hitherto been practised. A and B are two rulers of mahogany a foot in length, 1 inch broad, and half an inch thick, joined together with a joint in the same manner as a common foot rule. The leg A has a glass tube filled with spirits all to a bubble, which is fixed on the upper side; the brass arch c folds into the leg B when put into the pocket; D D is a rod 12 feet in length, which is laid upon the surface of the road, and the instrument is laid upon it; there is a rack and pinion to bring the leg A to a level; the arch is divided into equal distances of 12 in an inch. That this road instrument may be rendered as easy and expeditious as possible, the inspector and contractor ought to be furnished with a table the same as the one annexed.

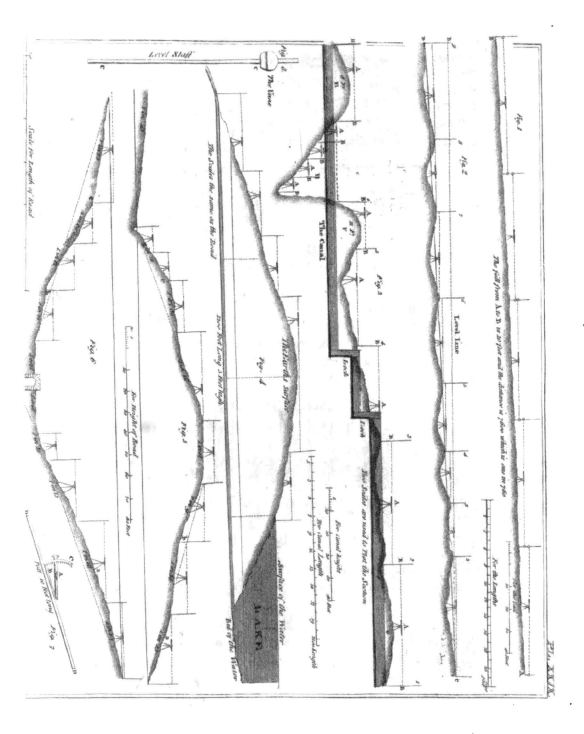

that the declivity or acclivity of any road they wish to know the pull of (as it is termed) may be exactly ascertained.

Divisions on the Arch.	One in	Divisions on the Arch.	One in	Divisions on the Arch.	One in
1	144	$7\frac{1}{2}$	19	14	10
$1\frac{1}{2}$	96	8	18	15	$9\frac{1}{2}$
2	72	$8\frac{1}{2}$	17	16	9
$2\frac{1}{2}$	58	9	16	17	$8\frac{1}{4}$
3	48	$9\frac{1}{2}$	15	18	8
$3\frac{1}{2}$	41	10	$14\frac{1}{2}$	19	$7\frac{1}{2}$
4	36	$10\frac{1}{2}$	$13\frac{1}{2}$	20	$7\frac{1}{4}$
$4\frac{1}{2}$	32	11	13	21	7
5	29	$11\frac{1}{2}$	$12\frac{1}{2}$	22	$6\frac{1}{2}$
$5\frac{1}{2}$	26	12	12	23	$6\frac{3}{4}$
6	24	$12\frac{1}{2}$	$11\frac{1}{2}$	24	6
$6\frac{1}{2}$	22	13	11	25	$5\frac{1}{4}$
7	20	$13\frac{1}{2}$	$10\frac{1}{2}$		

The following Table, by the help of the quadrant on the theodolite, is found to be very useful to a practical surveyor in ascertaining the pull that a road can be brought to, by a single observation, if the top of the rise from the bottom can be seen, or, *vice versa*, if the bottom can be seen from the top.

Degrees.	One in	Degrees.	One in	Degrees.	One in	Degrees.	One in
$0\frac{1}{8}$	228	$2\frac{1}{2}$	21	$5\frac{1}{4}$	11	10	6
$0\frac{1}{4}$	114	3	19	$5\frac{1}{2}$	$10\frac{1}{4}$	11	$5\frac{1}{2}$
$0\frac{1}{2}$	76	$3\frac{1}{4}$	18	$5\frac{1}{2}$	10	12	$5\frac{1}{4}$
1	56	$3\frac{1}{2}$	17	6	$9\frac{1}{2}$	13	5
$1\frac{1}{4}$	46	$3\frac{1}{4}$	16	$6\frac{1}{4}$	9	14	$4\frac{1}{2}$
$1\frac{1}{2}$	38	4	15	$6\frac{1}{2}$	$8\frac{1}{2}$	15	4
$1\frac{3}{4}$	32	$4\frac{1}{4}$	14	7	8	16	$3\frac{1}{2}$
2	28	$4\frac{1}{2}$	13	$7\frac{1}{4}$	$7\frac{1}{4}$	17	$3\frac{1}{2}$
$2\frac{1}{4}$	26	$4\frac{3}{4}$	12	8	7	18	$3\frac{1}{4}$
$2\frac{1}{2}$	23	5	$11\frac{1}{2}$	9	$6\frac{1}{4}$	19	3

Explanation of the Table. Set the theodolite level by the help of the screws B B between the brass plates, after having set the index at o on the quadrant; send one of your assistants to the top of the hill or rising ground with a piece of paper, or any other mark, which he holds to that part of his breast that the height of the telescope reached to when he was at the bottom; then elevate the telescope till you see the paper and the cross hairs in the telescope to coincide; look to the quadrant, and see how many de_grees and minutes the index cuts, which is 8 degrees; look for 8 degrees in the table, and opposite it on the right hand column is 1 in 7, that is to say, for every seven feet you go upon the road you ascend one foot in perpendicular height: again, if the index cut $2\frac{1}{2}°$ upon the quadrant, look into the table for $2\frac{1}{2}°$, and opposite it is 1 in 23. This shows that every 23 feet you go upon the surface you rise one foot in perpendicular height. If you wish to know the perpendicular height of the hill, measure the length from the bottom to the top of the rise, which suppose is 2162 feet; divide the number by 23, and the quotient is 94 feet for the height of the hill.

It will be necessary to observe here, that the different sections on *Plate* XXIX. representing the rail-way, &c. two scales are used, one for the lengths, and the other for the perpendicular heights. If they had been laid down upon the same scale, the perpendiculars on some of the sections would not have appeared on so small a scale; but to be very correct, it will be proper to lay them down upon a very large scale, that the perpendicular height may be ascertained by applying a pair of compasses to the scale the section is plotted by.

SECTION FIFTH.

COUNTY SURVEYING.

THE surveying of a large district or county is an operation so extensive and complicated, as to require the utmost exertion of the surveyor's abilities in every branch of his department; for in the exercise of it, he will find various difficulties to encounter; errors, if due care is not taken, will arise, and these will continue multiplying throughout the whole survey. The satisfaction, then, that the surveyor will have, both in the progress and termination of his work, must, it is evident, entirely depend upon the correctness, care, and caution he sets out with; and, added to this, the accuracy of his instruments. The choice and measurement of a base line, though in itself it appears a simple operation, is, however, when done with the nicety required, laborious and difficult, as a very small error (more particularly if the base is short) will affect the whole work *.

* The accuracy with which base lines have been measured in this country, is better known by those who are in possession of an invaluable work, entitled *The Account of a Grand Trigonometrical Survey of England and Wales*, carried on by Government under the direction of the learned Col. Mudge. In this work is contained the result of a series of great triangles, extending over almost all England, with the whole of Wales, and a part of the south of Scotland. Those triangles are again filled up by smaller ones. By this means the situations of all the principal objects are ascertained, including their latitudes, longitudes, bearings, and distances from the meridian, and perpendiculars to that meridian, with the heights of the several grand stations, and other remarkable hills, &c. besides scientific information concerning the measurement of the degree in this country. In a short time, then, a skeleton map, as it were, of the whole kingdom will be accomplished; however, in that part already com-

A person who undertakes the survey of a county, is apt to imagine, that to measure his base, and take his angles with expensive instruments, calculating his triangles by logarithms, by which means, laying down the objects by their distances instead of protracting them by their angles, &c. will take more time and expense than the advantage (if any) that may accrue from his performance will compensate for. It is perhaps more on this account than any other, that the proper method has seldom (till Government took it in hand) been pursued; and of course the reason why most of our maps are so erroneous; and though some, in the course of various editions, get rid of the most glaring errors, the skeleton, or boundary work, often remains the same. However, in the few remarks (elucidated by example) I have to make, I will attend as much as possible to the advantage of the surveyor as to the accuracy of his work.

First, I would advise the surveyor to make himself well acquainted with the district or county he is about to survey. This may be effected by riding or walking over it in various directions with a person well-informed of every particular part. By this means the names of the several towns, villages, seats, hills, and other remarkable objects, may be obtained, which will prove of the most essential service in the progress of the survey. Being possessed of this previous information, the surveyor will be enabled to choose a proper piece of ground whereon to measure a base; he will also be acquainted with the names of objects he sees at a distance from any of his stations. Having measured a base of a convenient length, bearings must be taken from its extremities, &c. all round; by this means intersecting every object of note with at least three or four intersections. Those

pleted, the surveyor will find bases already measured, and objects intersected, from which he can find no difficulty in surveying or filling up a district, however large. The public, besides, being possessed of such a valuable work, derive another advantage; maps are constructed on the basis of the trigonometrical survey, and regularly published at the tower of London, by the same gentleman under whose direction the various branches of such a laborious undertaking are performed. These maps are published in large districts, on a scale of one inch to a mile; and being constructed on trigonometrical principles, they have attained the greatest degree of perfection in respect to accuracy, besides their superior beauty of engraving. To a skilful surveyor this work may be termed an invaluable treasure.

objects being accurately determined with regard to situation, bearings must be taken from those that will be convenient for stations, to the former objects, and to as many more of note as may appear in view. The surveyor may find it convenient to measure the turnpike roads, &c. as he goes on; and, by this means, make use of his stations in the roads, to intersect objects also. This will be more clearly comprehended by an example.

Measure a base line (with your chain) of a convenient length, as accurately as you possibly can; but in order to have the utmost certainty of such accuracy, it will be proper to measure the base, at least two or three times over. Having thus completed it, suppose its length 400 chains, or 5 miles, as in *Plate 30*. Being provided with a good theodolite, which ought to be at least 6 or 7 inches diameter, to take the principal bearings with, (as for the road surveying, an instrument divided into every five minutes will answer all the purpose of one larger), plant the theodolite at the eastern extremity of the base, and, having levelled it exactly, which must be carefully done at every station you intend taking principal bearings from, take a bearing to the windmill, and a circle of bearings all round; repeat the bearing to the windmill; should it answer to what it was formerly, it proves the instrument has not shifted.

The theodolite is then to be removed to the west end of the base line. To put the instrument in the same position it was at the east end, the surveyor must be very attentive to observe what was the bearing from the east to the west extremity, *viz.* 270°, from which must be subtracted 180°; there remains 90°; set the index on the limb over 90°; turn the head of the instrument round, till you see the mark left at the east end; when the mark and the cross hairs in the telescope is seen to coincide, screw the instrument fast; take first a bearing to the windmill; if it answers to 270°, it is right as to the line; then commence taking your observations. In the following page is the Field-book, pointing out the bearings taken from both ends of the base. See *Plate* XXX.

OBSERVATIONS TAKEN FROM THE EAST END.			OBSERVATIONS TAKEN FROM THE WEST END.		
	Deg. Min.			Deg. Min.	
Windmill, ⁓⁓⁓	270.00	The base.	Higham Church,	90.00	{ And mark at east end.
	278.00	Old Church.	Wardlaw, ⁓⁓⁓	81.36	
	290.00	Billonhouse.	Huntershill, ⁓⁓⁓	66.40	
	293.30	{ Catcraig and Davieston.	Tippetlaw, ⁓⁓	48.36	
	299.48	Haggs Castle.	Tomkins and } High Pen in } a line, }	42.00	
	303.36	Pease Cairn.			
	310.40	Usie Church.			
	317.30	Broad Cairn.	Hags Castle, ⁓⁓	23.30	
	338.24	Tomkins.	Broad Cairn, ⁓	19.50	
	343.48	High Pen.	Pease Cairn, ⁓	347.00	
	353.06	Tippet Law.	Davieston, ⁓⁓⁓	330.30	
	18.48	Huntershill.	Old Church, ⁓	315.00	
	84.54	Wardlaw.	Windmill, ⁓⁓⁓	270.00	
	90.00	Higham Ch.		94.00	Red Church.
High Pike, ⁓⁓⁓	134.36			97.50	High Pike.
Parkhouse, ⁓⁓⁓	197.30			111.36	Parkhouse.
Torshill, ⁓⁓⁓	238.40			117.48	Dunscairn.
Windhill, ⁓⁓⁓	254.00			125.12	Torshill.
Dunscairn, ⁓⁓⁓	255.30			189.48	Windhill.
Red Church & } John's Church, }	265.30			237.00	St John's Cha.
				90.00	Higman Ch.

DISTANCES ON THE BASE.

	Chains.	
From the east end to a mark at a ⁓⁓	50	
Crosses a brook at ⁓⁓⁓⁓⁓⁓⁓⁓	63	
Crosses a road at ⁓⁓⁓⁓⁓⁓⁓	110	Byre Loan.
Crosses a road at ⁓⁓⁓⁓⁓⁓⁓	130	
Crosses a road near lower bridge ⁓⁓	170	
Crosses Till river ⁓⁓⁓⁓⁓⁓	200	
Crosses road at Longlee houses ⁓⁓	222	
Crosses road at Redhall houses ⁓⁓⁓	271	
Crosses road at Todholes houses ⁓⁓	350	
West end of the base line ⁓⁓⁓⁓	400	Or five miles.

Field Notes of the Road measured on Plate 30, from the mark at a to Davieston.

	Bearings			Chains	
	Deg. Min.				
	24.30	from a to b		29	Road goes off.
	301.30	do. b to c		45	
Road goes off,	337.30	do. c to d		38	Usie Town.
	313.30	do. d to e		45	Usie Village.
	272.00	do. e to f		50	
Road goes off,	255.30	do. f to g		28	
Hillhead,	279.00	do. g to h		54	
	311.30	do. h to i		62	
	279.00	do. i to k		38	
	265.24	do. k to l		44	
Upper bridge,	291.12	do. l to m		37	
Road goes off,	314.24	do. m to n		37	
	271.30	do. n to o		35	
Davieston,	248.48	do. o to p		32	Davieston.

Field Notes of the measure of the River Till, from N° 1. to King's Seat.

	Bearings			Chains	
	Deg. Min.				
	17.00	from N° 1 to 2		61	
Opposite Drembank,	276.00	do. 2 to 3		63	
	242.30	do. 3 to 4		62	
Opposite Bridgend,	358.00	do. 4 to 5		61	Cockfield House at 36.
	248.48	do. 5 to 6		42	
	210.30	do. 6 to 7		57	
	334.30	do. 7 to 8		66	Broadholm at 38.
	64.48	do. 8 to 9		45	
	340.30	do. 9 to 10		49	Tillbank at 24.
	51.00	do. 10 to 11		68	

Use the same method in protracting the above observations as is particularly described in p. 88. Farm of Tipperty, and Bonnyton, p. 89.; with this difference, that those farms were laid down with a semicircular protractor divided into 180 degrees, and the above must be protracted with a circular one divided into 360 degrees, or twice 180 degrees, according to the division of your theodolite. Should the surveyor use a semicircular, in this case he must subtract 180 from the amount, and the remainder will be the bearing. For my own part I would prefer taking the bearings with an instrument divided into twice 180 degrees, as it saves the trouble of altering the index and the limb on the theodolite, when it is removed from one station to another.   Besides, two verniers can be used on the limb, and a mean taken of their readings.   This is useful when the triangles are to be calculated by logarithms, as greater accuracy is attained.

To protract the observations, use the same scale by which you have laid down the bearings on the base line, suppose 1 inch to a mile. Should you not use a protractor of your own making, prick off all the bearings from the east and west end of the base, as described in p. 88, (Farm of Tipperty), and draw them all in with a black lead pencil; the point of intersection marks the distance to the stations where the respective bearings are taken; insert the name of the church, house, or hill, or whatever object you take your bearings to; let the same be done with all the other intersections, which will not only ascertain the horizontal distance from each end of the base, but the distance from one place to another.   The next thing to be done is to go to one of the intersected objects, suppose the broad cairn, and there erect the theodolite; look into the field-book for the bearing to the broad cairn, which was $317° 30'$ from the east end of the base; subtract $180°$ from it, and there remains $137° 30'$; move the index to that degree and minute on the limb, and turn the head of the instrument round till you see through the telescope the conspicuous mark built at the east end of the base line where you began; then screw the head of the instrument fast to the legs, and loosen the screw a little that holds the telescope and quadrant fast to the limb; then turn the pinion, and take a range of bearings from the broad cairn, the same as was done from the east and west ends of the base. If you take bearings from it to all the places you know you had bearings to before, when they are protracted, the three lines will meet in a point, which is a proof that your first intersection to those places are certain.   For example, the bearing to Hunters Hill is $108°$, that to Tippetlaw $89° 30'$, and to Pease Cairn $266° 30'$.   After protracting those bearings from the broad cairn, should they meet in a point with the former observations, you are certain thus far you are correct. You may then go to Hunters Hill, or any of the other intersected places where three lines meet in a point, taking another range of bearings all round, particularly to the north and east, and make as many intersections as you can; then go to the Pease Cairn, and take another range of bearings to the north and west.   After having subtracted $180°$ from $266° 30'$, the remain-

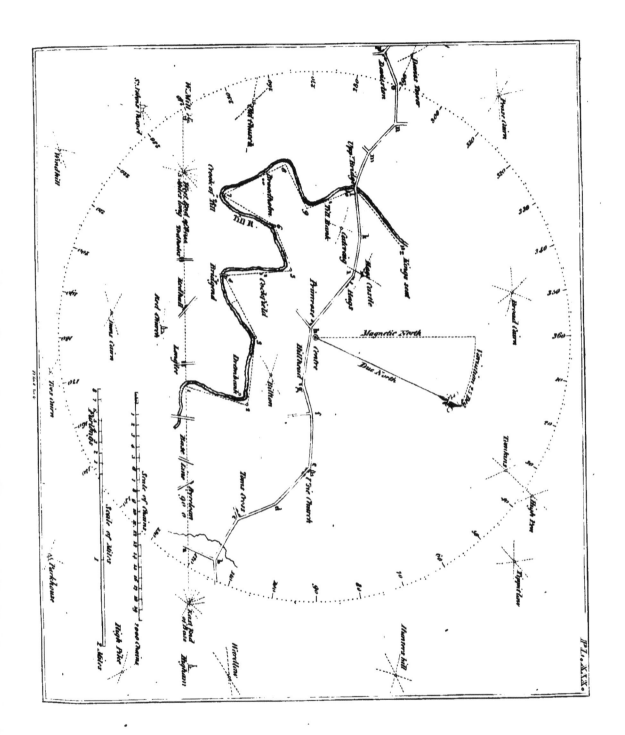

Magnetic North

Due North

Pl. XXX.

der is 86° 30′; set the index to 86° 30° on the limb, and turn the head of the instrument round with both hands till you see the cross hairs in the telescope to coincide with Hunter's Hill. Go from hill to hill, or any other convenient intersected place, where three or four bearings meet in a point, till you have got intersections to all the principal places in the county. By using a protractor of your own making you will very much facilitate the plotting, as every bearing is protracted from the centre. The work may be shortened in a great measure by using the T square and its companion, as particularly described in p. 78. by laying the chamfered edge upon the centre, and the degrees and minutes of the bearings you are laying off, and sliding the T parallel, by the help of its companion, to that part of the plan you are laying down the bearing from. In using those protractors made by land-surveyors, the figures denoting the degrees are only supposed to be inserted with a black lead pencil, which is easily rubbed out when the bearings and distances are all laid off. See *Plate* XIII.

From what has been said, it is hoped a surveyor will find very little difficulty in laying down the intersections of an inland county.

I have set down on the plan the base line, which is dotted from one end to the other, and marked where roads were crossed, and also the river Till, and such houses, with their names, as are near the base. After having protracted all the bearings, make marks thus ⊙ where the black lead lines intersect one another; which may be drawn in if you think proper. This I have avoided, in order that the diagram may appear less complicated. A road is also measured and protracted from a mark left on the base line at a to Davieston, and also the river Till, from another mark where the Till was crossed to the village of Kingseat. I have merely inserted the road and part of the river, to give the surveyor of a county a notion of the labour he may expect to meet with. Some surveyors prefer the plain table in filling up the vacant spaces between the great intersections, as they can draw in upon the table all the little angles and distances upon the spot, which indeed saves much time in plotting, as it is very tedious to lay down the bearings and distances with a protractor and scale.

In surveying the roads, the best method that a surveyor can adopt is to measure to one or more fixed points, as the road, when plotted with those points at its extremities, can be extended to the respective points from the

same scale on the skeleton work of the plan ; if it agree, the stations in
the road ought to be pricked through, and the sides of the roads formed,
leaving the offets, &c. to be laid down on the fair plan. This is the most
regular method a surveyor can adopt in any survey of a large extent.

Plate XXXII.

Is a chart of part of the sea coast, laid down from a scale of one inch to
a mile, and the bearings taken with a theodolite divided into twice 180°,
and the distances measured with a gunter's chain of 66 feet. This chart
will give a surveyor who is employed in the survey of a county some idea
of the labour in a work of that kind, as the whole coast must be measured
and planned, as represented by dotted lines from one station to another ;
but numerous other bearings besides those on the stations, including all
the roads, rivers, brooks, towns, farm-houses, and all remarkable objects,
must be inserted, in the same way as represented on the chart, in their
true situations ; and all inaccessible objects must be intersected, as may
be seen by examining the chart. For instance, take bearings from station
5 to the broad island at a, and another from station 8 to broad island at a,
and, in order to be certain, take another from station 10 to the same place ;
do the same to all other inaccessible objects as represented on the chart.
If you have a tolerably long base, the intersection of two lines meeting, if
not too acute, may be trusted to church steeples, gentlemen's houses, farms,
remarkable trees, windmills, &c. &c. till you have an opportunity of check-
ing them in the course of the survey. To get an idea of every little oc-
currence that is requisite in taking the survey of a large district or map
of a county, being a combination of the various branches of surveying, can
be attained only from a consultation of the whole work. The hills are
generally done by an eye-sketch upon a blank corner of the field-book, or
by a sketch in passing them, drawn in a rough manner in the blank leaves
of the book ; but if you are upon a hill, place the theodolite so as the index and the limb corresponds with the needle in the compass box, and take
bearings to two hills you know, and sketch in their likeness. The plain
table is an excellent instrument for this purpose, as you can sketch in the
likeness of a hill in truer proportion with it than by a guessed eye-sketch.
If you prick as many intersections off as the plain table sheet will hold,
and when you plant the table, lay the thin edge of the index upon the hill

you are upon, or any other hill or place you know, and turn the table round by the socket on its axis ; the needle will play over the *fleur de lis* in the compass box if you have laid the meridian line of the great triangles parallel with the longest side of the plain table.

But the most accurate method of sketching hills is, after having plotted a part of your plan, trace it through upon oiled paper ; and by going over that particular part of the country represented by the plan, you may sketch in the hills from point to point with great accuracy.

Plate XXXI.

Is the field-book of the survey of that part of the sea coast, see *Plate* XXXII. The survey was begun at a, and bearings and distances measured to *b, c, d, e,* &c. till such time as the letters were all exhausted ; recourse was then had to numbers from N° 1. to N° 17. If the soundings are to be taken, you may proceed in various ways. One method is by heaving out the log, and noting how far the boat sails in half a minute ; the boatmen having got previous notice to row as near an equal sail as possible, and to sail in a straight line from one point to another. Suppose the log run out 20 fathoms in half a minute, this is at the rate of 2400 feet in 10 minutes, or 36 chains 36 links ; so that if a sounding is taken every 10 minutes you prick off upon the chart 36 chains and 36 links, and insert the depth upon the chart. Again, if you take another depth in 22 minutes from starting, prick off 80 chains, or one mile, and so on till the boat crosses the bay.

Another method, which is much practised, is to sail in a direct line from one point to another, and take a sounding every 4 or 5 minutes ; measure the length upon the chart, and divide that length by the number of soundings that are taken, suppose 5, and the distance 4 miles. Another method is, by ordering the boatmen to keep the boat steady, and take a bearing with a sea compass, first to one place, then another bearing to another place, both places being at a considerable distance from one another, and both objects particularly marked on the chart ; protract those bearings from the meridian, and where the intersection meets ; insert the sounding at each intersection you make all along the coast and middle of the bays.

5

The above methods are all liable to error, although they are much practised.

A better method is by placing the theodolite at any part of the shore where you had a station, and order the boatmen to sail from one point to another in a direct line ; and, when a sounding is taken, to put up a flag. As soon as you take a bearing to it, set down the hour and minute ; the assistant in the boat sets down the sounding, and the minute when it was taken ; the same is done at every time the flag is put up. When one line is done, another must be begun in a different direction, and so on with several other lines till one bay is finished ; then remove the theodolite, and place it up on any part of the shore where you have a good view, and give the boatmen orders to sound another bay in the same way ; to protract the soundings, draw a black lead line upon the chart to represent the line the boatmen sailed on from one point to another ; then lay off the bearings taken to the flag, which will cross that line ; then observe the hour and minute the sounding was taken, which will correspond with the time you took the bearing ; set down the depth of water ; do the same with all the other lines on which the boat sailed till you have finished.

When you cannot sail from a direct point, order the boat-men, at each place he puts up his flag, to put himself in a line with two objects upon the land, which you have marked upon the chart. Place the theodolite in the best situation you can find, that the bearings you take may intersect the boat, so as the angles may not be too acute ; to protract the soundings, draw a black lead line by laying the edge of the ruler upon the two objects, and lay off the bearings from the meridian, and insert the soundings.

Another method, which is preferable to any of those described, is to have three memorandum books, and three watches, all set to the same minute at the beginning. Your assistant has one theodolite and you have another, which are placed at least a mile separate, or more if it can be got, where each of you have a good view of the bay or coast you intend to take the soundings of : the assistant in the boat sets down the minute and the depth of the sounding the moment the flag is hoisted ; you take one bearing, and your assistant takes another, and you both set down in your book the minute of time it was taken. After having taken a number of

1

Plate XXXV.

FIELD BOOK

of The Survey of a Sea Coast

Begins at Bottom of the
LEFT COLUMN

Left column

Bearings	From	Chains	Opposite
117°	from x	53	Booker Castle
108 . .	from x to z	32	
100 . ..	from z to z	62	
30 . .	from y to a	52	
128 . 20	from w to y	68	
107 . .	from v	128	
60 . .	from v		
97 . 30	from w to v	27	
76 . .	from w		
76 . 30	from z to w		
40 . 30	from z to w	30	
133 . 15	from v to w	72	
109 . 30	from t to v	70	
88 . 30	from s to t	103	
54 . 40	from r to s	53	
26 . .	from q to r	38	
63 . .	from p to q	51	Crow Point
138 . 30	from o to p	94	
83 . .	from n to o	60	
17 . .	from o to n	30	
76 . 30	from m to n		
13 . 30	from m		
131 . .	from m	70	Old Church
2 . .	from l to m	94	
88 . 36	from k to l	84	
99 . 30	from k to either	33	
2 . .	from h to k	27	Nippan 52
147 . 40	from g to h	100	Wait Water
116 . 30	from c to g	37	Dam of Deane
42 . 42	from e to f		
66 . 30	from e	50	Horse Shoe
88 . 30	from e to d	24	Horse Shoe
53 . .	from c to d	65	Little Island
2 . .	from c to d	108	
112 . .	from b to c		Little Island
60 . .	from b		Little Island
40 . 30	from a to b	50	Little Island
179 . .	from a		
177 . .	from z to a	175	

Begins at Bottom

Right column

Continuation

Bearings	Chains	Places
64 . 12	from d to A	54	
166 . 12	from c to d	50	
65 . 36	from b to c	51	
206 . 36	from a to b	53	on Broad Island
of A an interverted point			
Begun again			
246 . .	Long Island	82	Long is 8 wide
48 . 18	from 16 to 17		
110 . .	from 16		
98 . .	from 16		
24 . 30	from 16		
2 . 30	from 15 to 16	50	
21 . .	from 14 to 15	31	
127 . .	from 14		Long Island
68 . 40	from 14		Long Island
145 . 30	from 13 to 14	63	
53 . 30	from 12 to 13	55	
120 . 30	from 11 to 12	67	
134 . .	from 10 to 11	60	
166 . .	from 10		
134 . .	from 9 to 10	47	Branston
53 . .	from 8 by 9	45	
121 . .	from 8		
2 . .	from 7 to 8	66	Deserthet
63 . 40	from 6 to 7	82	
20 . 30	from 5 to 6	88	
112 . .	from 5		Broad Island
61 . 12	from 5	46	
107 . 30	from 4 to 5	104	
76 . 30	from 3 to 4	93	
173 . 3	from 2 to 3	52	
43 . .	from 1 to 2	68	
			Chains

In a Survey such as this, the Coast and the Distances are inserted in Chains

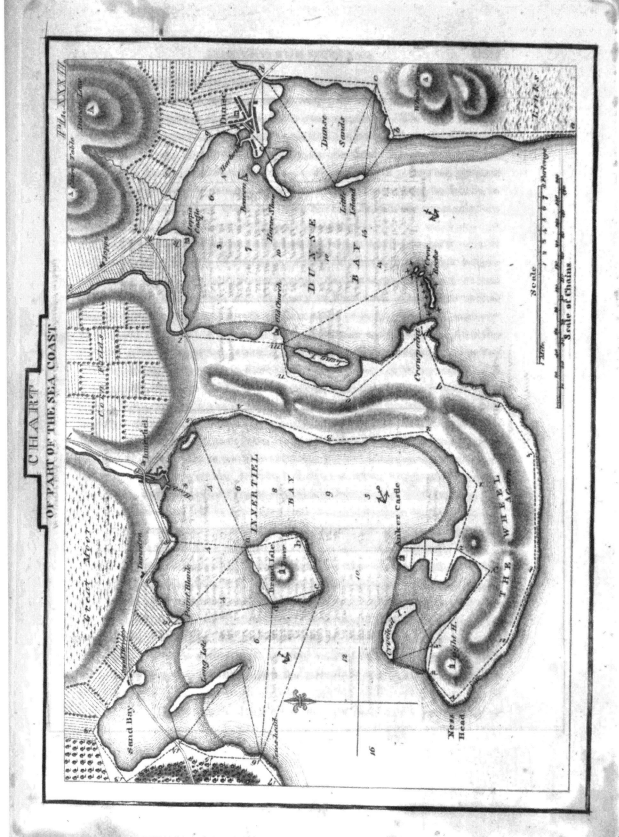

CHART
OF PART OF THE SEA COAST

Pl. XXXIII

Scale

Scale of Chains

soundings in all directions, all three compare books. The observations are then to be protracted, and laid down and plotted on the chart, and the soundings all inserted at their respective intersections. The same method of protracting is used as the chart is plotted by, and need not be again repeated. Be very particular in making an allowance for the fall and rise of the tide in all the different methods above specified; for this purpose a man ought to be watching at an index, such as are at most harbours, to set down on paper how much the tide rises or falls every quarter of an hour during the time the soundings were taking.

From the remarks I have made upon county surveying, a surveyor will find very little difficulty in surveying and making out a map, after having had a little practice in both departments. As the survey of a large extent requires great minuteness, it is necessary to have such instruments as will measure angles to a great nicety. A sextant of large radius, so contrived as to read every minute distinctly (and the angles to be observed with the greatest accuracy), and a triangle formed to a distant object, and calculated by logarithms, so as to have that distance very correct, and from it a range of bearings taken to various distant objects, is of great service. Few surveyors are at so much pains, resting satisfied when three bearings meet in a point. It frequently happens, that from two stations, another that you wish to make a station of, cannot be seen from the one you are at, and it is necessary to intersect it; in that case, measure a distance from where you are to where it can be seen; there plant up the theodolite, and take a bearing to it, and another at some convenient place, and so intersect it. It is necessary that a land-surveyor should take the latitude of some of the principal places by observation. This may be done by observing the altitude of the sun at 12 o'clock exactly; and, by a table of the sun's declination, you find the elevation of the equator in that place, and the compliment of this angle is the latitude required. Unless you have a well regulated watch, set by a time-piece, the hour of 12 cannot be exactly ascertained; therefore it is necessary that a surveyor ought to know how to find a true meridian line by observation taken with his theodolite. Choose a clear day, an hour or two before 12, take the sun's altitude, and in the afternoon you have to observe when the altitude is the same.

In the forenoon, suppose at 10 o'clock, the instrument is set level, the index over o on the limb, and the needle set over the *fleur de lis* in the compass box; move the index horizontally and the quadrant vertically, till you see through the telescope the cross hairs and the centre of the sun as cut in four quarters; observe what degrees and minutes are cut on the limb by the index, which note in a memorandum book, and also the angle of elevation cut by the index on the quadrant. In the afternoon, observe that the instrument is not moved from the level, and that the index and the quadrant correspond with the angle of elevation it was in the forenoon. Then move the index on the limb horizontally, and watch it till you see the cross hairs in the telescope as dividing the sun in four quarters, and note the degrees and minutes cut by the index on the limb, suppose 38° 30′; from the afternoon's observation subtract that made in the forenoon, which was 7° 30′; there remains 31°, the half of which is 15° 30′; to this half sum add the morning's observation, 7° 30′, and the sum is 23°. Let the theodolite remain in the same position, and turn the pinion about till the index cuts 23° on the limb; look through the telescope, and if the cross hairs coincide with any particular mark at a distance, it is in the line of the meridian. If no mark is seen that you are certain of, you must then set up a pole, or something else, by way of a mark; put also a mark where the instrument stands. By this means you may also know the variation of the magnetic needle, by observing what degree it cuts in the compass box when the index is placed exactly on the meridian.

The latitude of the place may be taken thus: After you have found out a true meridian, plant the theodolite level; bring the quadrant and telescope into the line of the meridian, and let the index remain at the same angle on the limb; then elevate the telescope towards the sun, and when the sun is in a line with the meridian, and the cross hairs in the telescope appear as if they were cutting the sun in four quarters, note down for the sun's meridian altitude the degrees and minutes cut by the index on the quadrant, which suppose is 42°, and for the sun's declination by an ephemeris for the same day, suppose 4° 2′; if it be a north declination, subtract this from 42°, the meridian altitude, and the remainder will be 37° 58′, the co-latitude; but if the sun hath made a south declination, it must be added to the meridian altitude, and the sum will be the co-latitude; by subtracting which from 90° you have the latitude of the place, 52° 2′,

SECTION SIXTH.

MILITARY SURVEYING.

As the art of arranging armies in order of battle, regulating their movements in such a manner as may be deemed most proper for attacking, defending, or retreating to the greatest possible advantage, must depend in a great measure upon a perfect knowledge of that part of the country where those movements are to take place, surveying and sketching ought to be made one of the most essential parts of a military education, as it is often necessary to sketch the ground in the neighbourhood of an encampment. I have inserted a military sketch, *Plate* XXXIII. out of the reach of an enemy. The ground may be regularly measured, and a map made of the same; when otherwise situated, it is sometimes paced.

Although this work does not require so much care and attention as other surveys where the content and area is required, a few lines may be measured, and a quantity of bearings taken, and intersections made of particular points, with any instrument for taking angles, and the rest of it sketched in by riding or pacing the ground. The plain table is an excellent instrument for a work of this kind, particularly as every thing can be sketched in upon it on the spot in better proportion than by the eye. It cannot be expected, that a person belonging to the army can take theodolites or plain tables along with him to the field of battle; but a snuff-box sextant, as represented on *Plate* 8. *Fig.* 7. being of small compass, can be easily carried, and will take an angle with great exactness. There is one thing very necessary that an officer in the army should be well acquainted with. He may know how to lay off squares, parallelograms, &c. very well on paper, but may be at a loss to do so in the field. The sextant, if the index is put to 90°, reflects a perpendicular; the optical square does the same. We shall now suppose you begin at A, and place a pole there; then go to any other part of the ground, suppose B, and measure the length from A to B; stand at B, and look through the sextant, the index being at 90°, and cause one of your men to go in as straight a line as possible; if you cannot see him at first, cause him to move to the right or the left till you see the pole at A and the man's pole to coincide, which will be exactly perpendicular from B to C; measure the distance to C, and then go to to A; then measure the same distance to D as is from B to C, which forms a rectangular long square for the encampment. With the sextant take an angle from A to Hill Pike, and another to a cairn on the hill-top nearest you; then go to B, and take an angle to Hill Pike, and another angle to the cairn that you observed from A; next go to C, and take an angle by reflecting the pole D to the park of artillery; then take an angle by reflecting the park of artillery to the fort. The angles are represented on the sketch by dotted lines, merely to show where they were taken from. Again, take an angle by reflecting the park of artillery to the Jew's farm. The best method of laying these angles off upon the sketch is with a protractor or line of chords (both of which are contained in a case of mathematical instruments), and where the intersections meet is the distance. The other parts of the plan may be all done by pacing, and other parts sketched in with the eye.

The following Table, for reducing the common pace of $2\frac{1}{2}$ feet into feet, will be found convenient in laying off the distances upon the sketch.

Paces	Ft. In.	Paces	Feet	Paces	Feet	Paces	Feet	Paces	Feet
1	2.6	30	75	230	575	430	1075	630	1575
2	5.0	40	100	240	600	440	1100	640	1600
3	7.6	50	125	250	625	450	1125	650	1625
4	10.0	60	150	260	650	460	1150	660	1650
5	12.6	70	175	270	675	470	1175	670	1675
6	15.0	80	200	280	700	480	1200	680	1700
7	17.6	90	225	290	725	490	1225	690	1725
8	20.0	100	250	300	750	500	1250	700	1750
9	22.6	110	275	310	775	510	1275	800	2000
10	25.0	120	300	320	800	520	1300	900	2250
11	27.6	130	325	330	825	530	1325	1000	2500
12	30.0	140	350	340	850	540	1350	2000	5000
13	32.6	150	375	350	875	550	1375	3000	7500
14	35.0	160	400	360	900	560	1400	4000	10000
15	37.6	170	425	370	925	570	1425	5000	12500
16	40.0	180	450	380	950	580	1450	6000	15000
17	42.6	190	475	390	975	590	1475	7000	17500
18	45.0	200	500	400	1000	600	1500	8000	20000
19	47.6	210	525	410	1025	610	1525	9000	22500
20	50.0	220	550	420	1050	620	1550	10000	25000

The sketch is frequently drawn in with pen and ink in a rough manner, but so as every thing can be easily read, and all the different characters perfectly understood. Forts and fortified towns are represented as on the sketch, the outline of which is generally made bold, and the buildings shaded with red, or dark with Indian ink, according to fancy. Batteries are of various kinds, viz. batteries with embrasures, batteries en barbete, masked batteries, where the cannon are placed behind hedges, mortar batteries, and open batteries. The embrasures are represented shewing the breast work, which is shaded; and the place left white is where the cannon are placed. In batteries en barbete the guns or howitzers fire over a breast work; mortar batteries have a breast work, and the number of guns they contain is expressed by small circles behind the breast work; an open battery has no breast work, and is represented on the sketch with one stroke and two shorter ones on each side, to represent a cannon: an abatis is represented by a quantity of trees laid before cannon, without leaves, to keep off an enemy; pallisades are represented by vertical strokes; frases are represented by small strokes laid horizontally before a battery; a chevaux de frize is represented by a line drawn across a river with oblique crosses. Troops of infantry are represented in small parallelograms crossed by a diagonal, the one half shaded dark and the other left light; the light part is sometimes coloured according to the colour or uniform of the regiment. Cavalry troops are likewise represented by parallelograms, but, for the sake of distinction, are commonly made broader than infantry troops. Encamped troops are represented the same way; but in place of erecting the standards upon the front line, they are placed at a little distance before it. Park of artillery is described by a square, crossed by two diagonals, one half shaded and the other half left white; its front is shewn by a strong line. The evolutions of troops are represented by dotted lines and arrows, representing the way they are moving and marching.

From what has been said with regard to making out a military sketch, an inspection of the Plate will greatly assist the surveyor in becoming acquainted with the characters.

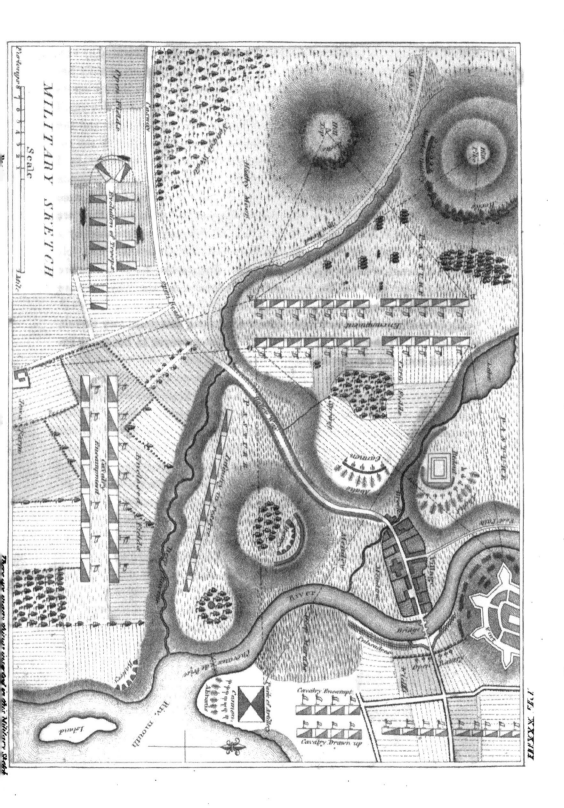

MILITARY SKETCH

Scale

PL. XXXII.

SECTION SEVENTH,

OF REDUCING AND DELINEATING PLANS.

ART. I. OF REDUCING.

THE *reduction* of a figure, design, or draught, is the making a copy of it either larger or smaller than the original, still preserving the form and proportion. This may be accomplished in various ways; but it may be necessary to mention that each has, more or less, its defects. *Plate* XXXIV. *Fig.* 1. represents a plan, which is to be reduced by means of squares. This is performed as follows; divide the original into little squares, and divide a piece of paper of the dimension required into the same number of squares, which are to be larger or smaller than the original as the map is to be enlarged or diminished. This done, in every square of the second figure draw what you find in its correspondent one in the first, as in Fig. 2. same *Plate*, which is reduced to one half of the original, or one fourth in extent.

The proportional compasses, or, as they are frequently termed (from their use), compasses of reduction, are of great use in reducing. *Plate* XXXIV. *Fig.* 8. represents a pair of those compasses, which are made use of as follows: move the slider A till such time as by trials you find the number of extents of the one end of the legs CC, contained in one extent of the other end B B. The number of extents indicate the proportion in which you are to enlarge or diminish. From this the application must appear evident. The instrument is generally sold divided to your hand, which renders it still more convenient.

Plate XXXIV. (*Fig.* 4.)

Represents a proportional scale or fan, which answers exactly the same purpose as the proportional compasses. It is constructed as follows : Draw two lines at any angle you please from D ; then take a pair of compasses, with either the drawing pen or pencil, and put one foot in the angle D, and draw a number of segments of a circle at as nearly equal distances as you can guess, and number them in the same manner as ts on the figure ; then divide the farthest arch from D into three equal divisions, and draw a line from D to the second division, which makes that part on the left only half of what is on the right. To use it, take any length from the large plan, and apply that length in the compasses to the right side of the fan, by moving them down till you bisect the line drawn through the fan. Turn the compasses round, and press in one leg, till the point just reaches the left line on the fan, which gives one half the distance, which apply to the copy that you are to reduce. This method will be found equally expeditious and as correct as the proportional compasses. It can be drawn with a black lead pencil upon any part of your plan, which can be rubbed out when convenient.

Plate XXXIV. (*Fig.* 6. and 7.)

Is the plan of the mouth of the rivers Esk and Dee, which has a large flat of marshy ground between the river Dee and the sea. On the east are broad sands and a bold shore, with steep rocks ; above the rocks is gently rising ground, with a clump of planting ; opposite is the village of Esk, with some open fields, a plan of which is made on a reduced scale by means of squares ; the proportion is as three to four, that is to say, three squares on the large plan is to be divided into four squares in the smaller one, or three chains from a scale upon the original plan will measure four on the reduced one. If you make each square on the large plan two inches, each square on the small plan must be an inch and a half. If you use the proportional compasses, let them be set so as two inches betwixt the largest legs may measure only an inch and a half in the short legs.

1

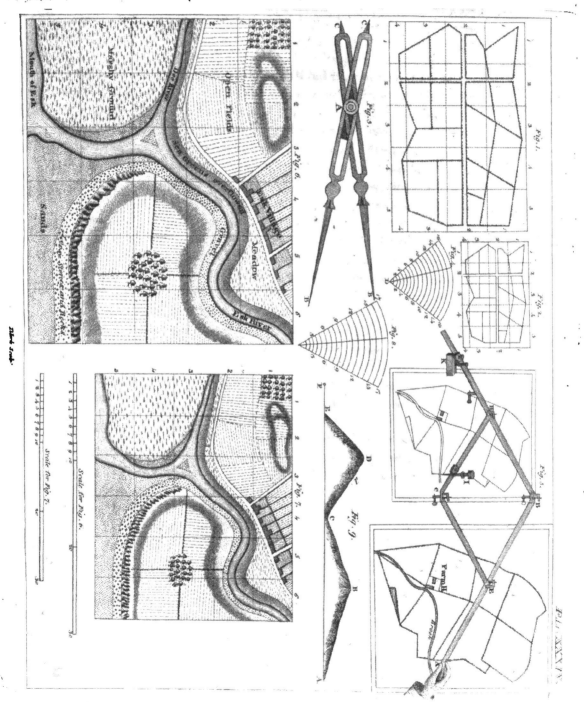

Plate XXXVI.

Should you prefer a proportion, let the middle line be in the same proportion as three is to four. (See the fan *Fig.* 8.)

Plate XXXIV. (*Fig.* 5.)

Represents a pantographer at work. Of all instruments that have hitherto been invented for reducing, copying or enlarging plans, the pantographer is by far the best; not only for being the most expeditious, but the most correct, as every straight and curved line is copied with the greatest exactness. It is as useful to an experienced draftsman, as to those who have had but little practice in drawing. It saves much time, either in reducing or enlarging plans of estates, and with equal facility may be used for copying figures, sea-charts, maps, profiles, landscapes, &c. This, like all other good instruments, most mathematical instrument makers lay claim of having made improvements upon. Those instruments are in general made of brass, from one to four feet in length; it consists of four flat bars, about half an inch broad, and about one eight of an inch thick, two long, and two short. The two longest are joined at the end B, by a double pivot, which is fixed to one of the bars, and works in two small holes placed at the end of the other. Under the joint is a castor, with an ivory roller, to support this end of the instrument. The two smaller bars are fixed by pivots at E and H, near the middle of the longer bars, and are also joined together at C by a double pivot. By the construction of the pantographer, the four bars always form a parallelogram or rhombus. There is a slider on one of the larger bars or arms, and another on one of the shorter, which moves upon the arms till they are put in a line, which is known by taking a piece of thread, and applying it to the tracing pin A, the pin in the weight, and the pencil tube; and are fixed to the arms or bars by means of milled screws. Each of the boxes has a cylindric tube, to carry either the pencil point I, or the weight K, which is made of lead, and covered with leather or silk. On this weight the whole instrument moves, and every part is in motion when at work, except the weight, which holds the pantographer fast to the paper by means of four prongs in the under side of it. The instrument is supported upon castors with ivory rollers to facilitate its motions. The long tube, with the pencil, moves easily up and down in a socket, within another tube, to give way to any unevenness in the paper. There is a cap at the top, for putting in a piece of lead, to encrease the strength of the pencil mark. If the original plan is of large dimensions, and the pantographer cannot take it in all at once, the operation must be done at two, three, or four times, by drawing a line from one point to another, upon the large plan with a black lead pencil; the same line must be taken off from the large plan upon a new sheet, which will correspond with the line drawn upon the copy. The original plan must be removed into such a situation, as to allow the reducing or enlarging the remaining part. In this manner, by frequent shifting, a pantographer is made to reduce, enlarge, or copy a drawing of large dimensions, by joining the parts together.

To avoid the trouble of setting the weight, pencil, and tracer, each time, two of the bars are divided into ten or twenty of the most common proportions; by which divisions the sliders are to be fixed. When the machine is used, a fine string is fastened in the pencil case; the other end has a loop, to be fastened to the finger of the operator, by pulling which he can raise the pencil when he does not wish it to mark.

No surveyor should be without this machine, as his plans will have to be reduced to a smaller scale than the rough sketches he makes out for calculating the contents, particularly if the estate is large.

Hitherto I have only given directions for taking surveys, and making out rough plans and sketches. I now come to point out the methods used by practical surveyors for copying and drawing plans with the greatest facility, at the same time with as much ease and exactness, as the nature of the work will admit of; and to transfer the rough copies to be drawn upon clean paper or vellum. Some surveyors use a pair of compasses with a third leg annexed, which takes off a triangle at once. With the same extent it is applied to the clean paper, and the lines drawn immediately in upon the copy with a black lead pencil. They go over the whole drawing in the same manner, till such time as it is all taken off from the rough drawings and transferred to the clean paper.

Another method, which is more expeditious than the three-legged compasses, is by laying the rough plan above a sheet of clean paper, and with a needle pricking all the angles and curved lines through the rough plan, and the marks made by the needle are left perceptible upon the clean paper or vellum. It is then drawn, first with a black lead pencil, to see that nothing has been wrong done, or omitted; then inked in with Indian ink. The straight lines are drawn with a ruler and drawing pen, and the curved lines with the hand.

Another method, is by a copying glass, which is fixed in a frame, and is lifted up from another frame, which it is fixed to with hinges, and is supported at any elevation with two pillars, which rest in nitches made in both sides of the under frame. The plan that you have to copy is fixed to a sheet of clean paper with pins, sealing wax, or wafers, at the corners; the plan is laid next the glass, which you see distinctly reflected upon the clean paper. If the drawing paper is very thick, put a piece of white paper next the under frame, which will make it more transparent, run over the whole with a black lead pencil, and ink it in.

Another method is, to rub the back part of the rough plan over with black lead dust, and lay the back part of the rough drawing next the clean drawing paper; and with a blunt etching needle, trace over all the lines on the rough plan; when done, take it off, and you will have an impression upon the drawing paper; you then ink it in. If you wish to preserve your rough plans from being damaged by rubbing them with the lead dust, take a sheet of thin paper, and rub it uniformly over with lead dust; lay the rubbed side next the drawing paper, and the plan above it, and let them be all kept fast with pins or weights to prevent shifting; press the tracing point pretty hard upon the rough draught, and when you have gone all over it, take it off and ink it in.

If you have a plan to copy that has been drawn upon very thick drawing paper, or a plan that is pasted on linen, or a plan to make a copy from that is highly finished, which the tracing point would damage, get some sheets of cambrick or fan paper, both of which are very thin, and rub them over with nut-oil; then lay the oiled paper between sheets of blotting paper, and it will be fit for use in a few days; lay the oil paper, after it is thoroughly dry upon the original, which must be kept down with weights; then with a pen or a black lead pencil go over all the lines, till you have copied the whole of the plan upon the oil paper; then take the oil paper, and lay it above a sheet of black lead paper, and with a tracer trace through the oil paper, which leaves the outline of the plan upon the clean drawing paper, and you will have the outline of the plan, which afterwards ink carefully in.

ART. II. OF DELINEATING PLANS.

A proficiency in delineating and making out neat drawings cannot be acquired but by practice. For that purpose, those who are desirous to improve themselves in that art, should at every leisure hour be copying or making out drawings, either from drawn plans or copperplates; and should also study the different tints necessary to give drawings effect.

Indian ink, of all colours, is more used by a land-surveyor than any other. A well finished drawing with Indian ink has a fine effect, and is esteemed by many persons to excel those done in colours. But it requires the hands of an excellent draftsman to finish a drawing with Indian ink alone; to give it all the different tints necessary, it is more tedious than delineating a plan with colours; and when colours are used, Indian ink is the chief, as all the outlines and deep shading must be done with it.

Verdigris is much used by land-surveyors, as well as all other draftsmen. It answers better than any other colour, for shading lakes, tarns, or lochs, rivers, brooks, and the sea, and when mixed with a little gumbouge, makes a fine green, either for pasture, meadows, bogs, morasses, trees, &c. &c. Carmine and lake, are best for shading buildings; umber, burnt sienna, and bistre, give different shades of brown; Prussian blue is often used for giving dark shades to the sides of rivers, and the sea shore; gumbouge a fine yellow, and when mixed with lake, is a good colour for shading roads. These are the colours generally made use of by surveyors.

The most expeditious method of delineating a plan, is to draw all the straight lines with a ruler and drawing pen, the curved lines with the hand, hedges, trees, bushes, and shrubberies, with the pen and Indian ink. Use a hair pencil, and weak Indian ink for hills, for the first tint, and wash the top and bottom off with clear water and a clean brush, before the first coat gets time to dry. Some surveyors mix a little bistre with their Indian ink, which gives them a brownish tint: others mix a little Prussian blue with the Indian ink, which gives them a fine effect. If the hills are very steep, add another coat or two, and shade them according to their steepness; let each coat dry before another is put on, and never neglect to wash off the edges with a clean brush and clear water. The Indian ink brush should be at one end of the pencil stick, and the water brush at the other end of it. If there are a number of hills and rising grounds, do them all in the same way, with one coat, and those that require to be touched up steeper will be dry. Begin again, and give them a second coat. Go from hill to hill till you have finished; and begin again, and give them a third, and so on, till such time as you bring them to the tint required. If the hills are very large, as in the Highlands of Scotland, Yorkshire, Westmoreland, or Wales, use large brushes, and give the rocks a tint, resembling the colour of the stone by shades. (See *Plate* XXXIII. Military Sketch).

Moors.

Make first the representation of a few scattered hillocks with the pen, or a fine hair pencil, according to the nature of the moor. If the moor is flat, the small hillocks should be omitted. Draw in with the pen a few tufts of furze, if there be any on the moor; then with a hair pencil, touch up each hillock on the right side with Indian ink, and wash the edges off with another brush at the other end of the pencil stick, on the left and bottom part, with clean water; give each furze a touch with Indian ink, and shade them off with the hair pencil towards the right; you may then mix a little Indian ink and bistre, and lay on some broad shades promiscuously, very light, on different parts of the moor; then mix up a little weak Indian ink, and Prussian blue, and lay shades on those parts of the moor where no colours have been laid on, washing off the edges to keep them from appearing harsh. Mix Indian ink and a little lake, both very weak, and lay on shades here and there, so as to interfere as little as possible with the tints already laid on; then take a little weak yellow and green, and fill up any vacant spaces that may have been left untouched with the other colours, which will give the moor a variety of shades, after all is gone over. If it is heath, shade it over with Indian ink. If there is pasture and heath mixed, shade it with light green all over, with a large hair pencil. If the moor is of a brownish nature, shade it all over with very weak bistre. In observing the above directions, you will be enabled to give the moor a resemblance very near its natural colour. The furze, whins, or fuzins, as they are termed in different places, look well if you give them a touch of green on the right side, and a touch of yellow on the west side, which should be laid on last, which will give them the appearance of being in blossom.

Morasses.

Take a fine pointed hair pencil, with Indian ink of a pale colour; and draw with the hand short horizontal lines, pretty close to one another, some short and some long, which do as quick as you can, till you have gone over the whole; and with the pen, insert rushes, reeds, and herbages, and shade over the whole with a pale green, inclining a little to blue; then touch up the rushes, reeds, and herbage, with a strong green, which shade off to the right, with a tint of lighter green.

Meadows.

With the pen, or a fine pointed hair pencil and light Indian ink, make a few strokes, some long and some short, none to exceed the 6th part of an inch in length, all over the meadow, as they are represented on *Plate* XXXIV. *Fig.* 6. (plan of Eskmouth), and wash the whole of the meadow with light green, inclining to yellow.

Pasture Grounds

Are sometimes represented by sloping and upright strokes, very short, none of them to exceed the 50th part of an inch, as in *Plate* XXXIII. Military Sketch. But most surveyors content themselves with washing the whole over with green, something darker than the meadows, and running over the whole with horizontal shades of Indian ink; which if used should be tinted before the green is laid on.

5

Sands upon the Sea Shore.

Wash them all over with a little weak carmine, and gumbouge, mixed neither too strong nor too weak. Some surveyors dot them all over with small dots, as is represented on *Plate* XXXIV. *Fig.* 6. with a pen, but this is only done on high finished drawings, particularly if the sands and scale are large, as it is very tedious to do them with dots.

Trees

Ought to be done very neat, upon a plan, as they give a drawing a fine appearance, (see *Plate* XXXIII. Military Sketch), or any of the following plates. They are expressed by a vertical stem, with a horizontal shade at bottom, and made broad at the top, and shaded with the pen on the right or east side, or with a touch of Indian ink, and coloured green on the left side, with here and there some with a little brown, others of the trees yellow, for the sake of distinction and variety.

Rocks

Upon a hill side are made to appear rugged, as on *Plate* XXXIII, and those upon a bold shore as represented on *Plate* XXXIV. *Fig.* 6. and 7. Houses are often shaded with carmine and lake, and frequently dark with Indian ink, and they are in general shaded darker on the east and south sides, see *Plate* XXXV.

Rivers, Lakes, and the Sea Shore,

Are shaded by going round the edges on both sides of a river with a strong liquid blue, which is softened off with a hair pencil, and a weaker blue towards the middle. Some surveyors prefer shading the edges of the rivers and sea coast with Indian ink, which is softened off with a pencil and clear water, and when dry, shade the whole of the river, lake, or sea, with water blue. This method makes the water look bolder at the edges, than when it is all shaded blue. Surveyors that have time, and wish to excel in drawing, frequently draw in the whole of the river with bold lines near the edge, and fainter towards the middle, in imitation of engraving. The sea shore is shaded in the same way, but much broader, and washed off with a large pencil and clear water. When the Indian ink is thoroughly dry, a coat of strong blue is laid above the ink, and washed off with a weaker blue, with a large hair pencil and clear water.

Corn Fields

Give a plan a fine appearance, if they are neatly shaded. The common way is to draw parallel lines as near as you can guess, at equal distances, either with the hand, or with a parallel ruler and a drawing pen, and weak Indian ink, or with the colour you intend to shade the field with, to represent the ridges; when that is done, with any colour you think proper to make the divisions of the field, suppose yellow, take a little yellow in a hair pencil, and run down the ridges, and before the colour is quite dry, wash the edge of it with the hair pencil on the other end of the stick with clear water. Do the next field in the same way, but a different colour, and vary the colours so that two fields adjoining should be of different colours, till you have gone over the whole plan, some brown, and others blue or red. But most draftsmen prefer making all the fields at least something betwixt yellow and light brown.

Plate XXXV.

Is a design for a new town, which was proposed to be built in the same way as represented on the Plate, where every corner house has the benefit of a garden. In most towns the corner houses are in general the best, but often deprived of a garden, when the interior houses have the advantage of one. To distinguish the gardens belonging to the corner houses, they are coloured upon the Plate with different colours, merely to shew how they are situated from the house they belong to. This plan is introduced principally to give an idea how gardens are generally tinted and finished upon plans. After the outline of the whole is drawn with a drawing pen and Indian ink, before any colours are used, take a fine pointed hair pencil or pen, run over with weak Indian ink the lines to represent the different beds; then draw in bushes along the sides of the walks, and here and there some bushes at the divisions of the different beds, and some scattered trees, if there are any in the garden, which should be done in a neat style, and shaded dark with Indian ink on the right cheek, and let the left

1

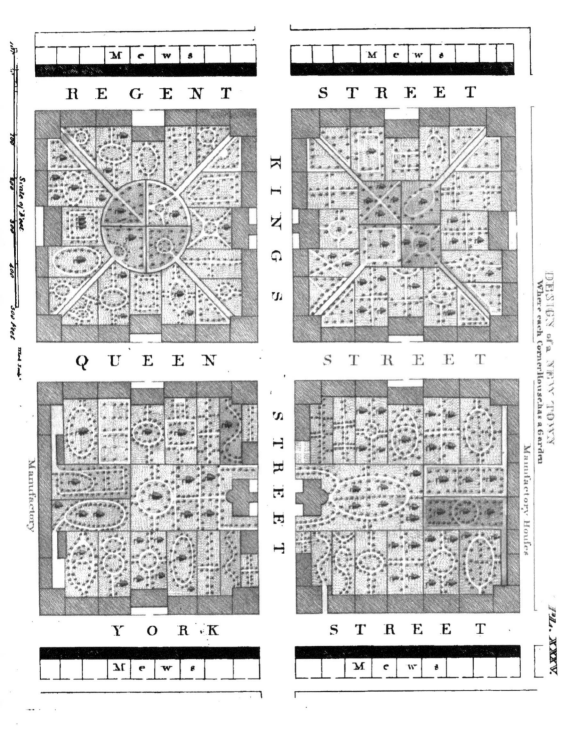

DESIGN of a NEW TOWN
Where each Corner House has a Garden

Manufactory Houses

Pl. XXXV.

sides of the trees be left white ; they should all have a shade at the bottom, which is commonly done on the right hand from the roots. Houses are sometimes shaded dark in plans with Indian ink, but more frequently with carmine, and on the east and south sides with lake, which is something of a darker red than carmine. The carmine should be diluted with gum water ; the best kind is to be bought in powder or in cakes. If Indian ink is used, which some surveyors prefer to carmine or lake ; draw a dark line on the east and south side of the buildings, pretty bold, as is done on the Plate, which gives a good effect to the drawing. The beds of the gardens should be tinted with very light and pale colours, such as green, yellow, red, and any other colour you choose, to make a small distinction of one bed from another. The gravel walks are shaded brown, and the grass walks green. The bushes and trees should all have a tint of green, brown, or yellow on the light side, some one colour and some another, but most of them green, which gives a pleasant effect, if they are tastefully laid on. The streets in a town are commonly left white, although some surveyors prefer giving them a tint of very light blue, to represent the causeway ; and if the town has a flagged pavement, it is coloured brown in general.

Plate XXXVI.

Is the plan of a pleasure ground as it is now finished. The gravel walks which are numerous, are made of Kensington gravel, and laid out very tastefully round beautiful fish-ponds, and the shrubbery, which is extensive, kept in the finest order ; the whole sheltered with plantations of considerable extent. A few corn fields are represented, which gives an idea of the method of laying down fields and hedges, adjoining a pleasure ground, and what way to make out a finished drawing. But observe, the dotted lines on the Plate representing the ridges, should be drawn with a drawing pen with light Indian ink, or with colour on your plan, the same as you intend to shade the different fields with, which should be bolder than the faint colour with which you shade the ground. This gives a fine effect to a drawing, if smoothly laid on.

Plate XXXVII.

Represents a park with the village of Duddingston adjoining, which has been finished for a number of years, and is kept in fine order. The garden is

M m

in the middle of the grounds, and finely sheltered. This, as well as *Plate*
XXXVI. is upon a small scale. Both Plates are only made out to shew,
what way the drawing of pleasure grounds ought to be finished. In order
to get an idea of taking the survey, pointing out the numerous distances
and angles, recourse must be had to various parts of the treatise; let it
suffice, to observe, that by what has been already described, if a pupil has
made himself acquainted with the different methods of surveying and
making out his protractions, he will find little difficulty either in taking
a survey, though ever so intricate, or making a plan of the same.

The drawings of the pleasure grounds would require to be plotted upon
a scale three times the size they are laid down on the plates, which would
give sufficient room to colour all the roads and gravel walks minutely.
To avoid confusion, they are left uncoloured on the plates, which are only
represented by double lines, which can be easily traced. When a pupil
improves himself in drawing, he will soon be enabled to make out a neat
plan, by following the directions given in delineating, from page 240 to
245. Those who wish to excel in drawing, should provide themselves
with good Indian ink, and with a set of Reeve's colours, which can be purchased ready prepared in small cakes, very finely ground, and may be
had at any of the colour or print shops. A very fine liquid blue may be
made, by mixing three ounces of verdigris and one ounce of cream of tar-
tar, with half a gill or a nuggan of vinegar. Put the mixture into a vial,
and shake it two or three times a day till the verdigris is dissolved, and
you will have a fine water blue, which, when mixed with a little yellow, is
a beautiful grass green. The above two colours are more used by land-
surveyors, with the addition of Indian ink, than any of the other
colours.

A land-surveyor who undertakes the survey of a county, ought to study
attentively the method of laying down and transferring his rough draughts
and sketches with accuracy, and to copy them very minutely and very
neat upon his clean drawing.

Before I close this Treatise on surveying, I shall offer a few remarks
which may prove useful to the surveyor in the delineating of high ground on
maps, viz. mountains, fells, hills, and knolls; which appellations are made
use of according to the altitude, which in general is determined from the
level of the sea at low water.

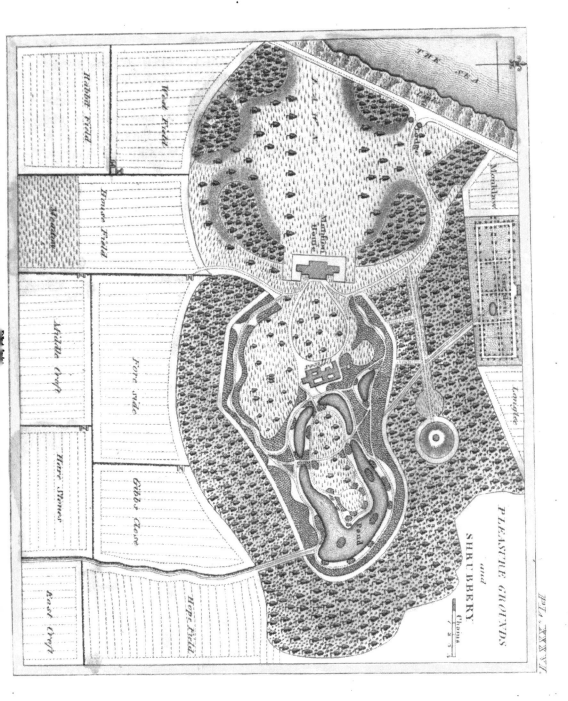

PLEASURE GROUNDS
and
SHRUBBERY

Pl. XXXI.

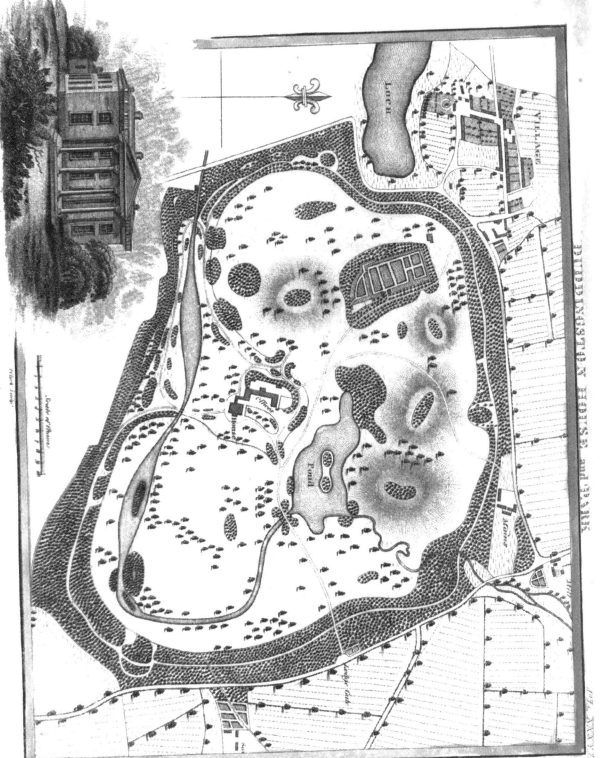

DUDDINGSTON HOUSE and PARK.

Of all the methods that have been invented for drawing high grounds, although many are used, yet none is more generally adopted, or indeed of greater utility, than those represented in Plates XXXVIII. and XXXIX. The former is more particularly adapted to close or complete a country, the latter where it is high and open ; yet the principle in both is exactly the same, and simply consists in what is in general termed a *bird's eye view*, the eye being supposed at a distance from the ground. The greater the altitude of the hill, the deeper the shade. It being impossible to place the eye in that position, recourse must be had to sketching the ground from eminences, commencing first at one side of a mountain or hill, and going all round, so as to introduce as little as possible any perspective view ; thus will every part of a hill or mountain have a proper extent, and will be in their proper situations with regard to horizontal distance. If the hill is perfectly flat on the top, it is left white as on the plates. Although many surveyors prefer perspective methods, which, when executed with taste, may please the eye on account of their landscape appearance, and though I have always admired and commended fine drawn plans; yet it is my opinion (as maps are not merely for shew) accuracy ought to be preferred. I must here mention, that in no pub-lication on surveying has any thing been said of the drawing of maps. This has induced me to introduce these two plates as specimens; the one for the various parts of the outline, such as towns, rivers, roads, and sea coast, &c.; the latter for high ground and the heads of rivers; and I may venture to affirm, they will afford more information on the subject than the most lengthened detail. However, I shall shew the method I have made use of in sketching the hills. After having done all the outline work on the plan, the best way of introducing the hills with accuracy, is to trace on part of paper the plan of the outline, and fasten it upon a plain table, and sketch in the hills ; which again take off the table, and trace the hills upon the outline plan, and shade them according to their steepness ; then do all the other smaller hills in the same way. When the work runs off the plain table, use more traced paper, till such time as you have gone over the whole map, taking care to notice all cairns, burrows, or rocks, which are situated on the hills, and shade them as far as they have a de-clivity towards the rivers or brooks. Great care should also be taken to

N n

trace the various ravines and brows of hills, which will give a true representation of the country ; and to have it well drawn, has a fine effect. The draftsman should take care not to labour the hills too much ; for it frequently happens that greatly laboured plans lose effect, and drown the most useful part of the plan, (the outline).

It will sometimes be necessary, particularly if the scale is large, to determine the falls of hills by levelling (for which see page 200) ; but an accurate eye-sketch is sufficient for all scales connected with county surveys.

Some draftsmen use the hair pencil for hills. It is in my opinion best, as it gives more spirit than with the pen ; yet I have seen a few drawings with the pen only, in imitation of engraving, exquisitely finished. Notwithstanding, from the very few good specimens, it is an art in which very few attain to any degree of perfection, but which if they do attain, is an excellent specimen to the engraver. In a plan, one of the greatest recommendations I know of is good writing ; and nothing tends more to deteriorate a map or plan, even if accurately surveyed and well drawn, than bad writing. The young draftsman ought therefore to practise the various hands as represented in Plate XXXVIII. which will not only be a good specimen to himself, but an excellent one to the engraver.

When a land-surveyor has finished a plan of a nobleman or gentleman's estate, in as elegant a style of drawing as he is capable of, if the scale he has adopted is large, he will upon his plan have several blank corners ; one of which should be filled up with a neat wrote title, another with a table of contents ; he should also, on any convenient place, insert a scale, and on another blank space a compass ; and if there is any other blank corner remaining, it may be filled up with a view of the mansion-house, as in Plate XXXVII. or an old ruin of a castle, or any particular building, if there are any on the property (see Plate XL. by way of specimen). If neatly drawn, and like the building, it is a fine embellishment to a plan.

Having now brought this Treatise to a conclusion, I feel no hesitation in saying, that, with proper attention to the various methods of surveying, and minute inspection of the Plates, the young surveyor, with perseverance, may soon become master of his profession.

FINIS.

Edinburgh :
Printed by John Brown.

Plate XXXVIII.

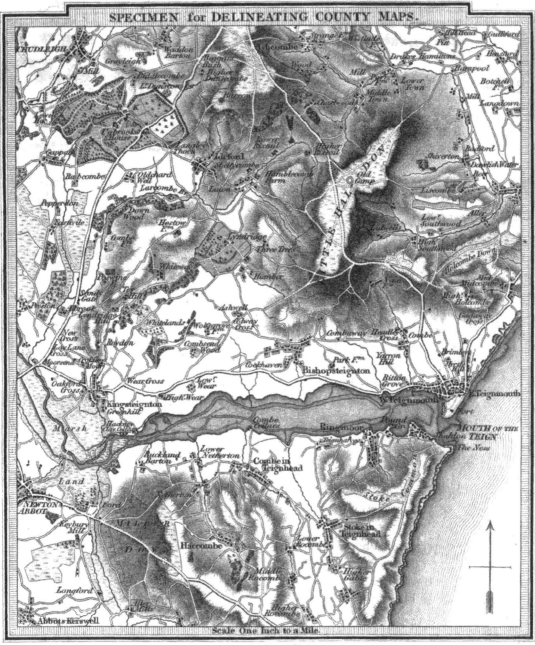

SPECIMEN for DELINEATING COUNTY MAPS.

Scale One Inch to a Mile.

Engraved by R. Knight London.

Plate XXXIX.

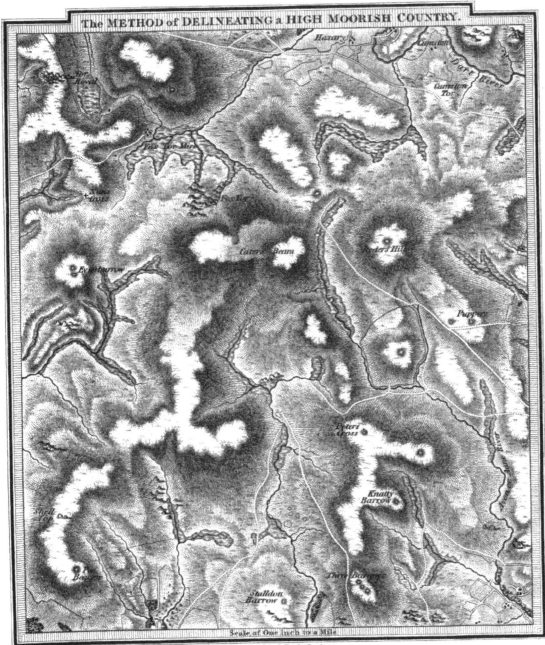

The METHOD of DELINEATING a HIGH MOORISH COUNTRY.

Scale of One Inch to a Mile.

Engraved by R. Knight London.

DIRECTIONS FOR PLACING THE PLATES.

The binder will observe, that when the Plates are to be placed face to face, the head of the second should always lie at the bottom of the first, as they are intended to read on.